One Hundred Voices

Volume One

Centum Press

One Hundred Voices Volume One
Copyright © 2016 Centum Press

For information contact :
Centum Press
http://www.centumpublishing.com
email: info@centumpublishing.com

ISBN: 978-1-945737039(paperback)
        978-1-945737046(hardcover)

LCCN: 2016916045

Edited By Destiny Rose Editorial Services
Cover Design by J Asheley Brown Designs

First Edition: September 2016

10 9 8 7 6 5 4 3 2 1

WHEN WORDS FAIL

HANNA ABI AKL

We were still together at that time.

I'd taken her to our favorite place: a rocky plane with a nicely-drawn path carved in stone that led to a cliff overlooking the ocean.

It was her favorite spot.

She once told me she could be anything here: a singer, a celebrity, a rocket scientist, an actress, a princess…anything without the world judging her or tearing her down or laughing in her face.

She felt invincible just by standing here. And I felt invincible standing next to her.

Strange how deeply another human life can affect us; I'd always believed that life was meant to be carried out alone – that you were born alone and spent your time alone until your final day. I never believed in sharing my moments with anyone. I never believed in sharing my soul with anyone.

But she was different.

She was brilliant, intelligent, sharp and beautiful…and she had that little devil that danced within her occasionally, setting her apart from the other smart and beautiful girls I had met in my life.

She loved music – and she loved to perform – which made our favorite spot all the more special: she'd run over to the cliff, twisting and turning while galloping across the pathway until she made it to the end.

There, she'd sing with her loudest and most melodic voice, and I'd close my eyes and forget all the dark nights I spent alone drinking in front of the white pages. I'd close my eyes and forget the whorehouses and the smokes and the fights in the alleys and the rent money and the food and the dirty clothes and the endless tiring jobs. I'd be transported and soothed by this angelic voice, a voice that was pure and compassionate and beyond human greed and contempt.

I'd look at her and see her under a new light every time she'd sing another song; I'd look at her and think, '*Damn, there isn't a single moment I could imagine being turned off by this.*'

And so I'd postulate the odds, the odds of an old bum like me winding up with a maiden like her, the odds of a failure meeting a spark that would reignite it, the odds of a madman driven to the grave by booze and words finally meeting peace and salvation.

I'd contemplate the odds – because the odds were themselves oddities that struck a man's mind and turned it upside down. The odds were themselves strange and weird and mad and crazy and forbidden and unrealistic; the odds challenged reality and the truth of the matter and everything else in this life which clearly showed a person like me could never end up with a woman like her.

That's why I contemplated the odds – because they were scary and full of hope.

And hope was an oath I swore never to take.

The sun was coming down on this pleasant day and we sat down contemplating the raging ocean waves on the cliff's edge.

"Why do you never write about me?" she asked me with her sweet voice.

Her eyes were filled with sparkles and were close to tears.

I didn't answer her. It wasn't because I didn't want to – it was because I didn't know how. I didn't have an answer for her question – and I didn't have the cure for her heartache.

She was struggling to control herself and fight back the tears.

"You've always said you wrote about the things that matter...the things that influence you or amaze you or inspire you or drive you crazy...the things that count in life...why don't you ever write about me?"

Then her voice disappeared.

She moved closer to me, sticking her body to mine, gently placing her right hand on top of mine, looking at me again with those pearly eyes as if to drive me to submission, before asking again, "Why don't you ever write about me? Is it because I don't mean anything to you?" There was another cold silence.

I tried to summon every power in me to answer her, but at that very moment, words – usually my closest allies in times of need and darkness – deserted me. I sat there with nothing to say.

She took my resignation as a sign of acceptance, withdrew her hand and got up, stared at me one last time with those big eyes – like a person who had run out of reasons to not hate someone – and walked away.

I watched her leave down the stone pathway, in between the giant carved rocks, her body shining with the colors of the sunset before she finally disappeared.

I was still frozen in place, my lips sealed tightly together, my mind blank with fear and confusion.

The worst had happened; I had lost her.

I had lost her over a conversation; I had lost her over an answer; I had lost her over a few words.

I got up, dusted myself, put my hands in my jeans pockets and started walking down the pathway.

If only she knew, I thought, *the reason why I never wrote about her…*

It had finally dawned on me after all this time: I'd never mentioned her in my writing, I'd never written a single sentence about her, I'd never tried my hand at a poem dedicated to her…

If only she knew…that she was the thing that mattered, the thing that influenced me and amazed me and inspired me and drove me crazy – the thing that counted in life.

She was the one thing I could never write about – she was the only thing I could never risk defacing or ruining or breaking or hurting or degrading with my art.

By the end of the day I had the answer she was burning to hear: I couldn't write about her because I didn't want to turn something beautiful into less than what it was.

THE ADVENTURES OF RABBIT

EDWARD AHERN

This is a reprint, having been published by Beorh Quarterly about three years ago.

This is a retelling of a folk tale recorded by Charles Leland in <u>The Algonquin Legends of New England</u>, published in 1884.

Of the old times.

Some indian tribes called him Mahtiguess, the rabbit, but the Micmac called him Ableegumooch, master rabbit and this part of rabbit's tale was told by the Micmacs.

Rabbit lived in hard times in a wigwam with his grandmother, waiting for things to get better. It was a brittle cold winter, with ice on the river and snow on the plain, and rabbit could not find food.

One day, while running through the forest and leaving deep tracks in the snow he saw a solitary lodge. Inside was Keeoony the otter. Otter's wigwam was on the banks of a river, with an ice slide from the door of the lodge to the edge of the river.

Otter welcomed rabbit into his wigwam, and offered to cook him food. Rabbit was skinny from hunger and quickly said yes.

"Wait here in the warmth of the lodge," otter said, "while I catch dinner."

Otter took down hooks he used to hold the fish he caught. Laying down on his belly at the top of the ice slide, he pushed off and slid down the slide and deep into the water. In a little while he came out of the water with three eels on hooks. They quickly cleaned, cooked and ate the eels.

My life, thought the rabbit, *this is an easy way to live. Fishers do little work and eat well. I am cleverer than this otter, I must be able to do this.*

And rabbit was so confident that that he asked otter to come visit and eat with him- adamadusk ketkewop- in three days time.

The next morning rabbit called to his grandmother. "Come, we will move our wigwam down to the lake."

And they moved their wigwam down to a bank on the lake. Rabbit poured water to make an ice slide, just as otter had. When otter arrived, rabbit called to his grandmother," prepare for dinner."

"But what am I to cook, grandson?"

"I will see to that."

Rabbit grabbed a nabogun, a stick for stringing eels, and hopped over to the ice slide.

But rabbit was not made for sliding, and as soon as he got onto the ice he swerved right, then left, then tumbled tail over head until he fell into the water.

And things got worse. Rabbit fur is not otter fur, and rabbit began to freeze in the cold water. Rabbit also is perhaps the worst swimmer of the animals. He lost his breath, struggled and began to sink.

Otter was looking down the bank at these thrashings. "What is wrong with this fellow?" He asked the grandmother.

"He has seen you do this," said grandmother, "and is trying to do as you do."

"Ho," yelled otter," come out of the water and hand me your nabogun."

Rabbit crawled, shivering, out of the water and up the bank. He gave his nabogun to Otter and limped into his lodge to get warm.

Otter slid down the bank and plunged into the lake. He surfaced again in a few minutes with several fish held on the nabogun. Otter was angry at rabbit for attempting what he could not perform. He threw the fish down at the entrance to the wigwam and went back to his lodge without tasting a single fish.

Rabbit was embarrassed and disappointed, but not discouraged, for he never gave up. One day in spring he was wandering in the woods when he came to a wigwam filled with several pretty girls, all wearing red headdresses and looking just like birds. And no wonder, for they were woodpecker sisters.

Rabbit may have been rash and over confident, but he also had good manners. He and the girls talked together so happily that he was invited to dinner, which he immediately accepted, for rabbit was still very hungry.

One of the red-capped girls took at wooden dish, a woltes, and seemed to run right up a tree. She stopped here and there, tapping now at this spot, now at that, picking out insects called rice, apchel-moal-timp-kawal, because the little bugs looked like rice grains.

These bugs, for those who like to eat them, are very tasty. The woodpecker sisters quickly boiled the insects and they all sat down to eat.

And rabbit thought, *how easy it is for some people to live.*

"Girls," he said, "come over and eat with me the day after tomorrow."

When the woodpecker sisters arrived rabbit took the pointed head of an eel spear and tied it to the front of his face. And rabbit started to climb up a spruce tree. But rabbit paws are not made for climbing and rabbit did not get very high. He began banging his head against the tree trunk, but rabbit did not know where the insects were hiding. And rabbit's face began to get bruised and bleeding from the pounding of the eel spear head.

The pretty woodpecker sisters laughed loudly and asked rabbit's grandmother what he was doing.

"Ah," said grandmother," I suppose he is trying to do what he has seen someone else do. It's like him."

One of the woodpecker girls stopped laughing and yelled up at rabbit," Come down here and give me your bowl, your woltes." She grabbed the bowl from rabbit and hopped right up the spruce. Pecking here and there she soon had a bowlful for them to eat.

But it was a long time after that before rabbit's face healed and even longer before the tree tapping sisters quit reminding him of hitting his head against a tree with the tip of an eel spear.

Even after this, rabbit still thought about living as other animals do and not as a rabbit does. For rabbit was very strong of will, and once his strong mind was set he would almost have to die before he changed it.

One day, while wandering in the woods, rabbit came to a bear cave, and Mooin the bear invited him in.

And rabbit asked Mooin," I have heard a story that you are able to live during the winter by sucking on your own paws. Is this so?"

Mooin did not explain, but only said, "Join us while we eat."

The bear Mooin took a huge pot and put it over the fire. He filled the pot half full with water. Then he took a knife and cut a little slice from a pad under his foot. Mooin threw the slice into the pot and it boiled and grew into a huge chunk of meat which was served to rabbit and the bear family. And there was a large piece left over which was given to rabbit to take back to his lodge.

Truly, thought rabbit, *this is a thing I can do. For it is told in wampum beads that whatever a bear can do a rabbit can do better.*

Rabbit turned to Mooin the bear and asked him, ketekewopk, to dine with him the day after tomorrow.

After bear had arrived rabbit said to grandmother, "Noogume Kuesawal wohu, set your pot to boiling." Rabbit whetted his knife and started slicing at his feet. But rabbit's soles are small and thin and he got almost nothing despite all the cutting and pain.

"What is he trying to do?" growled Mooin.

"Ah," sighed the grandmother, "something he has seen someone else do."

"Ho! You! Rabbit!," growled the bear, " give me the knife."

Bear took a small slice from his sole, which did him no harm. He threw the slice into the pot and they all ate. But rabbit was in considerable pain, and even after the pain went away he was embarrassed to remember trying to feed Mooin.

Rabbit began to understand that he was bad at imitating others, but good at persevering. He quit trying to do as others did and did as he was meant to do. Rabbit studied and gained magic power, *m'teoulin*. And it was good that he did, for he fell into great trouble with Lusifee, the wild cat. But that is a tale told by the Passamaquoddy, for another time.

THE COLLEAGUE

FARAH ALI

Mona leaned against the counter, folding her arms across her chest as she absently tapped her heel to the rhythm of the copy machine while it shot out her photocopies. Her students had a quiz next class and she only remembered this morning to print them off. As the machine continued at its staccato pace, Mona's gaze shifted out of the copy room and onto the closed door across the hall. Immediately, she felt her heart rate quicken as a knot formed in her chest.

It was her first time in this part of the building since the school year began last week, and her first time seeing that door since last May. It was a regular office door, not unlike the other office doors in the building, but it had been stripped of its previous ornaments – event flyers and a miniature print of a Picasso painting. Mona didn't know the name of the painting, only that it was definitely a Picasso, and that the woman portrayed in it had been Picasso's lover. Mona had become accustomed to seeing that painting whenever she went to the copy room, her glance impulsively falling on the distorted image, the sharp edges and bright colors almost soothing her eyes. Occasionally, the door was left open, blocking the painting from her view as she walked to the copy room, but Mona didn't mind. The open door gave her butterflies. It meant that *he* was in there. Not that they spoke much; when he was in his office he rarely ever looked up from his work, and she never had the courage to interrupt him. Their interactions happened randomly, usually in the copy room. He would occasionally run in between classes to reheat his coffee in the microwave sitting on the table adjacent to the copy machine. Considering that photocopies took about five minutes to make and reheating coffee took exactly one minute, Mona considered it an exciting treat in statistical probability whenever their coffee and copying needs coincided.

Their shared minute was always the same: he would bypass Mona to get to the microwave and set to reheating his coffee, while Mona pretended to be interested in whatever she was working on. Once the timer was set on the microwave, he would immediately turn around and smile charmingly at Mona. He would ask her how her day was going, his Boston accent cutting through the quiet humming of the microwave.

He would compliment her appearance, telling her from time to time that she looked especially nice that day. He would ask how she was settling in, if she liked the university and the town. Sometimes they would recommend movies to each other, and a few weeks later would discuss said movie. They occasionally discussed art – and in one instance Mona ventured to tell him that she loved the Picasso print on his door. He asked her once if she was single, to which Mona answered as nonchalantly as possible that she indeed was. She hoped that such a question meant that a date was in sight, but it never happened.

The Picasso was gone now – taken down by personnel, perhaps.

Mona looked at the nameplate on the door. It read "*J. McPherson.*" And the sudden image of the previous name plate – sitting at the bottom of a trash bin, probably – tightened the knot in her chest. She could deal with the fact that the janitorial staff had rearranged the furniture in her office over the summer. She could deal with the department's sudden decision to give every faculty member a photocopy quota in order to save money. But passing by the transformed door every time she needed to make copies was not something she wanted to deal with.

He had left at the end of the school year, after receiving a better job offer in Los Angeles, nearly two thousand miles away. His departure was announced at their end-of-term faculty meeting. He sat a few chairs away from Mona when the department chair broke the news, and while she clapped along with the rest of her colleagues to congratulate him, Mona felt her heart sink. They had probably spent a collective total of thirty minutes in each other's company, and that would be it.

Mona imagined him out in L.A., surrounded by noise and culture and people. Neither of them was meant to live in the provincial little town she lived in now, and for that Mona envied him a bit. He was starting over with a fresh slate, much like she did the previous year. She imagined him redecorating his office, her mind wandering back to the Picasso. Perhaps he took it with him. Mona ruefully fantasized about him giving it to her as a final, romantic gesture – a memento by which to remember him. But he did no such thing and the resulting chagrin Mona felt at inventing such a silly fantasy did nothing to soften the blow of his parting.

Her surroundings went quiet. Mona glanced back at the copy machine. Her quizzes were ready. Grabbing the stack of papers, she walked out of the copy room, slowing down in front of the closed door in order to take a quick glance through its tiny window. She wanted to see the antique map he had put up on the wall adjacent to the window. Or the hat rack he kept by the bookshelf. She wanted to see some trace of him left behind in his office. But the room was bare save for a clean desk and an empty bookshelf. Mona took a deep breath and exhaled, hoping to push some of the tension out of her chest. She kept walking.

Mona paused at the end of the hall, where the faculty mailboxes were lined up. She wasn't in the habit of checking her mailbox regularly, as most university communication could just be done electronically. In fact, she hadn't checked her mail at all since returning for the fall semester.

She pulled the knob on her box and found a small pile of flyers. While she hadn't been expecting anything, she immediately felt her heart sink. Opening a mailbox – personal or work, physical or electronic – was always disappointing when it was filled with junk mail.

She pulled out the colorful sheets of paper and shut her mailbox, glancing down at the small pile. A bright yellow flyer advertising the Spanish Club's end of the semester party…from last April. A department notice on red paper reminding faculty that grades were due May 10th. There were four duplicate flyers advertising the same event – a poetry reading being hosted by the English Department upstairs.

Mona grimaced and folded the stack of flyers in half, pressing them at the crease as she searched for a trash can. Just as she spotted one at the other end of the hall near the copy room, a smaller, thicker piece of paper fell out of her stack, face down. Mona bent down, realizing that it must have gotten stuck between one of the event flyers. She picked it up, furrowing her brows as she noticed that a small bit of tape had been stuck to the back. She turned it around and immediately broke into a smile. It was the Picasso.

THE BEAUTY OF ANOTHER WOMAN

FEYISAYO ANJORIN

I am usually fascinated by the unknown. It gets me curious, stirs the explorer in me, calls me to shine a light in the darkness. It invites me to a dark cave with its possibilities of treasures and of danger. If there is really a God as some people would want us to believe – I'm not talking about a democracy of gods according to the Yorubas and the Greeks; I mean one omnipotent, omniscient God – I don't think I would want to be that kind of being.

Sometimes I consider the burdens that would come with knowing everything. It could be boring; I guess one could be stuck in a rut with that kind of knowledge.

It is impossible for a being with limited knowledge to imagine unlimited knowledge accurately.

This idea could take hours, or even days to break down; this thing about the unknown would take the dedication of Socrates and Aristotle and Plato and those long gone guys who seemed to have all the time in the world to discuss complicated things. A friend of mine would say those ancients must have been encouraged by a particular plant. It's a possibility, isn't it? One would need their type of discipline to gain deeper insight into the unknown. If we could sit down like those philosophers, we would definitely grow enough beards to cut and trade with companies that sell hair extensions.

We would never know how many road accidents happened because a man could not take his eyes off an attractive woman.

A few years ago, I crashed my car against the fence of a compound because of a woman in miniskirt and stilettos; but I didn't reveal that to the police officer who investigated the accident. I blamed the brakes. When I got home without the car, I looked into my wife's eyes and blamed the brakes.

That is what humanity does. Sometimes, we never get to the root of things; we hardly ever get beyond facades; we depend too much on the things we can see.

Something gets our attention. We ask questions and gather facts, we get the remnants of an explosive event. We gather bits and pieces, we reason and draw conclusions. Sometimes we experiment, we observe, and then we draw conclusions; as if our brains could reliably figure everything out by observation. Where would prejudice feature in this? Where would the error of judgement feature? Where would the unknown feature in this? With experiments, how many car crashes must happen – with my ready-made blame for the brakes – before the authorities (law enforcement officials and my wife) realize I've always been distracted by beautiful women's bottoms?

What then should we do? Depend on things we cannot see? Would we not be fools to do that? Fraudsters, perverts, serial killers, mass murderers, ritual killers, all sorts of normal-looking mentally unstable people; we've seen a lot of them pointing to a god, or a voice, or a spirit, maybe a demon, as their director.

That is an aspect of the unknown I would rather not get to. I might have crashed my car because I applied my brakes when it was too late to do so; which could equally have happened if I had been admiring the clear blue sky. Why tell my wife or anyone else that I had my eyes on a curvy woman before the car went off the road?

Talking about seeing it all – or unlimited knowledge – I am not a kind of man that would prefer a naked woman to a scantily dressed beauty. A skimpy dress would make you see shapely legs as far as possible, but the invitation wouldn't have lost its magnetic mysteries. A push-up bra could do wonders for a body-fitted blouse with a low neckline – another invitation.

So, why would I not protect myself from possible persecution for the natural curiosity I have? Why not distort the truth if my natural attraction to the beauty of another woman makes my wife sad or uncomfortable?

One cold evening when the sun was already like an orange ball in the grey western sky, I was driving in an air-conditioned car along the ever-busy six-lane road that connected Akure's east and west end. The streetlights were already on, glowing behind me and ahead of me. I saw this voluptuous light-complexioned girl in white spandex miniskirt and high heels standing by the roadside. I stopped beside her, rolled down the glass and lowered my head towards her direction so that she could have a good look at my face.

She was in the car with me before I could ask where she was going – you have to understand that I was in a brand new car in a country where people throw wild parties for buying ten-year-old cars – and I could perceive that she would go with me, wherever I wanted to take her. But my pregnant wife was waiting at home. All I wanted to do that night, with the girl I got in the car with me, was lay the pipes so when I feel the need for some release, I would just dial her number and name the place.

When I was able to have a proper look at her breasts, I imagined her on top of me, moaning with a slack mouth as I grab her breasts.

"You are very beautiful." I said, swallowing like a hungry man beside his best food in a clean plate.

She gave me a slow, sleepy-eyed appraisal and smiled. "Thank you."

"You are the most beautiful woman I've seen in recent times."

"Really?"

"Yes. I know it sounds cliché, but's true. I'm not the kind that stops to pick women by the roadside. I just can't help the magnetic pull of your beauty."

"Thank you."

"What is your name?"

"Lola," she said and pouted. "What's yours?"

"Tunde."

I tried to keep my eyes away from her silky smooth laps, wondering why the night should end with just an exchange of numbers when I could just drive to a dark lonely street to seal the deal.

"Nice car."

"I just got it last week." I lied. It was my wife's car.

"You live in Alagbaka?"

"GRA."

"Oh, great." She nodded. "Tunde, thanks for your kind words and your timely help. You know, some people just drive past as if one is a ghost. And taxis hardly ever stop there. I definitely like to know you more."

I felt a sensation between my legs. It must have been the way she spoke, the way she said my name; it must have been the calm confidence, and the softness of her voice, as if I was already a lover. I felt like a rare kind man in a world full of selfish idiots. Her words reminded me of that popular Yoruba song in political rallies: "Even if you don't talk, you have won". *Boo tie soro, o ti wole.*

"Thanks." I said. "I would like to know you more you too."

I made up my mind.

She seemed a bit surprised when I turned to a darker lonely street that I knew very well. She seemed surprised but not afraid, and obviously not offended. "Where are we going?"

"I know somewhere we can park." I said with a wink. "I have a joint, and some beer in the boot."

"Wow. It's my lucky night. A man who knows how to have fun."

"Lola, this could be history in the making for the two of us."

The smile on her face, her eyes, her easy surrender, all seemed to say she was not the kind that makes any effort whatsoever to stay within rigid bounds of religion and morality. This one would suck any lollypop as if her life depended on it. I was sure.

I decided not to worry about a condom; I parked under a mango tree with many unripe fruits, and looked around to be sure we were alone. I took my phone and switched it off to make sure my wife would not interrupt the flow of things.

I got the joint from the glove compartment and got down to get the beer from the boot. That was when her voice changed; that was when she showed me the gun. That was when she jumped in the driver's seat like a gymnast.

That night, as she drove off with my car – with my heart pounding like a jungle drum and the thing between my legs already shrunk to the size of a twelve-year-old's – I knew I would have to come up with a convincing mix of fact and fiction; for my wife, and for the police.

THE FLOOD

CLARE BABBIDGE

The rain belted heavily on the window as the cool air engulfed the damp and musty room. Warm yellow lights darted sporadically through the darkness of the Georgian windows, as cars slowly made their way through the ever increasing stream of water running down the road. My head was heavy, dizzy and deafening from a high pitch ringing in my ears; my heart hit my chest rapidly and with force I had never experienced before. Screeching tyres outside broke my lull, the headlights of the speeding car glistened on a knife, the long black handle just about visible in the thick dark blood.

The lifeless face was enough to shake me from my daze, the lazy green eyes transfixed on the wall behind me, a cheekbone floating in blood, hair that was once strawberry blonde, now almost stained black. I had to escape, the clock struck 11pm, and I must have been here for at least an hour. I left the party just before 10pm. I knew it wouldn't be long before I was missed, or more importantly he would be missed. I had killed him; his blood was seeping into my white tuxedo jacket, matching my burgundy cummerbund. I tore it off, launching it towards the sofa, his eyes remained disapproving as I began to think of getting off the island that was now surely becoming isolated from the rising dirty flood water.

Life was for living and I had taken one. My own survival was now a finite option. I grabbed the knife as I stood up and rushed towards the window, wiping the blood from the blade in the bulky curtains, the stillness outside being at odds with the panic that remained inside of me.

I turned and stepped over the widening pool of blood, my hand shaking as I placed the knife in my trouser pocket, the echo of my shoes hitting the floor in the quiet of the room. The heavy wooden door was closed. I grabbed at the bulbous handle and turned it gently. I had no idea if the house was empty and the sound of my own breathing was overwhelming my ability to listen to my thoughts. Coats hung in the hallway. I pulled one off the hook and raced for the front door, my long thin frame stumbling over a rug. I opened the door and ran out into the driving rain. Water soon engulfed my feet up to my ankles as I was fiddling with the zip of my coat, my fingers too wet to grip tightly. My mouth covered by the turned up collars, the coat, too large, only really served as a temporary relief from the rain as it ran down my neck, soaking my waistcoat and shirt beneath it. I headed for what I hoped was the bridge. My suit was not the attire for a trail run.

The muscles in my legs throbbed. I took respite in a dark doorway. The island was almost deserted, the lights of what appeared to be a late night petrol station flickered in the distance; we had driven past it when we arrived. I ran my hand through my short fringe, tidying it in a bid to look less dishevelled, my breath becoming more laboured as the warm air hit the collar of my coat. I groped around my back trouser pocket, now soaked from the rain and the water lapping at my legs, I let out an audible sigh as I felt the comforting protrusion of my wallet. I sped off in the direction of the petrol station, desperate to get out of the rain.

The petrol station looked abandoned, dark with intermittent lighting, a corroded sign, and no discernible humanity. I couldn't remember having had a single logical thought since I was at the party. All I wanted was to make everything right, but I couldn't. I couldn't take any of it back. A violent ring from the entrance bell reverberated through my ears as I clattered through the door. An old man woke up with a start. The gold bell still swinging from the force of entry.

"Sorry we are closed," he announced, barely raising his body as he slumped back into the chair.

"Shouldn't you have locked up then?" I was indignant, rain water spitting out in front of me as I tried to straighten my sopping wet clothes.

"Shouldn't *you* have chosen a better night to come into a petrol station without *a* car?" his eyes remained closed and he gently rocked the stool.

"I simply wanted to make sure I was on the right road to the bridge?"

I leaned on the counter, feeling my presence, his eyes narrowed as he looked directly at me. I didn't even know if there was any blood showing. His speech was slow, the crooks in his unshaven face moved gently as he ground his teeth.

"The bridge is shut, has been for hours," his eyes met my knuckles, the blue and yellow was beginning to show.

"How do I get to the mainland then?" My voice cracked and I had to clear my throat.

"Buy a boat," his wrinkles lifted to a smirk. His shirt collar, formerly white, was almost black. He would be better off in the rain than me.

Without uttering a word I turned as a small amount of dust rose from the confectionary, the magazines dog-eared and left as clutter. People clearly didn't come here for anything other than petrol. When Sartre said Hell was other people, he wasn't wrong. I pulled the door and felt sorry for him as that shrill bell rang again; it must be enough to drive anyone into their own personal Hell.

I headed towards the structure that appeared through the fog, by now we would been missed from the party, people would be looking, people would know. Gasps of surprise from women in ball gowns, men in suits newer and better than mine would puff their chests and come looking for the culprit.

I kept moving, a solitary figure desperately fighting against the water at my feet holding back my pace. Suddenly, my arms and torso splashed heavily in the water, my breathing was hard and tight through my lungs and chest. Unsteadily I raised myself up onto my feet; pain shot through my forearm. I stopped, my mind was running faster than I ever could and wearing out my muscles harder than the gym. What would become of me? I had to get off this island and I was slowly losing the will to find my way.

My feet heavy and cold, my vision blurred, the oxygen struggling to make its way round my body. It wouldn't be long before they found me, someone found me.

Finally as the raging storm swept me over inside and out, I approached the grass banking alongside the bridge. The tall uprights jutting high into the sky, the road under a torrent of water. He may have been a grumpy old man, but he was right. I could only make out the other side of the bridge in the distance by the slowly circling blue lights. It had to be the police or coastguard, an emergency service that under normal circumstances are like a hug from an old friend.

The smooth soles of my shoes made it increasingly impossible to grip the grass; to attempt a crossing would be surely fatal; to stay and be caught would also be catastrophic. I hadn't meant to kill him and I knew that, but circumstances had overtaken me. He had raped my sister and he told me of that fact. I could never prove that to the police, not now and not then when he was alive. He had avoided justice and was mocking me for it. My suspicion about having a block of knives in the kitchen was proven right. Returning from a visit to the toilet I entered the kitchen and picked one up, hiding it behind my back as I returned to face him.

My tears were disguised by the rain as I sat slumped on the side of the river bank, the swell lapping up around me as I looked up in the sky. The stars glistened through the heavy rain, oblivious to the events below them, like a permanency of life watching down on mortal beings.

"Excuse me," I slipped as I tried to gain some purchase off the mud, fearing the worst.

"Come with me."

DYING FLY

PAUL BAMBOROUGH

FLY.

A curtain blows, scratching across the pane glass like animated scorpion tails in some old desert dream. The tiny grains of midnight sand pebble-dashing a drum roll in their skittering wake. What is it about glass that so readily holds half forgotten childhood terrors and randomly casts them into the pool of awakening consciousness? Broken through into the cold ice of awareness, the mind's cold journey back into light. Back to this place.

If there were a device to measure and compare the weights of ants and human beings on this planet, they would be exactly equal at this moment, an equilibrium of existence.

Diffused light spills out the colour of mother's milk, seeping over harsh surfaces swirling across metallic bends a dull sheen a patina of layered time dawn lying upon dawn.

The air turns invisible patterns of rotation hinting at dust's vanishing colours.

(Sigh.)

I've been trapped with a fly for 17 days now. Seems like an eternity. Initial hatred and fervent prayers for its demise have dissipated into this numb tolerance.

I have no direct knowledge of entomology, or anything else for that matter. But I'm pretty certain that flies have a shorter life span than the 17 days this tenacious demon has existed. Exist though, it certainly does, punctuating these long hours with its incessant buzzing and whirring, occasionally throwing in an irritating click as it attempts to co-exist with the glass of some unseen window.

(CLICK !)

The temperature today is as indeterminate as is the time of day or night. It is, as usual, neither cold nor hot.

The only certainty is this existence has recurred for 17 days, and so has the fly!

Sound of fly buzzes in. Fly appears and alights on nose.

Ah here it is now.

Lying here immobile, unable to move even a finger or toe. I am never the less, quite comfortable. That may be an exaggeration as both comfort and discomfort are alien notions to me. I feel neither.

Noisily, like a bread knife slicing week old bread, the fly perches, rubbing its legs together. Its persistent leg rubbing fractures my thoughts. Damn the creature and this unscratchable itch! Curse its random circling and this residual vertigo seeping into me!

I attempt movement yet again, to no avail.

When I first awoke, frantic panic gripped me. Had I been in some terrible accident, left here paralysed with amnesia? But there is no hospital smell. No undercurrent of disinfectant lying like a blanket over everything. No bodiless echo of corridor feet. No directionless squeak of rubber trolley wheels. Nothing at all. The air feels solid and as quiet as molecules, stirred only by hideous insect wings.

The ceiling above looks quite high. There is a gaping hole in its alabaster whiteness. The cracks around it seem to vaguely recall familiar topographical contours. Perhaps the past is a forgotten country. Shadowy memories gnaw at my mind like frantic rats' teeth. The hole appears to beckon a dark future, drawing me toward its echoless void.

My situation makes no sense. 17 days alone with no food or drink. I should be crying for water at least but I feel nothing, not even a bloody pulse from deep within me.

But what explains the irksome fly? What does it need to survive?

Sugar? Shit? Water? None of which seems in abundant supply in this pristine place. Yet survive and thrive it certainly does!

The fly re-alights upon my nose and continues its mesmerizing and aggravating leg rubbing.

Everything is now and of this moment. I exist neither before nor beyond it. In these 17 days there has been no minute that has not been identical to its twin, unless you throw the fly into the ointment.

No person or place dwells in my mind; just this vapid void. No clues to whom, or even what I am. Where have I come from to be here? Am I the only one? All I know is that I came to be 17 days ago, and that this is my life. Perhaps I am in a cocoon state halfway between transformations, but from what, into what?

Once more my thought pattern is broken by the fly's buzzing. In staccato flight, it hovers overhead before darting somewhere behind me. I have a burning sensation of its eyes, like giant glitter balls searing into my mind with malevolent intent.

Maybe I am being tested, or punished. I am past caring and wishing. I feel I could welcome death now. Access a switch to turn off the light within me, I know I would welcome death, to just turn off the light within me. Unbidden, a choked sob fills my throat, but the sensation passes.

The light here never changes. No days or nights, with no way of separating time. Somehow though, I know I have been here for 17 days. Every elasticated hour, each aching minute and endless second of it.

A dull echo seems to sound in the distant reaches of my mind. Perhaps that's what I am, some form of a sophisticated chronograph. But I can discern no mechanical clockwork playing understudy to my silent heartbeat.

I long to sleep, to dream, and fall into some other land scape. Instead, rolling my eyes in my head just replays an image of the ceiling's gaping hole, bible black and foreboding. An empty orbit in the Reaper's skull.

A quiet bubble of envy swells within me for this dread fly! It's mobility in flight, its ability to flit from place to place, even though it seems to be as fettered here as me.

I would give my eyes for a different perspective, an alternate angle, a change of ceiling. A different crack, a prettier hole. This is how small my ambitions have fallen. I don't ask for the moon or even a glimpse of it, just a pleasanter view. Or failing that, another noise to replace the tiny wind of insect wings, and their incessant buzzing!

A pulsating, far off hum approaches, growing in intensity.

What wonderful eyes has the fly, a veritable honeycomb of black lattice triangles, a myriad of geometrical designs. It must see hundreds of the same image simultaneously. That's a lot of input going somewhere, where? Do flies have brains? The thought is both ludicrous and intriguing. Do brains in turn signify sense? If so, then this one has more than I, lying here immobile and mute, while carefree and unthinking it flits hither and thither.

I yearn to call out! To scream, or make some sound other than this voiceless, internal sighing.

What was I before this? A nurse, a child, dancer, soldier, queen, king, murderer?

A collage of eyes, seemingly familiar, swim and merge in revolution carousel by my mind. I don't care what I was before, I just long to be some other. But things could be worse.

My companion could be a spider or a centipede, seeing my exposed nostrils as some ideal home.

My nostrils? How am I breathing? My lips feel sealed. Am I breathing? Perhaps this is death, this vapid void. A soulless limbo.

I sense a hot sensation probing inside my mind like an alien presence.

FLY:

MOVEMENT TWISTING, MOVEMENT, MOMENTUM, CONSTANT VIBRATING MOTION, HEADLONG, FLIGHT TWISTING, TURNING, SPINNING, SILENCE,ICE ON GLASS, SLIDING, MOMENTS STRETCHING ETERNAL, TRANSIENT,FIGURE EIGHT, SKITTERING, UPSIDE DOWN, TOPSY-TURVY, AERONAUTICS, PLANES FLAT, UNI-DI-MENSIONAL, GRAVITY, DEFYING, DARE DEVIL GYRA-TIONS, KALEIDOSCOPIC IMAGERY, DIAMOND VISIONS, FRANTIC, FRENETIC, FAST FORWARD, FANCY, FLEEING, FOOTSTEPS, FEARLESSLY, FOOTLOOSE, AIR IN CON-STANT MOVEMENT OF ITSELF, FLICKERING COLOURS, ABSTRACT PATTERNS IN PERPETUAL MOTION, MERRY GO ROUNDS OF DENSE SWIRLING FORMLESS SHAPES, ETHER CHAMELEON CHANGES, OZONE, A VERITABLE CACOPHONY OF BLOCK FUGUES, HELTER SKELTER, HELIXES OF PASTEL RAINBOWS, DELICIOUS SENSUAL SENSATION OF PREENING, HAIR AGAINST HAIR, EACH SEPARATE VIBRATING FOLLICLE EXCITES AS IT RUBS AGAINST ANOTHER, SENSING AS AN INDIVIDUAL STIM-

ULI, ANY TINY MOVEMENT IN THE FLOATING UNIVERSE OF THIS MICROCOSM THAT MAY BRING DANGER, PYROTECHNIC TRANSLUCENT FIREWORKS, EXPLODING SOFTLY AS THE FIRST BLOOM FLOWERS, SWIMMING IN THE DRY SEA OF FLOWING THERMALS, LOOSELY BOUND TOGETHER IN RIBBONS OF CURRENT, DRIFTING HAPHAZARDLY ON THE WHIMS OF CHANCE, UNBOUNDED BY LAWS OF PURPOSE OR REASON, UNLIMITED, THE FREEDOM OF CLOUDS SET AGAINST AZURE SKIES, MOVING IMPERCEPTIBLY IN THE GRANDEUR OF A MOMENTOUS INEVITABILITY, ALL THE TIME I AM THE DANCER, SPEEDING PAST AND THROUGH, A LIVING BULLET PROPELLED ONLY BY THE DESIRE TO SEE AND BE PART OF THE GOSSAMER CANVAS OF ITS UNFRAMED GLORY, FIRST ONE WAY THEN THE OTHER, A PROJECTILE ON INVISIBLE TRACKS.

HAR HAR! I BUSILY CRY. I AM, WHAT I DO - I AM FLY!

A strange confusion of thought holds me transfixed like an astral projection or too specific an imagining, transposing me into a dimension of my nemesis. But almost as soon as it is upon me, it dissipates. The experience drifts into the background, replaced by the endless cycle of these prickling thoughts.

Temporarily the fly returns to my nose, before seconds later, like an antiquated helicopter, the devil is airborne again.

An increasing deepening despair seeps into me. The crack above now takes on a baleful, glowing, malevolent grin.

Wait...what's this? A strange humming, undulating rhythm, like far off water lapping from some distant shore. A fleeting image of kneeling in the summer sands as a childhood seaside memory washes over me.

The silence enshrouds me, somehow feeling heavier now.

Lying bathed in this total emptiness fills me like a meditation, a rhapsody, a perversely empty pleasure, drowning me in the consuming nothingness of the moment, before the fly returns and turns all thought into wisps of empty black smoke.

Suddenly, an all-consuming rage burns in me; a hollow flame. An unrequited longing to burst forward, to scream and kill the creature. But ironically I remain as motionless as the creature is animated. This helplessness tips into me and fills me with disgust! I can feel my rage turning back in on me. An unutterable sigh builds, before shattering like glass in my mind. I am again left lying here, impotent, cold and bleeding out this desperation.

The fly turns on my nose like a dog settling in its circle.

FLY:

PINKS, MERGE IN WHITE, SILVER, GOLD, ULTRA VI-
OLET, AQUA MARINE, TURQUOISE, PURPLES, TURNING,
SPHERES ORBITING, MICROSCOPIC PLANETS, TWIRLING,
GLITTERING, FLOATING, TWISTING ON UNSEEN AXIS,
ZIPPING THROUGH A CANDYFLOSS SOFT CONFECTION-
ERY OF REFLECTING JEWELS, HYPNOTIC AND IRRESIST-
IBLY SEDUCTIVE, SKITTER AND SKELTER, SKIMMING
INTO THEM AGAIN AND AGAIN, FUSING AND BLENDING
TOGETHER, THEN APART, PASSING THROUGH THEM AS
THEY PASS THROUGH ME, DELIGHTFUL TRIANGLES,
DIAMONDS AND INVERTED PYRAMIDS, SQUARES AND
RECTANGLES, CHASING AND CHANGING, TURNING TO
FILL INVISIBLE HOLES WITHIN THE SHIFTING MELEE.

I REJOIN THE ETERNAL COSMIC MOLECULAR DANCE.
A SMALL NOTE WITHIN THE MUSIC OF THE SPHERES,
UNDULATING ROLLER COASTER MICROCOSMIC RIDE.

As I come back to myself the sense of a separate existence dissipates, but far off sounds of lapping water somehow return more insistent this time, a throbbing in the stillness.

The fly senses a changing too. Its whirling and swooping appear even more berserk.

Excitement and dread rise up in equal parts before recoiling back in restraint. A temporal climax looms, outstretched upon a passionate horizon.

The fly flits in and out of my vision, a disconcerting, flickering strobe of motion. The very air about me becomes agitated. It whirls and eddies on invisible tides.

Suddenly! I am awash in a glowing luminescence, as two angelic figures all in white, loom over my view.

The fly flees before them, and I can sense my salivation. At last, a human voice breaks my reverie.

(Moments before);-

TWO MEN IN WHITE STERILE BODY SUITS ENTER

THE ANIMATION CHAMBER. A FLASHING STASIS SIGN
BY THE DOORS THEY HAVE ENTERED BLINKS 'BREACH'
AS THEY WALK IN.

They walk straight over to the girl lying on the bed, surrounded by
tubes and dials. The plastic case covering her has a large hole in it, over
her head. As one of them presses a button to release the damaged cano-
py, a fly dashes up between their startled faces.
The elder of the two looks to his assistant, face red with anger.

"Davis! This deck is supposed to be sterile! How on earth has that
fly gotten in here?"

His assistant returned the look with a furrowed brow. He shrugs
before looking up at the damaged ceiling where a piece of dislodged
concrete reveals the inner darkness of the room's
structure.

"I've no idea sir."

Walks over to figure on bed
Looks up at hole in ceiling then down at the head.

DAVIS:

"Oh Shit!"

MORTON joins him, inspecting the head. They jointly peer into
the exposed brain, the girl laying bone still on the suspended animation
bed. An oozing mass of grey matter has become re-animated by the
mass of crawling maggots inside.

MORTON:

(Appalled & disgusted)

"Great Caesar's Ghost! How in the name of all that's holy..."

DAVIS:

(Timidly)

"It must have been that quake 17 days ago."

Points at ceiling.

MORTON:

(Shouting)

"You mean you haven't checked in here for over two weeks?"

DAVIS:

(Alarmed)

"It's been hectic Sir, what with the…"

MORTON:

(Interrupting)

"I don't care man. Get this cleaned up."

Turns to leave.

MORTON:

"And kill that bloody fly!"

Momentarily…I wonder silently…what colour is dust?

END?

A NORMAL LIFE

CHRISTINE BENEDICT

Debra's hands were small, delicate, the kind of hands that could fit inside a mayonnaise jar. She had bitten her fingernails down to the quick. She had picked at her cuticles and bit them, too, tearing fine strips of skin. She wanted so badly to stop. It was ugly. It hurt. But she bit them anyway.

Through heavy traffic she got lost, driving through a blowing rain. The wind whistled through a window that wouldn't close all the way. A brick building loomed ahead. Her stomach tightened. She could feel her hands shaking. They'd told her shock treatment therapy was standard treatment for the most baffling cases, the first step to a normal life.

The facility towered over a barbed wire perimeter where a long stretch of field surrounded it. She parked and somehow found herself in an elevator. She pushed the button for the 23rd floor, the psychiatric ward. The elevator ascended higher and higher in conjunction with Debra's rising pulse. She inhaled, slow and deliberate. She exhaled, easy and purposefully. She had lost count of how many times she was taken away as a child and placed in a foster home. Doctors would play with her mom's medication and she would seem okay for a while, so social services would give Debra back. Then her mom would start drinking again and would stop taking her meds because she said she was fine, and it would start all over.

33

An armed guard frisked Debra like a common criminal, guided her through an iron gate, leaving her on her own to find room A312 down the long narrow hall, the heaviness of her heart, thumping, pulsing. She passed the nurses station, the cage that surrounded it.

Debra tried to nudge past a big-bellied nurse and an unkempt man who took up the whole hallway. An unlit cigarette in his mouth, a lighter in his hand, his vacant eyes where shadowed in black.

"No. You can't smoke right now," The nurse commanded. "Wait 'till I take your temperature."

The man grunted a word, his voice too low to hear. The nurse snatched his lighter, and she shoved the thermometer in his mouth.

He bit down hard. Debra heard the glass break.

"What did you do? Spit that out!" The nurse yelled, fighting against his hands. "Call Doctor Strong! Stat!" He didn't fight back so much as he kept his mouth shut.

"Calling Doctor Strong … Calling Doctor Strong – Ward five," echoed over the PA. Suddenly an armed guard rushed in, then another. Debra crept further away, watching them strong-arm the frantic patient, watching the guards pin him down. Amid the yelling and screaming, she made her way to room 312. In the doorway she looked inside, and saw the cot-like beds in the cramped room were bolted to the floor. It was eerie seeing her mother string beads there, as if each one were a rare jewel. Hardly recognizable, her hair was pinned up, white strands at her temples.

"Mom?"

Aida jumped, startled, spilling her box of beads. "My… my … m…" She seemed stuck on one word. She stopped, her glazed eyes fixed on the wall.

"Mom, it's me." Debra said from the doorway, suddenly feeling guilty but not knowing why. Aida dropped to her knees, chasing beads under the bed. The woman who shared her room scooted inside the doorway behind Debra.

"They messed with her brain, you know," the woman informed, digging in a used-up Kotex box on a shelf. "Do you have a match?" she asked, fingering a cigarette.

"I don't smoke." Debra kept her eyes on her mother.

"Poop. Everyone else has a lighter, but they took mine. Isn't that asinine? All I did was tell that idiot scrub woman that I could set fire to these curtains just as good with a lighter as I could with a match."

"Really?"

"She told me to hand it over. I told her I was allowed to have it. I told her it was mine. She tried to take it away. It was mine. Do you know what they did then?" The woman's straw-like eyebrows straggled to the wrinkle lines in her forehead as she spoke; the fat on her arms swayed with every move of her hand. "They called Doctor Strong. You know what that means?"

Aida broke in, her words monotone, "Every able bodied man – get to the psyche ward." Aida seemed to know where she was now. "They jumped her all at once and crucified her to a gurney. They've done it to all of us. It was just your turn," she said to the woman, a haunting laugh lingering. She turned her head to Debra. "Wait 'till it's your turn."

Debra couldn't be fazed. At least she wouldn't show it. Aida rose up. She came up close.

"You smell like me," Aida sniffed.

"That's wild," came from Debra. This didn't seem real.

"Don't get smart with me. I'm still your mother," Aida worked hard for each word. "This is your fault."

Debra's breaths came in stops and starts. She blamed herself. It wasn't her fault but she blamed herself just the same. Aida claimed she killed Bill to protect her. Aida pled insanity at the trial which brought her here. And maybe she was insane. Debra kept quiet. Insane or not, trying to reason with her mother was the same as trying to reason with a drunk. She just didn't get it, no matter how much she wanted her to. "Mom," Debra said calmly. She would put a spin on it. She would turn it around. "I love what you've done to your hair."

"Just who do you think you are?"

Debra smiled politely, her insides wrenched. "It was nice to see you again. I have to go now," she rounded up a seemingly cordial visit, turning her back. It hurt so badly, first to see her mother this way, and then be assailed. Her mother's memory would awaken in bits 'till she could accept her lot in life. That was the call to come. Debra was one of those bits.

"Debby I'm sorry. Don't go." Aida wrung her hands nervously, prattling on. "Please. Don't do this. I'm your mother. Please don't leave me here."

Debra focused straight ahead, the click of her shoes echoing within the hall as she walked away. She would be strong. She would blink back the wet in her eyes, and she would be strong.

"Debby. Please. I love you. You're all I have."

Debra stopped. She bounced a glance off the gate and at her mother. This was the woman who would knock her to the floor. The woman who would sit on her chest, grab her hair and pound her head on the floor, in a psychotic frenzy.

But that was another life.

She returned and told her mother she loved her. She said she'd stay longer next time. "Next time you'll feel better." Looking into Aida's eyes, she could see they were empty now, electric-shock empty.

A guard unlocked the chain-link door. Debra kissed her mother, and squeezed through the door.

Inside the ladies' room, she brought herself back to the present. 'Aida's insanity belongs to Aida. Not me.' She took deep breath. 'Disconnect. Disconnect.'

'A mentally ill person is like someone who's drowning - they'll drag you under. You've got to let go.' The caseworker told her so. She splashed cold water on her face telling herself, 'settle down.' Drying, she mindlessly tugged at her lashes until a tight bunch fell down her cheek. She rubbed her fist in her eye, stopping herself from pulling out any more. In the mirror she filled in the bald spot with eyeliner, like always.

Out in the corridor a nurse came up to Debra. "It's hard. I know it's hard." She took Debra's hand. "Aida is stabilizing. She's coming around." The nurse's hand was soft, her skin loose with age, small like Debra's.

"Aren't they done with shock treatment? You'd think it'd be illegal in this day and age."

"Oh Honey. You're thinking about the movies. It's not like that. They get sodium pentathlon just like they would for any surgery. She'll get her memory back, a little at a time, until it's all manageable for her." The nurse cradled Debra's hand in her own. "You've been through a lot. Haven't you?"

Debra looked down and back. "I'm alright now."

The nurse studied her face, her hazel eyes. "How did you get to be so normal?"

'Normal' was more like a trick that she'd learned to master. She would pull out her eyelashes. She would bite her cuticles 'till her fingers bled. It was as close to normal as she would ever be, so she said the only thing that made any sense, "By the grace of God." And she meant it. She meant every word. Her life could have been so different. She could have been like her mother.

CHANGING SARAH

TRACY GARDNER BENO

"Why is he here?" I peer across the hall into room 186. My new patient lay facing the wall, lying under the thin hospital blanket.

Gina looks at me. "What do you mean, here?"

"Here. He's from … I don't know, the middle east? How did he wind up here?"

My coworker pulls her log from her scrub pocket. "I told you. He's like, a captain or something in the army over there and he got blown up. They had to reconstruct his whole shoulder and right arm. Part of his jaw. His right leg was shattered. I guess he needed the specialists here."

I don't speak the angry words on my tongue: what earned him the use of our surgeons? Fighting in a war I can't understand, one which has cost me so much?

"Whatever. Thanks lady, get out of here and get some rest," I toss over my shoulder, heading down the hall to start my rounds. The day-shift nurses are wrapping up, giving report and scrambling to finish charting.

"Sarah," Gina matches my stride. "He doesn't know a word of English. And he's pretty miserable with all the drains and hardware," she motions around her right side, neck to fingertips. "Just keep close, okay?"

I soften. "I will. Don't worry."

Gina looks mildly relieved. She's new; only been here a year. She doesn't know me, not really. She doesn't need to warn me. I am a good nurse.

I'm just not in a hurry to meet my new patient.

An hour later, when I get to his room, he is sitting up in bed watching the doorway as I enter. He looks like an animal – a wild, cornered animal, eyes wide and black, mouth drawn down grotesquely on the right from the swelling and sutures that extend from his collar bone to his reconstructed jaw. He is thin and lanky, one boney knee drawn up under the sheet, making him look much smaller than before.

I stand at the foot of his bed, shrugging off the guilt that tries to snake up my spine at leaving him for last; he is clearly in pain. He cradles his bandaged right arm with his left hand, body rigid. I see, poking out from the gauze at his wrist, the external brace the surgeon created just for him: metal talons extending out over each finger, 5 small titanium pins securing each hinged rod through the back of his hand to the bones.

My eyes meet his and I could cry. He hasn't said a word, but I am not sure he can. "I'll get your pain medicine."

When I return, he is in the same exact position, perfectly still. I inject the morphine through the port in his IV line, and watch, gratified, as I see his posture relax within moments.

I know I spend more time than I have available helping him get comfortable. A heated blanket, a pillow to prop his damaged arm upon, and ice chips on the bedside table, which is bare but for the hospital brochure and a Styrofoam cup. No cards, no flowers. No family in this country.

I place the call button in his good hand. "Push this if you need anything."

He frowns at it, at me. Sets it down on the bed.

Well shit. Has nobody been able to make him understand how this works? No English. Bet we don't have a translator on hand. Later, around midnight, I'll learn that we have Spanish and French, despite the requirement we be able to communicate with all patients. I try again.

"Safet," I start, and he pats my arm.

"Sah – fet," he says, his voice hoarse and gravelly, and he places a hand on his chest. Emphasis on the "fet." I try it out, and he nods. Safet points to my name tag, raises his eyebrows.

I notice now that his pain has finally diminished, that he is a nice looking man. Or was. The right side of his face is still swollen and raw, and his head is mostly shaved on that side. But his eyes are kind, no longer those of an animal caught in a trap.

I point to my tag as well. "Sarah. Sarah," I say, slower, and he repeats it. "You've got it. Listen," I put the call button back in his hand and close his long fingers around it. "If you hurt …" I grip my own arm, making a face, hunching over. "Push this," I say, straightening up and touching the red button. "If you hurt, I will come."

He nods at me, testing it out.

"Yes." I hit the reset switch. "Okay, Safet?"

I get a lopsided smile for my efforts. "Okay," he tells me, a whispered agreement.

***

Safet watches me tape the poster to the wall opposite his bed. It is his third day here. I am off tomorrow. Someone else will be his nurse. I can't draw. The pictures next to each phonetically spelled word could have been rendered by a five year old. It works anyway.

"Juice," he croaks, pointing at the chart, my crooked glass colored in with yellow marker. "Please," he says, and I stare at him. That one isn't on the list. I want to say I won't see him tomorrow, but can't quite figure out how.

When I return on Saturday, I find him up in a chair, casted right leg propped out in front of him, and a pencil gingerly clutched in his broken hand. The external traction barely allows it, but he is somehow sketching. I startle him, he is so deep in concentration; over his shoulder I see the faint outline of a woman's profile, strong jaw, soft lips. His wife? I realize I know nothing about him.

"This is so good," I nod to the paper, and he looks up at me.

"I was …" he sighs. He lets go of the pencil, frowning. "I was …." Safet makes motions in the air with his good hand, long strokes, painting.

"A painter? An artist?"

He nods. "Artist. I was." He swipes his hand across the paper, then crumples it and drops it into the trash can, eyes cast downward. I can feel frustration coming off him in waves.

"You are," I say, waiting until he looks at me. The unfinished portrait he made with his broken hand was better than anything I'd ever been able to draw. "You still are."

I know he doesn't understand. The next day, I round the corner onto my unit with excitement and head straight for his room. I can't wait for him to see what's in the small cardboard box under my arm: charcoal pencils, heavy drawing paper, paints and a few brushes.

The sight of him stops me in my tracks. Safet is sitting in bed, eyes on the wall-mounted television, tears streaming down his face. His good arm is wrapped around his knee and his shoulders shake with sobs I can hardly hear. I move to his bedside, looking to see what in the world he is watching.

It's war footage. It's a live feed on some news channel: chaos, screaming, women and kids and buildings on fire, gunshots in the background. The streaming caption across the bottom declares a state of emergency, citing numbers: dead, wounded, civilian casualties, too many numbers.

I pick up the remote to turn it off and he stops me, gently covers my hand.

"No." He looks at me, tortured, and then back at the screen, shaking his head.

I pull up a chair and press a tissue into his hand. I rub his back, making slow circles, trying to soothe him. It is all I can do. He's mourning someone, maybe his whole family, and punishing himself for being here, safe.

When he finally sinks back into the pillows, turning on his side, I wait until his eyes are closed and turn off the news. I am blissfully, woefully unaware of what Safet and his family have been through. I can imagine it, but I know only my own sad piece of the tragedy happening there. I pull the blanket over his curled up frame, frown still painted between his brows in sleep. The cardboard box stays where I dropped it, on his nightstand.

***

Safet is going home. It isn't home, but it will be. Housing is arranged just outside Detroit. Yesterday I watched him read the letter detailing how his wife and daughter have safely fled, will arrive in the city soon.

I remove the last of the bandages, marveling at his hand. It, like the rest of him, bears scars. But it works. Safet captures mine between his.

I meet his eyes. He is leaving, and leaving me changed.

"Thank you Sarah." He places a small painting in my hand: a watercolor bird, bright and vivid against a dark gray sky.

STIFF AS BOARDS

S.B. BORGERSEN

The line of wash crackles in the freezing salt wind. "Stiff as boards," Ma says as she unpins the ice encrusted flannel shirts, letting them fall like planks of cedar into the old tin bath she uses as a laundry basket.

How her fingers don't freeze to its metal handles as she hauls it back across the frozen waste that is our lawn in summer, I'll never know. But in she comes, cheeks the rosiness of the huckleberry pasture in the fall, lips as blue as Da's old coveralls, kicking the kitchen door behind her with her booted foot. She plonks the old tin bath on the floor and repeats herself, "stiff as boards."

"Just smell the sea." She grins, "smell Da's ole shirt, isn't that just the smell of The Narrows?"

Then she thrusts the 'stiff as boards' clothes under our noses and we, as we know we must, smell. With loud sniffs to please her. Nicky snorts, he sniffs so well. Benny laughs at him. A broad laugh showing all his teeth; looking more like Da every day.

Then we sit around the table while Freda, good and steady Freda, butters the mountain of hot tea biscuits she's taken from the oven just moments ago. Arms reach, as they have done since we were little kids, in competition to reach the platter first. To grab the hot biscuits and cram them in our mouths before the butter melts. Before it trickles down our chins.

Freda smiles and pours steaming tea from the big brown pot into our blue enamel mugs that all say 'Admiral' on the side.

Da won them in a dory race years ago. Back and forth across the gut, ten times. Middle of summer. Arms muscle-bulging. Face redder than the rosy knobs out on the island. Sweat pouring down his bare back like the Niagara Falls. Or at least like the pictures I've seen of the falls in last year's calendar. The day he won was a day for celebration. And he came home with the box of mugs, giving one to each of us four kids and Ma. "Well," he said, "I can only drink out of one at a time, cannot I?" And with that he turned to the jug of screech and poured himself a healthy dose, downing it in one before collapsing with exhaustion on the old swing chair on the stoop.

I can see him now, and I know Ma sees him every day too. We miss the old guy. Drunk or sober, we miss him. That's why we all still wear his shirts to this day. So we can feel him close, remember the good days, and forget the day he went out on the scallop dragger to the George's Bank. It was the 30th January. The day it went down. 14 hours out so heavy with ice it just sank with all five crew. Including Da.

"Come on now Callie, let's not sit here dreaming. Help me give this lot a shake out so we can fold 'em," says Ma.

I get up from the table and as I shake and fold the frozen wash, I smell the sea. And Da.

LIKE A SOUL

KAREN BOVENMYER

This story was first published in The Stonecoast Review 8/1/13.

Me and Mamma went to see the pod in the hayloft just before sunrise—it spun out of the shadows ever so slow, sheen glittering in the pale light, all black and dotted with gold. The pod looked like a little jewel, something a rich man wore on his neck, but when I reached to take it down, Momma caught my arm and hugged me close. "Leave it. Butterfly gonna hatch out of it."

I didn't know what she meant, not then, because hatching wasn't ever a good thing. Not here. Not with the Clickers.

We moved quick when we came down, so the Overseer wouldn't catch us. Everyone had to be outside the barn by sunrise. If somebody weren't on time, or was maybe drunk or sick, he got whipped. If somebody went missing and the Overseer thought he'd ran off, his kin were whipped until he was found. Almost nobody took a chance like that.

The Clickers hung Jefferson from a tree when they thought his brother was gone—him gone only two days, and the Clickers killed Jefferson just to show everyone they could. Then they found his brother anyhow. Lettie said he went for a piss in the night and fell down into the river and died—but Momma said maybe he jumped. Maybe he thought he could swim past the Clickers. But nobody ever got away. We were trapped, waiting like that butterfly inside that pod, maybe fixin' to hatch into something else. Anyway, both of them were dead for no reason at all. All the Clickers stomped up a big fit, snapping their saw-tooth jaw-bones, clacking their graspers together.

But they didn't eat no one, and nobody hatched. Not that time.

When Jefferson hung from that tree, the morning rays lit up a sheen in the sweat across his thick face. But there weren't no gold dots. And there weren't no jewel at all about Jefferson. Lettie said it's been goin' on a year or more since someone split open to show a Clicker living inside, all white bones and graspers and grabbing arms. An uncommon long time and time for it to happen soon. Clickers hide deep inside folks, and nobody knows until someone starts screaming and the Clicker splits out and scares everyone. Then the big ones come to take the new one away. Lettie said it doesn't matter. Someday we all gonna hatch Clickers, because that's how they make young. That's what we're for.

Momma said that didn't have to be true, that we aren't all going to hatch into Clickers. She said so up in the hayloft when she saw that pod.

"Rudy, do you know what's in that pod?" We watched it together.

"Butterfly," I said, just like she told me. "He's gonna fly out of here."

"That's right," she said. "Fly up, up and away. Like a soul."

"He's gonna die?" I knew souls were things that flew away from people when they died, God said so. Lettie said a soul and a Clicker can't live inside a person at the same time.

"Yeah. He's gonna die. But first he'll fly up out of this pod and look over the whole wide world. He'll find a girl butterfly and make babies, and then he'll die, just like he ought to." Then she hugged me again and rubbed my arms.

But I thought about that. Jefferson had no business being hung. Letty said so, and she got a slap 'cause of her mouthin' off. But she only said what we were all thinking. If the Overseer had just waited, the Clickers would'a only lost one man, not two.

"Why does he have to die?" I said.

"'Cause that's what God made him for."

"Then why'd God make Clickers?"

She didn't answer, just hugged me to her again, so I decided maybe God wasn't the one who made them. "Nothing lasts forever, Rudy. Not you, not me, not the butterflies. Not even the Clickers. Everyone has to say goodbye sometime."

I nodded my head against her chest, hearing her heartbeat under my ear, feeling the drops of her tears tickle the back of my neck. But I didn't want to listen. I didn't want that butterfly to hatch and fly away and die.

That night, I walked in the dark and I stole the pod. I wanted him to stay black and beautiful and glittering. I wanted him to stay safe in my palm. So I carried him around with me, in my pocket.

I had him with me through the long hours of working in the field. I hid him during bath time. I tucked him in my pocket when it was time for cookin' and eatin'. I even put him in my mouth once when the Clickers came and touched us all with their forearms, poking and rubbing, spending extra time on me like they knew I was hiding something. He tasted like dried leaves. At bedtime I held him close to my ear to see if I could hear that soul inside getting ready to fly away.

He was in my pocket the morning Momma was gone.

They looked for her everywhere. They tied my ankles to a stool in the middle of the yard. I felt so bad my stomach hurt something awful. Every time a search party came back with no Momma, the Overseer hit me real hard trying to make me scream. If she was hiding, she'd come running.

I tried not to—but I screamed after all, and loud too, because the Clickers came and snapped and poked at me. But they didn't string me up, just left me tied there and hurting.

Lettie limped up and gave me some water when no one was looking, and gave me some bread, but she couldn't do more—and I couldn't eat it anyway, my guts feeling all upside down. I had to stay there tied to that stool 'til they found Mama.

At night I cried. Then I found the little pod in my pocket and turned it over and over again, waiting, just like that butterfly, for sunrise.

In the morning I held it up to the light and the sun shone right through it. I saw all that glossy black was thin as paper. Something started pushing the sides like a flower blooming, coming out striped orange and black. A crumpled ball sort of fell down like a drop, its wings soaking wet like it was in the river. It clung to the pod in my hand and rocked there, the wings getting bigger, flatter, fanning themselves, while the sun got higher, brighter.

I heard a *click, clack, clack*. I looked over into the edge of the woods and saw a big group of Clickers coming, carrying something black that glistened in the light. It was Momma, but she was all wet. She was all limp and her eyes were staring. She wasn't split open and there was no Clicker wiggling out of her. She didn't move at all.

I looked back down to the butterfly in my hand. I didn't want to look at Momma. The wings were full flat fans now.

Lettie came over to me with tears washing her face and the Overseer took off his hat and nodded his head. Someone untied me from the stool.

I looked at the butterfly. It fanned its wings and took off, flying up, up over my head and above the barn. Like a soul.

And something deep inside me cracked open.

DILEMMA

JOE BROADMEADOW

My cell rang. I didn't recognize the number. Thought about ignoring it, then decided to give the telemarketer some shit.

"Hello."

"Tommy, this is AJ."

"AJ? What's this a new phone?"

"I need your help." AJ's tone imparted a more serious patina to the four simple words.

"You always need my help," I answered. "What is it this time, did you get thrown out again?"

"Come outside, I'm parked in the lot across the street.

"Why are you parked across the street?" I asked. Silence. After a moment, I realized he'd ended the call.

Grabbing my jacket, I walked to the door. "Where are you off to?" My wife questioned.

"I don't know. That was AJ, said he needs help with something."

My wife put her hands on her hips, "Tommy, I don't care what he's done this time, no money. Promise me."

I smiled, "No money, I learned my lesson with his last scam," I opened the door, the cool fall air rushing in. "I'll be right back."

Walking down the driveway, I looked across the street. AJ was leaning against the hood of his car, arms folded around himself from the cold, staring at the ground. As I got closer, he heard my footsteps and stood straight.

I've read that ninety percent of communication is non-verbal. AJ's body was telling me this was not one of his ordinary, self-created problems.

"Hey man, what's up?"

"Tom, Tommy," AJ stuttered, glancing around. "I need help buddy. Big time. Can you take a ride with me?"

I saw something in his eyes I'd never seen before; genuine fear. This was a man who once took on three bikers in a bar and got his ass kicked. He returned two days later looking for the three bikers. The same thing happened. He went back several more times, but the bikers never showed up again.

They must have recognized crazy. AJ wasn't afraid of anything.

"A ride, where?"

"Please man, just come with me." His body language was now in full alarm mode.

"Ah, okay. Let me call Karen. Tell her I'll be gone for a bit. Where we going anyway?"

"No," AJ shouted, then glanced around. "No calls."

"No calls?" I replied. "If you want me to go with you I will after I call my wife. A philosophy you should have adopted years ago and saved yourself a ton of trouble."

I could see AJ's mind racing as he paced back and forth. "Okay, tell her I need help moving something, that's all."

I stood there a moment, holding my phone, studying my now frantic friend. Shaking my head, I pushed the call button. "Hey, it's me. AJ needs me to help him move something. What? I don't know, hang on," holding the phone away from my ear I asked him, "She wants to know what you need moved. How long will it take?"

AJ threw his arm up, slapping them back to his side. "I don't know, something heavy. You'll be back in, ah, a couple of hours."

"There's a bunch of stuff, I guess. Won't take long," listening to her response I smiled at AJ. "Yeah I know, no bars and no scams; I don't have any money anyway. I'll call on the way back." I walked to the passenger side. "Okay AJ, tell me the story. What'd you do?"

"First, turn off your cell."

"I'm not turning off my cell, asshole. What is this about?"

"Look, trust me on this. You'll understand shortly," pointing with his hand at my phone. "Turn it off and pull the battery. Then I'll tell you what this is about."

I did as he asked, but kept questioning as we drove.

"You what?" I said, shaking my head and looking out the window. "I don't believe this. You're kidding," trying to gage the look on his face.

"I'll show you," he said as we pulled into a dirt road used by off-road vehicles.

"You can't drive this thing down here," I said, my hand on the dash as AJ dodged the ruts and dips in the dirt track.

"Yes I can, I checked this out before."

"You checked this out… I don't believe this."

Checking the rearview mirror, AJ drove several hundred yards. Making sure we were far beyond the houses bordering the property.

"Ready?"

"AJ, please tell me this is all bullshit." "Look," he said, opening the door.

I watched as he walked around to the back of the car, motioning for me to join him

I opened the door, put one foot on the ground, glanced over my right shoulder at AJ as he looked all around the area.

I got out and stood next to him. "Ready?"

I laughed. "Okay, you got me. What's the joke?"

I heard the click of the trunk release, watching as it popped up. AJ reached over, opening the trunk.

As I looked in, my mind went into denial.

I looked from the trunk to AJ and back. Voices in my head screamed, '*Run, you idiot, run.*" But my legs remained paralyzed in place. I tried to speak, but my throat was sand. I tasted the adrenaline rushing through my body. The fight or flight response to my brain was recognizing a problem.

A big problem.

"I had to do it, Tommy. He beat her, put her in the hospital. He molested my granddaughter."

Words eluded me. I backed away, trying to absorb the reality. "Tommy, I need you to help me here. I need help getting rid of it."

For fifty years, AJ had been my best friend. We had grown from GI Joes and baseball to girls and beer to married with kids, together. We'd spent twenty years together as cops, righting wrongs, trying to make a difference.

He'd been there when my first wife died of cancer. He held me in his arms, covered in my blood from the bullet wound in my arm, when they drove me to the hospital.

Never leaving my side.

But this? This was beyond it all. This was too much. I knew the stories. The hospital visits to see his daughter. The on again off again boyfriend sliding through the system.

But this? They say friends will be there when you most need them. But this?

As my heart rate slowed, the rationale me resumed control. The panic passed and the realization of the choice I faced came clear.

I knew what I had to do.

I looked at my friend. The tears welled up, the emotions uncontrollable. I took a deep breath and walked back to the car.

"AJ, I'm sorry." I reached into my pocket and pulled out my phone, walking to the side of the car, away from my best friend.

His eyes showed regret as the enormity of what he asked of me, of what he'd done, set in.

I tossed the phone on the seat. Reaching into the back seat, I grabbed the two shovels and the bag of lime. I'd spotted them when I got in the car. Hoping I was wrong.

Walking to AJ, I handed him a shovel. "That's what friends are for."

KINDNESS

MATTHEW BROCKMEYER

When Jack and Margie returned home from the funeral, they found that someone had spray-painted *BE KIND* on the asphalt outside their brownstone.

"How could they?" Jack asked. "After all we've been through."

"Get over it. Not everything is about you," muttered Margie, lighting a cigarette and pushing past him with a vitriolic sneer, her black dress rippling behind her like spilled ink. As she stepped through the large, ornate doorway of their townhouse, she let the door slam shut behind her. Jack was left alone on the curb. He struggled not to weep, shaking his head causing bits of grass and dirt fell from his disheveled hair.

She was treating him this way because of how he acted at the funeral: moaning, breaking down, sobbing uncontrollably, tumbling to the ground, rolling in the grass, and banging the ground with his fists like a toddler in the throes of a temper tantrum.

"Get up," she had hissed. "You're behaving like a child and demeaning the memory of my son."

But didn't he have the right to mourn as he saw fit? Dale had been his son, too. Jack was the one who took him to football stadiums, camping trips with the Boy Scouts, inappropriate R-rated comedies, and out to get cheese steaks, fries, ice cream, and their favorite: hotdogs covered in peanut butter and hot peppers.

51

Jack had once been a fighter—a boxer in his youth: Golden Gloves champ 1996—and had endured many pummeling fists. He ran businesses, terminated jobs, been audited by the IRS, but nothing compared to this dull, aching pain that rested inside him now. This impalpable affliction sat in his gut and burned behind his eyes like liquid fire. A torment that compelled him out of his own body, so that he was like an automaton, segregated from his husk, shambling around on autopilot.

He slipped another Xanax into his mouth, shuffled into the townhouse, mumbling to himself, directionless. He found her in the kitchen pouring a glass of wine.

"You don't think that graffiti was meant for us?" he asked.

"Probably just some dumb kids."

"It was a message for us. Had to be."

"There you go again. Are you going to blame yourself for his death again, too? Always the martyr, aren't you? Every little tragedy involves you. Your problem is, you're too fucking selfish to see beyond your own damn dilemmas. Everything is just about you, you, you."

"That's the wine talking. You don't mean that."

"The wine only makes me honest," she declared and stormed away, leaving only the echo of her heels clacking across the cold stone floor.

He got a bucket of water, splashed some bleach into it, and went outside, trying toscrub the words away, wondering to himself what they meant, why someone would put them there.

Could it be like Margie said? That it wasn't about him or about the awful thing that had happened to his beloved seventeen-year-old son? On his knees, pushing a scrub brush back and forth over those words, the scent of sunbaked concrete and bleach filling the air, the rough sound of the bristles scratching across the black asphalt, his Xanax addled mind reeled and he wondered: are all events just random and senseless? Is there any order to the universe at all?

Damnit! It wasn't coming off. It wasn't going away, no matter how much he scrubbed, it would always be there. Only time could remove those two words.

Then he saw them: two kids down the street on skateboards. Little neighborhood punks in black hoodies with patches sewn all over them. But it wasn't the skateboards he was looking at, it was their hands. Particularly the hands of the shorter kid with the long bangs and baggy pants. His hands were stained white. The same white as the words on the asphalt.

Jack got up and started towards them, his long legs quickly carrying him over the cracked sidewalk. When they noticed him coming they scrambled onto their boards and tried to skate away, but Jack was too quick, grasping the one with the stained-white hands by the collar and jerking him off his board and onto the ground.

"What the fuck, dude?"

Jack grabbed him by the shoulders.

"Why? Why would you write that? What does it mean?"

"Let me go, man! I don't know what the fuck you're talking about!" The kid stammered, his eyes wild orbs that dashed right to left, searching for help.

"The hell you don't! Tell me why! Tell me why he had to die and why you wrote *BE KIND* in front of my house! Why, damnit!" He was shaking him now, roughly thrusting the boy's shoulders forwards and backwards so that his head bobbled. Then the other kid was there, pulling on him.

"Dude, let him go! You're hurting him. Let him go, man!"

But Jack just kept on screaming into the kid's terrified face, "Why? Why? Why?" hardly noticing that the back of the kid's head was now making contact with the street, smacking down against it with awful thuds, a pool of blood forming and running down the cracks in the pavement.

And now the other kid was hitting Jack with his skateboard, slamming it against his back and howling, "Let him go! Let him go!"

But Jack was so engaged in the violent futility of demanding that a cold and uncaring universe answer *Why?* that he hardly noticed. Hardly noticed the screams of the horrified neighbors as they began pouring out onto their front porches. Hardly noticed the sound of sirens filling the air. Hardly noticed the kid had gone limp and the back of his skull was now cracked open, leaking chunks of brain. So lost was he in his anger and rage, seething in his ocean of pain and lake of searing heartache, he was also unaware that he was not being kind in any way whatsoever.

THE FRAME

FRANCES SUSANNE BROWN

Jacob's parents began work on his frame before he was even born. Together they shaped it, filling in the details on those quiet nights in front of the fire as Mother's belly swelled with him, Father reaching over now and again to place a hand on the place where the child grew.

"A perfect little boy," Father said. "We'll teach him how, from the first day."

In the nursery his parents arranged the frame carefully around the caged bed where the infant slept, so of course at first, Jacob didn't even know the frame was there. But as he grew, he learned of its presence. At first, in only little ways.

By the time Jacob was old enough to start school, he had learned to carry his frame with him, and proudly. Only every so often did Mother have to readjust the corners. She occasionally needed Father's help when the boy had tested the frame beyond its boundaries. But the frame remained in fine shape. It was well built and sturdy.

First days at school are notoriously hard, since everyone's frames are different sizes and colors and shapes. Although Jacob's classroom was expansive, there wasn't any way to fit all the frames into the space comfortably without bumping into each other. His teacher was smooth, though. She knew all about arranging new groups of frames. It didn't take long before the children learned to stack them neatly in a pile near the doorway. It was important that their learning day wasn't obstructed by their frames.

Years passed. Jacob tumbled over the brink of time into adolescence, along with his frame that had, by then, loosened at the corners and become wobbly. Sometimes he was afraid it would come apart completely. He feared his frame would splinter, leaving him buried in a pile of slats with sharp, pointed ends. But the frame held together, even though Jacob wondered if he might be outgrowing it.

He wasn't, really. Mother and Father had done a good job. Jacob's frame held steady and strong all the way until it proudly rimmed a portrait of Jacob in his cap and gown.

The boy had become a man, emerging with an official document as proof enclosed within his strong, well-defined frame. Life lay ahead of him with all the promise anything can possess—when viewed through a four-cornered window. Jacob struck out on his own, frame tucked under his arm like a hollow-cored shield. He began his life's work in a cubicle, working numbers on a screen, just like Father.

He wondered sometimes about his frame. Why had he been born with that particular one, and why did his parents always emphasize how important it was that he protect it so? But after twenty-five years the rigid boundary had become such a part of him, he couldn't imagine life without it. True, sometimes the frame was a hindrance. A nuisance that got in his way. But for the most part, Jacob's frame remained his comfort and his strength.

Naturally, Jacob fell in with a group whose frames were all very similar to his. It made things easier that way, since the stacks inside the door didn't topple over wherever Jacob and his friends got together. One would think that finding one's own particular frame might be difficult when it was time to leave, but that was never a problem. Everyone, including Jacob, knew exactly which one they belonged to as they carefully disengaged their frame from the group.

When Jacob was twenty-nine his grandfather died. Until then, he had avoided those awkward gatherings. But this time Mother insisted he go. Jacob had never known Grandfather well. The man had already traveled quite a distance ahead of him in time when Jacob was born. And Grandfather's frame, Mother explained, was very different from Jacob's. Grandfather had earned his living *with his hands*.

Which always puzzled Jacob. Both he and his father used their hands to make their living. On a keyboard yes, but still. What had Mother meant?

A sick feeling churned in Jacob's stomach as he walked up the paved path to the door of a building that looked much like the house in which he grew up. There were men in dark suits all around, strange men he didn't know. He couldn't understand why they were being so nice to him, and how they knew his name. One reached to take his frame at the door. Jacob backed away, shaking his head, and clutched it tighter to his chest.

In a room filled with flowers were many people Jacob knew, his Mother and Father, and many more he'd never seen before. All talked quietly, some cried, but not many were holding their frames. It was then Jacob noticed in the corner near the door were stacks of frames. Each pile appeared different from the other. He was surprised. For the number of people in the room, the different kinds of stacks numbered so few.

And then he saw his grandfather. In a small wooden box almost obscured by the jungle of blooms, he was perched on a pedestal between two easeled frames. Jacob stood and stared at the display in disbelief. The box holding what was left of his grandfather was very, very small, but that's not why Jacob stared. He couldn't believe his eyes—had Grandfather really possessed two frames?

Within one was a portrait of the man he barely remembered, looking so many years younger that Jacob hardly recognized him. In the other frame was a collage, a collection of snapshots with lots of people Jacob knew, his Mother and Father, and many more he'd never seen before. The frame around the collage matched the one around the portrait, perfectly. Jacob left the gathering very confused, clutching his frame tightly underneath his arm, wondering what it all meant.

That night he had a dream. In his dream he was visited by the grandfather he hardly knew.

"Grandfather," Jacob asked, "Why two frames?"

His grandfather scoffed, "Frames! You young people are so hung up on them. My life wasn't bound by any frame, boy."

"Of course it was. You had two! I saw them, and although they matched, each one held different images of you—of your life. Did you have to carry both of them with you?" Jacob asked. "All the time?"

"Those are just frames, boy. Not borders or fences, or boxes like the one I've got now." His grandfather shook his head, chuckling. "It's important to know your frame, and to keep it close to your heart. But for mercy's sake, boy, don't carry it around with you like a shield! It's hollow-cored, son. It will limit your potential and it cannot protect you."

The next day Jacob did something he'd never done before. He went off to work and left his frame at home. It was scary at first. He found himself looking around as he got off the train feeling as though he left something behind. He did the same thing when he stepped out of his cubicle for lunch, and again when he left the restroom. But each time he stopped and smiled, remembering that his frame was at home. Knowing it was safe.

On his way home Jacob saw things he'd never seen before since he wasn't busy maneuvering through a crowd with his frame. He noticed new faces—people with different colors of skin, different types of clothing and hair. Jacob couldn't believe he'd never noticed them before. The whole world looked new to him. Jacob felt a little giddy, and strangely free.

Two weeks later Jacob did something else he'd never done before. He signed up for a class in woodworking. And he smiled again when he saw the plans for the first class project.

The class was going to teach him how to craft a frame.

TABULA RASA

CAROLE BULEWSKI

Here I am on this train again; the same train, leaving the same nameless station.

I know everything that happens once the train reaches Frankfurt airport, its final destination – plane, taxi and my empty London flat. I've dreamed it over and over again. What I cannot recall is what happens before the train leaves the station and the days that follow my return home. I cannot remember what I'm doing on this train and why I'm crying so desperately.

I had this dream for the first time about a month ago. At first I thought it was because I was physically exhausted. These things are known to happen when you're tired; some tiny bits of your memory you thought had been irreversibly erased re-emerge. Just a temporary blip, nothing willpower cannot fix.

I was particularly busy at work, although working fourteen-hour days was nothing I hadn't experienced before. I just needed to buckle up and go with the flow for a while; it wouldn't kill me. Things would eventually calm down –they always did – and then I'd have all the time in the world to take care of myself, since I have no one else to take care of. I'd have time to meet up with people who don't have anyone else to care for either. We'd convince each other, but mostly ourselves, that we had it good; so much better than those poor sods who wasted their time caring for others. We too could have had people to take care of if we'd decided to, although we didn't remember who these people were. We made a conscious decision not to have these people in our lives, because we instinctively felt it was for our own good. The corrective surgery, the *Tabula Rasa* – from the Latin and meaning 'clean slate' – had erased the painful memories that were holding us back, and none of us ever regretted having the procedure.

Often, at one of our get-togethers at some gastro pub or Michelin-starred restaurant, we would remember those times when the only way to get over the pain was to work on yourself, maybe go through a few therapy sessions, take some medication in extreme cases. We who had the *Tabula Rasa*, we remembered those days – not in great detail of course, just the vague and uncomfortable feeling of it – and how nothing really worked. How the past would catch up with you eventually, preventing you from moving forward.

About ten years ago the understanding of the brain, of its intricate networks and its fragile chemistry, suddenly progressed immensely and in a short period of time, making procedures such as the *Tabula Rasa* possible. People complained at first, but then a few high-profile cases of psychologically damaged people who had found a new love for life following the procedure started shifting public opinion on the benefits of the *Tabula Rasa*. Eventually it became clear to most that if horrendous memories could be erased from people's brains forever, then the small things that hold us back in life – what we perceive as a traumatic childhood memory, a bad breakup or bullying at school – could be forever obliterated.

Not all procedures would go entirely according to plan, and some unlucky people would have some of their happy memories taken away from them at the same time as the dark ones. Clinical studies, however, showed that this effect could not directly be linked to the *Tabula Rasa* itself. I believed the studies. My case was proof that the surgery was entirely beneficial. Why I had it in the first place I could not remember, but what I knew was that I had never been so happy and productive than since having it.

Then the dream came. At first I thought it was because of the crazy hours at work, but when things calmed down and the dream didn't go away I knew there was something wrong with me. I knew it had to do with the *Tabula Rasa*, somehow. I needed help and I didn't know where to turn.

When someone, somehow, found out that your *Tabula Rasa* had not fully worked, your life was over. No one would have put you in front of a firing squad of course, but your life was over all the same. No one would touch you with a bargepole, socially or at the workplace. You became a pariah, worse even than someone who wouldn't have had the procedure. You were a failure and that was unforgivable.

The dream was the same, over and over again: a train leaving a nameless station, and my endless, irrepressible tears. Eventually I realised the reason why I couldn't erase this memory from my brain was that I didn't want this bittersweet, incomplete memory that was slowly turning into an obsession to go away. And every night before going to sleep, I wished the dream would reveal a little bit more.

I heard rumours about a procedure that would nullify the *Tabula Rasa*. There were no clinical studies to validate this second intervention. You just had to decide on faith.

The dream meanwhile remained unchanged and so I concentrated on the memories, somewhat altered, of what had happened after leaving the train station. I remembered boarding a London-bound plane at Frankfurt airport and the aircraft being hit by turbulence and I remembered thinking that if I died there and then, I wouldn't die particularly happy. I remembered a baby crying, and I remembered feeling broken at the thought that I would never have children of my own. But the memories of the following few days were inexistent, just as the ones from the moments preceding the train leaving the station remained inaccessible.

Despair engulfed me and eventually I decided to have the reversed *Tabula Rasa* performed on my brain. I was entering a world of shadiness.

I spent an entire week at an underground hospital. I could barely remember my own name at that stage and I thought I would remain in this hospital bed for the rest of my days, but on the morning of the seventh day, my head finally cleared up.

The dream did not recur in the first few weeks following the procedure. In fact, I did not dream at all during these first few weeks. I think I was happy, for a while. I went back to work and because I remembered how I had behaved before having my *Tabula Rasa* reversed, I was able to mimic my movements, words and demeanour of those days. No one noticed. I don't think anyone cared.

One day the memories resurfaced and I drowned. In this train station, the name of which I finally recalled, I had left someone I loved. Not the simplest of relationships, although at times it was. I had made certain choices, for the sake of my future and what I wanted it to be. I had decided to control my future, and the *Tabula Rasa* was certainly the way forward. I would forget him and the person I'd been when I was with him. I would concentrate on what was truly important: my career and my status in society.

The beautiful days and the ugly ones, the days spent with him, I had forgotten them all, but now I remembered the smell of freshly cooked rice pudding, the sound of a guitar played hesitantly, a book called *Steppenwolf* and many letters written on green paper. I remembered the colours and I remembered the smells, I remembered his voice and I remembered his lips. As the memories came back to my mind, things became more confused. Some days I would wake up not remembering where I was or what I had done the day before. I thought it was a side effect of having my brain tampered with so many times. And so I went back to the underground hospital because soon people, at work and elsewhere, would start noticing that something wasn't quite right with me.

I was told that nothing could be done to put things back in place inside my brain. "Actually," the doctor said as I was leaving, "there's something you should try." I asked what it was, because I was ready to try anything. "You should go and see him," the doctor answered, "the one you left behind. But nothing is ever completely certain," he concluded.

NOW THAT I'VE FOUND YOU

ROSS BURTON

I've been alone almost a year now. A year of soulless motel rooms, searching. Nearly gave up; thought I'd never find you, thought I'd be alone forever. Thought I'd die alone, never see you again.

But now I've found you. Just as well, I didn't know how much longer the money would last. But that doesn't matter now. Now that I've found you.

Was it chance, an accident that I saw her? No. When I found your house yesterday, I saw you both at breakfast in the kitchen. You had no idea I was there in the little wood, watching you. It was raining, I got pretty wet. But that didn't matter. I welcomed the discomfort.

A peck on the cheek from your faithful wife when you left for work. Did you know she smoked? I watched her go through her daily routine. She stood at the back door, having a sly cigarette. Thought she saw me, but no. I stood stock still in the wood. After cleaning the kitchen, making the bed, hoovering like a good little housewife, she got into her little car. I guessed she might be going to the Mall. I was right.

She was having coffee. I took the next table. Tiny tables, just enough for two people, ours were close together. Close enough for me to talk, engage her in conversation. She's very polite. A light voice, indeterminate accent. New Jersey? No, I'm being unkind. Somewhere in the east, though. Well brought up. From money. Is that why you like her? Can't be her conversation; she doesn't have any. No politics. No view on health care. No views on anything, as far as I could tell. Not like me. A view on everything, and not slow to share it.

Outspoken? *Moi?* At least I'm alive. Got an opinion. But you married her. Not me. Her. Is that what you want? Someone to host a vapid dinner party? Keep the idle chat going amongst the wives? The other empty vessels? I 'd have argued with your friends, the men. I guess that's why you preferred her. Preferred. Her. I am filled with anger. It suffocates me. I wanted you. Would have been a proper partner. Not some little mouse. Instead, here I stand in the dark woods, watching your silent, empty house.

She's quite pretty. Delicate features. A bit thin. I always thought you liked a bit more, how can I put it . . . substance. Heft. Not that I'm fat, just a bit more to me than her. In every way. I saw the way she looked at you. She loves you. As much as I do? Perhaps. Don't think it's reciprocated though. I remember the way you looked at me. Don't see that look on your face now. Don't you love her? Your lovely wife? Your slim, pretty, young wife? I know you. You don't love her the way you loved me.

The house is dark. You're out somewhere. The cinema? A meal with friends? I've been standing here a while. Doesn't matter, I've no pressing engagement to rush back for. My diary is free. Ah, there you are, you lovely couple. Had a nice time? Lights on in the living room. The fire leaps at the touch of a button, and you sink into pale cream leather. The couch looks comfy. Expensive too.

She's in the kitchen. Some wine, darling? Why not? Looks like Pinot Grigio. How appropriate. Bland, characterless, like her. We drank better stuff, when we'd sit and talk long into the night. There's the tv coming on. Big screen, high on the wall. A bit vulgar. What to watch? Flick, flick, flick; so many channels; so much rubbish. How about this, honey? House. Series 5, looks like. Think I remember this one. Look at you, side by side on the couch. Eyes glued to the big screen, not talking. Not even touching. Sad. I'll leave you to it. See you tomorrow.

Back to my crummy, lonely motel room for some R & R. Pull the nearly comfy chair over to rest my feet on the not at all comfy bed. Should I put the tv on? Join you in House, series five? Don't think I'll bother. Got myself some wine. A litre of the good stuff. Cheap, but good enough to dull the pain. Make this room look a little better. The shabby decor. The damp patch by the window. Curtains that don't keep light out. Cheap furniture - used, tired. A bit like I feel. I've travelled so long, searching for you. Rooms like this have been my way of life. But seeing your lovely home. Your spacious, well-appointed family home; this place looks like the shithole it is.

Another glass, madame? Don't mind if I do.

Good place to raise a family, your home. Big garden; nice, middle class neighbourhood; good schools. So why no kids? Waiting? For what? You're in your late thirties, she's a few years younger. But hey, that clock's ticking away. Tick tock.

Maybe she can't.

We know it's not you, don't we? I should have kept it. Big mistake letting you talk me out of it. We'd still be together. Sure, we were young, but others manage, don't they? Seem happy. Happy families. We could have been a happy family. Us in that house. Three, four of us by now. A boy and a girl. You're good looking, and I'm not ugly. Good stock; we could have made nice kids together. We'd have brought them up right. I'd have taught them not to assume that women were just there to keep house, be a mom. It might not have gone down too well here, though, in fucking Stepford.

Fuck 'em. Fuck you, and her. Why should I be the lonely one? I've drunk too much of this cheap, shitty wine. It's finished and I'm off to sleep, perchance to dream. Nighty night.

I was right. It's a nice couch. Comfortable. Luxurious. I could sleep on it; have a better night than I had at the motel. The room's nicer than it looks from the woods. I've made myself coffee with the kick-ass machine in the kitchen. Think I prefer nescafe, but hey, beggars, you know? I'm wearing one of her dresses. De La Renta, it says on the label. I've always liked Oscar's stuff. She's not as skinny as she looks, it fits just fine.

When I rang the doorbell I didn't know what I was going to say. She recognised me from the mall. Took fright. Somewhere in that empty head she realised I wasn't her friend, wasn't there for a cosy chat about the best place to get muffins.

But she was too polite to slam the door in my face. Hesitated. Too slow, too indecisive. Easy to push past into the hall, down to the kitchen; ignoring her shouting, telling me to get out, that she was going to call the police.

That she was going to call her husband.

That's when I got a little angry. She'd been preparing a meal. Steaks on a chopping board. Nifty little tenderiser; metal, heavy, the head studded with sharp-looking spikes

I finished preparing the steaks, shame to waste them. Got some potatoes baking. You used to like that. Steak, medium rare. Baked potato, butter with a little salt and pepper. Green salad on the side. We'll open a good bottle of red wine. It'll be just like the old days.

THE DYING DISASTER

JM BUSH

The horribly disfigured features of the hill giant's face were contorted with agony as his head sailed through the air, trailing blood and bits of gore like a comet does with ice and rock as it soars through space. Gorith the Walking Disaster, as the hill giant was known in the valley, fell to his knees as his decapitated ten-foot-tall body finally died, and then his headless corpse fell forward into the muddy courtyard in front the tavern.

All eyes in town rested on the strange dwarf who had ended the giant's 15-year reign of terror in the valley beyond the mountain stronghold of Kelgrond. Over the course of those long years, not one single request for help had been answered by the Queen. The dwarves in the small town of Dowtan had begged numerous times through emissaries and letters. Offerings were made to the ancestors and the Gods that kept them. No one ever tried to stop Gorith from tormenting the residents of this small, insignificant town.

Until today, that is.

There was not a dwarf standing in the courtyard, watching the death of their most feared enemy, who even recognized the unusual hero in their midst. No one in town had never seen him before today. He was not one of the kingdom's recognized heroes. He didn't wear the clothes of a hill dwarf. He didn't wear the armor typical of the royal army, either.

65

This stranger was dressed in such an odd assortment of items, when he had arrived earlier in the day, the residents of Dowtan mocked him mercilessly.

"Where'd ye get them silly rags ye be wearin', stranger?" the town's constable questioned as the stranger entered town that morning. Constable Toram grinned his broken smile and twirled his warhammer by its strap, as was his custom.

The odd dwarf only smiled, "I found them amongst yer mother's small clothes, officer. She bid me keep them for the good work I'd done on her the night 'afore." The newcomer had then spit at the constable's feet and continued toward the pub in search of a drink, all the while trailing that unusual weapon of his.

That was the most unnerving thing about this funny-looking dwarf. His bright red shirt was puffy with lace at the collar and wrists, his calf-high purple boots were hilarious, and his black pants were so tight you could tell his ancestry at a glance. But the massive sword he carried over one shoulder would be considered big if Gorith the Walking Disaster himself had carried it. On a four-and-a-half-foot tall dwarf, the sword was comically large. It dragged in the mud behind him, leaving a strange trail in his wake; two sauntering footsteps and a swerving line cut in the ground wherever he went.

Once he reached the pub the stranger didn't even order an ale, as was the custom for a dwarf in any land; mountain, hill, or sea. No, this outlandish fellow ordered an entire bottle of human whisky. He sat quietly in the corner, his gigantic sword leaned upon the table with the hilt in easy reach, and casually drained the entire bottle of booze over the course of two hours. His eyes flitted across every face that entered, as if he were searching for someone.

"Who are ye, then?" the buxom bartender had asked of this dwarf that stood out ever so much amongst her regular patrons.

"Why, I'm the fuckin' one ta save this shithole, lass. Now, do us a favour an' piss off, if ye don't mind," he replied with an unkind grin.

Merryander huffed and spun on her heels at such a rebuke, having never been spoken to as rudely by a customer. "I wonder what's up that one's arse," she muttered while storming off.

Around noon, per the norm, the resounding boom of footsteps of echoed through the middle of town. Gorith had come for his bribe.

The hill giant originally came to town years ago in order to kill and eat a few helpless dwarves once a week. Now, dwarves are a race bred for physical labor, making them strong and excellent fighters. But the people of Dowtan were farmers. They were never trained in the ways of war. Folks in these parts relied on the constable to protect them, but Shamrun had been the first to die those long years ago. The Queen, bless her majestic heart, had never sent more than a replacement constable to help. Toram arrived two months after Gorith's first attack. Having been trained as an officer, the new constable was skilled in negotiations, and so struck a deal with the fearsome hill giant. They would let Gorith have whatever he wanted and would not fight back, if he would refrain from killing any more dwarves.

Gorith the Walking Disaster agreed to this deal, and now only came once every other day, as he had for 15 long years, to eat freely from the market, drink as much ale as he wanted , and generally terrorize Dowtan. But at least he didn't kill and eat the townsfolk anymore.

The hill giant had not visited the town in three days and the people of Dowtan were hopeful he died in his sleep. Mothers, fathers, children, and the elderly alike all prayed to their ancestors and the Gods that kept them every night, asking for Gorith to fall down a ravine, stop breathing in his sleep, or ingest some bad mutton to die from a painful bout of dysentery. But today they all understood , once again, their prayers had gone unanswered, as the grotesque hill giant stomped into the town square around lunch time.

As he began demanding his customary lunch of several live sheep and three barrels of ale, Gorith slapped and kicked at any dwarf who was without that which he desired, if they were foolish enough to come his reach. The townsfolk ran and screamed as he threatened them, which made the hill giant roar with laughter. He turned his head to the side and blew a rocket of snot from his nose that covered the doorstep of the town's healer.

The elderly dwarf leaned out the window upon hearing the splat, and shouted to Gorith, "Ere now, that is fuckin' disgusting, that is! This be a place of healing and must be kept clean!"

The giant chuckled while pulling down his pants to squat in front of the windowsill where the healer had shouted from. Before he could produce an even more repugnant gift for the old dwarf, Gorith heard a name being called. A long forgotten name that sent shivers of fear through the huge creature.

"GRENDEL! GRENDEL, COME FACE ME!" The unusual dwarf called from the courtyard in front of the pub. His massive sword was now held out in front of him, and an odd shimmering glow surrounding the long blade.

Gorith stared at the dwarf without recognition, confusion clouding his judgement. "And who are you that uses the old name of my ancestors' tribe? Who are you, puny dwarf, who wields God's Feather, the bane of my people since ages past?"

As he said this, the hill giant stood and pulled his trousers back up, thinking to himself that he must come back after devouring this fool to finish shitting by this healer's hovel. Or maybe he would rip roof off and shit *in* the bastard's hovel. Either way, he needed to kill this idiot first. A dwarf who stupidly thinks he is actually one of the legendary Wolves of the Bay.

"I have been trained since birth by yer sworn enemy, Grendelkin. I know yer truth. I know yer no hill giant. I know what ye are, and I'm here to put an end to you. 50 years ago ye killed a dwarf with a golden beard while he worked the docks. Remember? That were me father. I was hiding behind a crate, monster. A member of the Wolves of the Bay came by later in search of ye. I begged her to take me along, and teach me how to fight as they once did. Ye see, not all of them are gone, although their numbers are few these days."

"Because we destroyed them, and feasted on their bones, fool. Just as I shall do with you now," Gorith said, his blood beginning to boil with the memories of what the Wolves had done to his people. And all because the Grendel enjoyed man flesh. Who cares about a few humans dying? There are so many of them!

"Nay, ye devil. I carry this blade because I earned it. Yer entire clan is dead and gone, Grendelkin. I killed them with this very sword after ripping it from within the crypt of your long dead chief. Yer the last one, far as I can tell," Yintal the Hunter said, baring his teeth in a snarl.

Wordlessly, full of rage, Gorith dashed towards this lying dwarf. As he did, Yintal leapt into the air and spun his body around, bringing God's Feather forward in a mighty swing. With a sound like a whip slicing through the air, followed by the thud of an enormous head slapping into the mud, Yintal landed by planting the sword tip in the earth, and using the handle to slow his descent, pulling it down with him. As his feet touched the ground, the sword now rested at an awkward angle, protruding from the courtyard.

Without even a thanks from the townsfolk, and not really wanting any, Yintal the Hunter grabbed the handle of God's Feather, pulled it out of the mud, and walked slowly away from Dowtan, leaving an unusual set of tracks in his wake. Two sauntering footsteps and a swerving line cut into the ground.

THE KEYS

MEGAN E. CASSIDY

The scent of burning pine needles drifted past, but whether it was from a small forest fire, or merely the rangers clearing out brush to make room for new growth, Olivia could not tell.

Mixed with the salty tang of the ocean, it reminded her of a small summer camp she had worked at ten years earlier. "The summer I was beautiful," she thought, looking down on her now softer, rounder figure.

The Summer of Beauty was six years ago, the season when she took first one lover, and then a second; the only two she ever had. They were very different men, either of whom she might have married had she met them separately. Now, breathing in the ocean spray, Olivia realized both men had long forgotten the memories she still clung to.

She had traveled to the Florida Keys to photograph a destination wedding, but stayed on a few extra days, hoping to add some nature shots to her portfolio. She chose this inlet for its obscurity, a small piece of protected forest cut through by a dusty trail, ending in a small beach. She had hiked the trail each morning, and found the beach empty every time, save for two rotting picnic tables and an unused fishing pier. Olivia found comfort in this routine, something she rarely found in a schedule that took her across the continent several times a month.

This afternoon, as the photographer approached the end of the path, she heard voices. Though resentful of the unwanted company, she doggedly plodded along, hoping that perhaps with her intrusion, the other party might become uncomfortable enough to leave.

Her efforts went unnoticed, however, and she plunked her heavy camera onto the table farthest from the domestic scene and slid onto its cracked bench. A young mother clad in a pink string bikini top and white denim shorts was unsuccessfully trying to sunbathe, slathering on suntan lotion with one hand while gently rolling a covered stroller back and forth with the other.

The woman's husband stood at the end of the graying pier, casting a fishing net into the waves. Moments later, he retrieved the empty net and shifted slightly before tossing it out again. He seemed joyous in the feckless task, showing off for his wife, who smiled appreciatively while lulling their whimpering baby boy.

The couple's daughter, a small girl of four or five, was dressed in a bathing suit the same color as her mother's, and ran back and forth between her parents. Pigtails whipping in the ocean breeze, she cooed at her little brother while pleading with her mother to play, then dashed back to her father, examining his net and beckoning him into the surf.

Finally, the girl's mother paused in her other tasks to open the large pink tote bag tucked in at her feet. The girl clapped her hands when she saw the bag, tearing out the plastic sand toys and casting the other childhood trinkets aside.

She set to making the base first, running to the water's edge countless times, using the molds for buckets, bringing them back, and pouring them out, splashing her mother's feet in the process. After she created the mud hole, she lay on her belly, stuck her feet up into the air, and gathered the sand to her chest as if playing with a treasured doll.

When the pile was sufficient, the tow-headed girl began to make turrets, deliberately packing the sand into the blue plastic boxes. Then mixing water carefully, she stuck the tip of her tongue out, and bit it gently in concentration.

Olivia watched this familial scene—the mother, minding the children and encouraging her husband's efforts; the father, hunting and gathering for his family; the daughter, now quietly focused on her endeavors. She gripped her camera, wanting to capture the moments, but she worried that as an adult alone without children or a companion of her own, they might view her interest with suspicion.

So instead, the photographer watched unnoticed, while pretending to be caught up in the sea. The waves seemed to grow more boisterous, despite the still-gentle breeze and uninterrupted sunshine. While the water slowly morphed from bright cerulean to a smoky indigo, Olivia saw that the little girl was satisfied with her creation and had run back to her mother. The girl's exuberance caused the calmed baby to wake.

The girl ignored her brother's cries and scampered over to her father, taking for granted as a part of everyday life the sound that grated the ears of Olivia, who was unused to babies, and felt an expansive anxiety clawing at the inside of her chest whenever she heard one crying. She felt her chest tighten at the sound, but stayed at the table's moldy bench, transfixed by the amused little girl.

"She'd be about Jenny's age," Olivia realized, thinking of the name she had given her almost-daughter, the phantom child she chose to relinquish after her one shining summer of love. Olivia shook her head, trying to erase the memory.

The girl's father had caught one or two fish and now ventured toward the shore to show the trophies to his wife. His daughter plopped onto the dock and began wiping golden grains of sand off her knobby knees.

Olivia decided to take this opportunity to surreptitiously slip into their midst, hoping to silently go around the girl to finally take some pictures of the pier and the azure sky beyond it.

She took out her camera from its case, and stood up, only to see the child standing in front of her, arms akimbo, gazing at her with a frankness the photographer was unused to.

"You like my castle?" the clear face tilted up at her.

"Um," Olivia stumbled, looking to the girl's preoccupied parents for assistance. "Why, yes. It's very nice."

"Watcha doin'?"

"I'm going to take some pictures."

"Why?"

"Well, it's very pretty down here. Don't you think so?"

The girl shrugged. "You wanna take a picture of my castle? It's real big!"

"I suppose so, if your mother doesn't mind."

"Where 'r your kids?" the girl asked suddenly. She darted behind Olivia as if looking for a playmate.

"I don't have any," the photographer replied, trying not to blush at the girl's guilelessness.

The girl tilted her head again in a sympathetic gesture this time, "Why not?"

Then the child's mother, squinting into the sun, interrupted, "Kelsey, honey, come over here. Stop bothering the nice lady." She offered the photographer a faint shrug and sympathetic smile as if to apologize for her daughter's boldness.

The girl grinned, waved goodbye to Olivia with both of her small hands, and blew her a kiss. Then she ran back to her mother's side yelling, "Mommy! That lady's funny. She doesn't gots kids!"

This time, Olivia did blush. Turning away from the pier, she packed up her equipment and slowly walked back down the trail without taking a single picture.

Upon entering the center glade carved out of the small patch of trees, Olivia paused and sunk onto a bed of brittle pine needles. She brought her knees to her chest, rocking back and forth in the silence, allowing herself to cry for the first time in six years. "It's time to stop running," she whispered into the wind. "It's time to go home."

A LITTLE EMERGENCY

GREGG CHAMBERLAIN

The Nanite slowly crawled down along the rough metal surface of the tunnel. Damp seeped through the fabric of his nanosuit. The bright white beam of his helmet lamp stabbed ahead into the darkness. A gleam of gold winked around a bend in the tunnel.

"Almost there," he muttered.

A few moments later his reaching hand wrapped around the smooth curved surface of an enormous golden ring. The Nanite tried an experimental tug. Nothing. The huge ring was wedged fast, top and bottom, at an angle against the curving surface of the tunnel. Glancing down at the base of the ring with his headlamp, the Nanite noted it appeared to be mired in some unknown viscous material.

"Merde," he grumbled. "Nothing's ever easy."

First making sure the magnetic clamps on his boots were at full power, the Nanite crouched down, braced his legs on either side of the ring, took hold and pulled back on it. Leg muscles straining, the Nanite heaved, muttering "thank God" as he heard a metallic scraping from above. The ring shifted forward suddenly, coming loose at the bottom with an oozy "sloosh" as it slid out and away from whatever had held it stuck.

Sighing with relief, the Nanite took a moment to recheck his foot clamps. One hand retained a firm balancing hold on the ring.

Standing up, he looped a muscular arm around the metal curve of his find and began slowly, carefully clambering back up the metal tunnel. The magnetic clamps on his boots made little metallic clicks with each slow step as he climbed. The great golden ring dragged down against the crook of his arm.

Emerging out of the tunnel mouth, the Nanite crawled onto a smooth, metal surface, the gold ring scraping along beside him.

A pair of giant fingers and a thumb reached down and plucked the golden ring from the Nanite.

He looked up. The giant fingers and thumb of a giant right hand were slipping the golden circlet over the ring finger of a giant left hand. Above the two hands loomed the giant dusky features of the Amazon, the Nanite's *Freedom Force* teammate, beaming down a big beautiful smile at the diminutive superhero.

"Ti-Jean, thank you so much," boomed the Amazon. "After losing my wedding ring for the fourth time now down the kitchen sink, maybe Nick will finally focus his *MechMan* mind on fixing the dishwasher."

"Fifth time, Kerima," corrected the Nanite, stepping away from the sink drain hole. "Let's hope so." He shrugged, thinking that Mister Mañana better described the procrastinating nature of his gadget-crazy comrade where mundane matters were concerned. A Gallic grin spread wide across his own face then as the Nanite also recalled the thrifty side of the cost-conscious member of *Freedom Force*.

"But, if you really want to get your hubby to quit tinkering with his blast pads and body armour," suggested the tiny titan to the Amazon, "and pick up a pipe wrench and soldering iron instead, maybe next time you should call a plumber and then show Nick the bill."

LIPSERVICE

DONNA CHESMAN

The door to the building was near impossible to find, covered by promotional posters for call girls and nearby nude bars. Sometimes, the women posted out front of the neighboring brothel would be kind enough to help newbies push their way inside. I didn't need any help, but I still stopped to chat up the fishnet-suspended women by the brothel door. Katherine had two daughters and a deadbeat husband, emphasis on beat. Alexandra was in thereabouts the same boat. Only one kid for her, though. Her son was nice. He would walk down the street sometimes after dark and bring his mommy flowers. Katherine had slept with a few of my friends. None of them believed me when I said I knew her name.

The building by the brothel was nothing more than a brick toothpick. Shaped like the boy no one wanted on their team in gym class, its interior was equally narrow. There was only one room, but perhaps calling it a hallway would be better. The ceiling was high and squared off, cradling a pool of calming darkness. Every few feet a simple light fixture jutted out of the wall, drawing out the rectangular perimeter of the long room. At the entrance stood a cheap plastic podium, painted over to appear wooden and sturdy.

"Hey, Friend." Jonathan greeted. He was the man behind the podium, the bookkeeper and the muscle. We go to the same pharmacy, but never make eye contact.

"I'm here for my one o'clock."

"That's right. I'd love to give you the usual, but Beth is out sick. Chelsea is here in her place, if that's okay with you."

I stared at him, taking a deep breath and considering my options.

"Their voices are almost identical, you won't notice a difference. She read your file. Her delivery is even better than Beth's" Jonathan assured. He made no promises, but he assured me with the type of confidence I found myself envying.

"It's okay with me."

Jonathan gave me the nod that I could go behind the podium and take my seat. I sat on one end of what could have been a mile long table. Even if I trained my eyes straight ahead, I had no way of making out Chelsea on the other end of that void, searching for me as well. We searched for each other for a few minutes, very quietly straining our eyes for nothing. Then Chelsea began to speak. Her voice, so similar to Beth's, stretched out from the dark and tried to reach me.

"You are a good person. Your children love you. Your friends are jealous of your success."

Things were said in threes and I had three minutes to take them in, to convince myself of them, to believe them. Once the three minutes evaporated, Chelsea continued with the script, speaking with a medium register and even pacing.

"Your family adores you. You are very attractive. Your parents are very proud of you."

Three minutes.

"You are a hard worker. Your boss appreciates you. You are not wasting time."

"Keep going," I interjected, digging into the quiet waiting space.

"Excuse me?" Jonathan turned to me, getting ready to explain the rules of *Lipservice* to me, as if it were my first time sitting at this table.

"I don't need three minutes. Just tell her she can keep going. Please."

He responded with a weary look, softened by the dim light placed next to the podium. Still, Jonathan told Chelsea she could keep talking. I could hear the sound of papers shuffling, the sound of her arranging the script so she could talk without pause. She wasn't very good at putting on airs. This wasn't the business for Chelsea.

"You have a nice house. You spend money wisely. Your car is handsome."

She hesitated.

"You are a good lover. You have a soft touch. You are easy to confide in."

And she hesitated.

"Your spouse loves you. Your spouse misses you. Your spouse feels blessed to be a part of your life." Then she hit her stride. "Your spouse has no regrets in regards to your relationship. Your spouse craves your company."

I rested my head on the glass table while she turned the page.

"Your spouse values what you do around the house. Your spouse remembers your anniversary. Your spouse is your best friend. Your spouse loves the life you have built together."

I shut my eyes and clenched my jaw. Things were brighter on the insides of my eyelids. Miles away from me, Chelsea could hear the lack of rhythm in my breathing. She could hear my crumbling and blubbering. And I could hear her turning the pages of my file and piling them together.

Miles away, Chelsea continued.

"Your spouse is excited to see you when you get home. Your spouse brags about you to their friends."

Then she found her confidence.

"Your spouse isn't cheating on you."

Miles away, Chelsea could hear the cracking in my voice, the coughing as salty tears trailed into my open mouth. I could hear Chelsea putting the papers she took from my file back into their manila envelope. I could hear Jonathan unlock the tin money box. I could hear him tapping his foot, waiting for me to get out my wallet and pay for my session. I could hear things coming to an end, but I stayed suspended and crying face down on the glass table.

And I cried.

No one was allowed to touch me until I was done crying. I could feel another side of Chelsea standing next to me. Then out the door. And when the door shut behind her, I cried harder. Buildings crumbling, cymbals crashing. Violently heaving, holding myself, and rocking myself; I cried. I cried because Chelsea had left me stranded, because as soon as I sat down I knew she was going to leave me. I cried because she was *such* a good liar.

COSTUME CONNECTION

SARA CODAIR

Paper balls assaulted Juliana as she navigated the overcrowded halls of Shelburne Middle School. The thick fabric of her Iron Man costume shielded her from the missiles and hid her headphones. The blonde-haired, blue-eyed Chester Davy glared. Last week, he tried to stuff her in a locker. His lips distorted into ugly shapes, but the Avenger's soundtrack blocked his words.

That same music muted the comments from the girls in her home-room. Juliana never fit in with them and as she got older, their comments got crueler. They had made fun of her scar all week. She just couldn't take it anymore, so today, she wore her Iron Man costume to school.

She couldn't hear the bell, but knew it rang when everyone rushed out of their seats. She waited for the room to empty before she got up and braved the hallway, where she imagined the other students were enemy planes shooting at her as they zoomed across the sky. She raised her palm and pretended lasers blasted the enemy fighters out of the blue.

When Juliana arrived at her first period history class, she sat at the back of the classroom and tried to make herself small so her teacher wouldn't notice her. It didn't work.

The gray haired Mrs. Winslow marched towards Juliana with rap-id-fire lip movements that didn't stop until Juliana removed her mask and headphones.

"I've said it dozens of times. You are not to wear that mask in my classroom." The teacher paused and looked around the room. "And if ANYONE makes a single remark about the scar on Juliana's cheek, you will have detention for a week."

Juliana slumped backwards, letting her fingers slide across the rippled skin, burned from the time her brother poured hot chocolate on it.

Mrs. Winslow's warning was mostly effective. All but one student had their eyes turned towards the whiteboard. Juliana didn't recognize the disobedient boy. He was thin, Asian, and decked out in Pokémon gear with Charmander sneakers, Pokéball t-shirt and the Pikachu-ear headband that restrained his silky black hair.

"We have a new student today," said Mrs. Winslow. "Hal just moved to Massachusetts from California."

Hal stood stiffly and waved to the class, but he kept sneaking glances back at Juliana. They made her squirm.

When class was over, she gathered her belongings and bolted.

"Juliana? That's your name, right?"

The slightly accented voice reminded her she had not donned her mask or headphones.

She kept walking.

"I like you costume," said the voice.

Juliana slowed.

"Iron Man is one of my favorite superheroes. He's got both brains and brawn."

She stopped and faced Hal. "Why are you talking to me?"

"You seem cool. Everyone else looks plain."

She squinted. "Everyone else hates me. They'll tease you if they see you talking to me."

"Then they're idiots." Hal walked away.

Juliana stood frozen in the hallway. Hal's final words and actions seemed contradictory. If he didn't care what they thought, then why would he walk away? She wondered if he wanted to be her friend, or if his intention had been to mess with her all along.

A sharp elbow to the rib snapped her out of her reverie, and the sight of Chester Davy's creepy grin sent her running the rest of the way to Social Studies.

#

Hal wasn't in her next class, or the one after it, but as Juliana was walking into lunch, she found him surrounded by a gaggle of snickering girls. Their ringleader, Felicia Bell, had his Pikachu ears clutched beneath her hot pink nails.

Before she let herself think too much, Juliana rushed the girls and snatched the ears.

"Mind your own business, Scarface," snarled Felecia.

"Hal, I warned you. If you talk to me, they will pick on you." Juliana handed him his headband and stormed away.

"Juliana," he called ahead of a storm of giggles. "I don't care what they say."

She stared at him with her head tilted; trying to figure out if he was serious. When she saw Felicia catching up to them, she started moving again.

"I meant what I said about your costume, I really like it. Would you like to sit with me at lunch?"

"You'll just mark yourself as a freak," she said, trying to get away from him.

"They already think I'm one." He was easily matching her fast pace. "And I really don't want to sit alone."

"Fine." Juliana shook her head as they stepped into the lunch line. Felicia and her clique whispered behind them, loud enough for Juliana to know they were gossiping about her, but soft enough for the elderly lunch ladies not to notice. "But your just making things worse."

"I disagree." Hal picked up his tray and followed Juliana to her usual seat near the emergency exit.

The cafeteria was a storm of voices. Some students were carrying on their own meaningless conversations; others were stage whispering about how Juliana and the new kid were two freaky peas in a pod.

Hal's voice cut through the tempest. "Do you ever LARP?'"

She shook her head as she sat down. "What's a larp?"

"LARPing is when people get together in costumes to act out a story. You do it to take a vacation from yourself and be someone else."

"That sounds nice."

"You're the first to agree here. Perhaps we'll be friends."

Juliana's cheeks burned as her shoulders relaxed. No one had ever wanted to be her friend before. "Do you wear costumes for LARPing?"

Excited to finally have a willing listener, Hal rambled on about the regalia and corresponding games, which seemed to include Pokémon, superheroes and mythical creatures. Juliana was so enticed by his voice that the other kids could have been calling her a loser or fat freak, and it wouldn't have mattered. She had finally had a friend of her own, or at least, a potential friend.

BETRAYED

SUE COLETTA

The splash echoed through my head when you plunged me into the depths of the unknown, covering your tracks, ridding yourself of extra baggage. I sunk lower…lower…floating, my arms reaching for the surface, longing for escape. Alone in the murky water, trapped between this world and the next, blood from my gaping chest wound washed away like finger-paints on a bathtub wall—erasing your betrayal, severing our bond.

Why did this happen?

When you pulled curbside everything seemed routine. I didn't know about the madman, or hear the rumors of the evil within, of the monster who claimed twenty and was hungering for victim twenty-one.

In my swampy grave the creatures waited, watched, bided their time till I descended into the dark recesses of their domain. Sound didn't exist. All that remained were visions of the moment when karma bit back.

Leafy algae waved me near, dared me to approach. I had no choice but to obey, my soul broken, my very being yearning for more. One last touch, kiss. One last laugh, joy. One last love with someone who wouldn't kick me out the door.

I worshiped every part of you, never judged, didn't complain when you had no time for me. Why couldn't I see the blackness inside? I reminisced about our first day, of your loving arms around me, of your whisper in my ear, "You're home. You're safe."

What did I do to illicit such hatred?

The years I spent behind bars were lonely ones. Then there you were, my savior. I ached for those words my entire life. For a long time, I figured my destiny had scrawled my ending into the Book of Life. Your kinds eyes gave me hope. Your giggle warmed my heart. You were my everything, my future, and my past. Not a day went by that I didn't welcome you home.

This made no sense. Were you in pain? If so, I could forgive. If you came back, I'd stand by your side. We could carry on, live our last days together.

Instead, I sunk lower…lower…to where the sun couldn't reach, warmth was nonexistent, and dubious peril lurked deep in the shadows. Maybe if I'd tried harder, you wouldn't have tossed me into an angry pit of despair.

For it was here when my outlook changed.

As I descended toward the murky floor, something wrapped around my ankle. What it was, I couldn't say. Pond monster? Seaweed? Something far more sinister?

I tugged, twisted, and tried to break free. That's when I witnessed what you'd done. Lined in a half-circle six corpses swayed side to side. Pastel gowns billowed with the rhythm of the water, long hair reaching for the surface. Around the women's ankles heavy chains secured their bodies to cinderblocks, not unlike the way you'd chained me many times. Papery-thin skin hung off their exposed arms, legs, and face, fish nibbling each morsel as if it were their last.

Motion from above startled me.

In seconds, a woman plummeted to the pond floor. Helping her wasn't an option. You'd already done the deed, her mouth gaped open in terror, eyes wide in disbelief, the ligature around her neck trailing her descent.

She looked familiar.

Recognition hit me hard.

My mind reviewed each day we spent together, each warm embrace, each song you strummed on your guitar—filling me with love and hope, more content than I'd envisioned. But then she entered our lives, the woman who took your time away, the home wrecker who shared your bed while you ordered me to watch. It wasn't fair. I'd loved you for so long. Yet there she was, living my dream, replacing my space in your heart.

Guess she wasn't enough for you, either.

When I squeezed my eyes closed to give into my fate, intuition re-awakened my senses. And there you were. Scuba gear from head to toe, a mask shielding the face I adored. One by one you tended to your sinful garden, stroking each soulless face, delighting in the madness you caused.

Summoning my last shred of strength, I paddled toward the surface. You never looked back, too busy with your maniacal den, the twisted kingdom where you reigned.

As my face crested the water, I struggled for air, my lungs denying breath.

"Over here!" a fisherman hollered before diving into the pond. He snaked an arm around my chest and dragged me into the rowboat. "She's been shot," he told his buddy. "Call the cops. Whoever harmed this beautiful Rottweiler must not be far."

THE IMPRESSION

KARA COSENTINO

The car puttered to a stop on the soft sand, groaning as the key was ripped from the ignition. Lillian grasped the box from the passenger seat. She took the ring out of the box; staring at the small dent it made on the ruby-colored felt. The small shadow, which would disappear within a few minutes, reminded her of his vanishing love. She disregarded the box on the sandy ground and walked towards the water. She admired the diamond she once found beauty in—just like her marriage. Then, tightly clenched her fist around the ring as memories flooded her mind, the past flowing as swift and powerful as the lake that flooded the valley earlier in the spring.

She had taken the ring off her finger over a year ago. That night, she slid it off, twisting it out of its trench in her skin and glided it over her nail, holding it up proudly so he could witness her determination. She would never see the green flecks in his blue eyes again. Or the dimple that appeared when he couldn't stop laughing. Or the clench of his fists when he got angry. Or the vein in his neck that erupted, just like him, when he was mad.

Five years of her life were gone; wasted, as she tried to make the marriage work. With Natalie, her therapist, and Dave the lawyer helping her through the painful time, Lillian finally felt like she was making progress. She hadn't called up any old friends, as Natalie suggested; but this morning, she did sign and mail the paperwork to Dave, officially ending her marriage. She was a single woman.

Lillian felt the ring rattle against her flesh in her fist as she walked through the sand. She paused to step out of the silver flats she wore and bent down to cuff her skinny jeans so they wouldn't get wet. She walked to the brink of the lake and pressed her toes into the sand as a small wave quietly lapped toward the shore. It was peaceful here. Around her, trees hid her location. A cliff of rocks, boulders, and pebbles ascended to her left. To her right, the edge of the lake expanded towards a line of trees until the water disappeared between their trunks. The sand was a light grey, not soft like the ocean, but course gravel not made entirely of rocks. The weather was beginning to cool down as October loomed in the near future. Lillian was looking forward to the brisk wind of Autumn and seeing the trees beginning to change colors. As if on cue, the wind strengthened, whipping her hair across her face, making her nails dig further into her palm.

Steeping forward, Lillian let the balls of her bare feet become engulfed by the waves. She shook the ring in her hand, feeling the diamond scratch her skin. Her life was forever changed now. She wasn't sure which direction it was going. Where would she end up? Lillian took another step forward. The water covered her feet. She jiggled the ring again. It seemed heavier now, weighing her down. Suddenly, she felt rage surging through her veins. The realization of all the years lost and of love underappreciated made her furious. Further, she was angry for being angry. For allowing herself to keep the hate for him locked inside. Abruptly, Lillian took a giant step forward, throwing her arm behind her, her fist closed so tightly, she could feel the diamond digging into her sweaty palm. She launched her entire body forward, her right arm leading. The ring flew from her grasp, sailing quickly up into the air. The wind pushed it high for a moment then plunged it back toward the waves. It disappeared from her view without a sound. She watched the waves lap over each other, like hungry dogs licking a bone. Then, she looked down at her empty, reddened hand with only an indentation left in the skin of her palm. She lifted her left hand and pressed her thumb into the center of her palm, covering the small circular dent left from the diamond. She noticed her bare ring finger. Although she hadn't worn her ring since the night she took it off, she was somehow surprised the ring was truly gone.

She thought she would feel a new energy, produced by the refreshing water washing over her feet. Becoming a new person. Letting go of the past. Starting something new. Everything the water was supposed to symbolize for her suddenly fell short.

And without her ring, she felt sadness crashing into her heart, much like the waves on the rocky shore.

THE GIRAFFE HUNTERS

MARIE HANNA CURRAN

Reaching up, I grab her hand following her indoors to weave between the assorted mix of people walking, riding in wheeling chairs and lying flat on slow moving beds.

"These people aren't like us." She says, "it's because they're special."

I think they're secret superheroes and begin to wish to be like one of them. She pulls me along the corridor for our visit in the special room, the one with the long name I can't read but looks like "Giraffe."

Opening the hinged door, the giraffes go into hiding behind the chairs of the special granny people. Knowing I can't go off and hunt, I sit beside my mother and the man she always speaks to during our visit.

As I begin to tell him about my new treehouse, two women approach me, calling me by different names, arguing over whose child I am. Then a man rushes over, telling the women I'm his; John's.

I laugh at them, knowing it's all a game. I don't have a father. My father's invisible.

When the funny adults leave, they begin looking behind chairs and under pillows. I want to join them, knowing they're on the hunt for the giraffes. Instead, I continue telling the man beside me about my plans for my treehouse. But he interrupts, asking when grandma will visit, saying no one visits him and he's all alone.

It's bad to lie and I tell him so, pointing out both me and mother who visit him all the time. Interjecting, mother explains his memory is bad but I know better; he's one of them and he is talking in code.

Sitting silently, I study him and realise he's younger than the rest of the adults in the room, more like mother's age than grandmother. Watching him, his head and eyes scan the room. I look too. No giraffes.

Saying goodbye, I wish the man good luck on his quest and as we leave the room, mother asks why. I tell her, "It's a secret."

WAITING FOR THE LIGHT

JEANNE DAVIES

Longchenpa slowly detached himself from the sphere of light. He'd just witnessed another life lost in the pursuit of truth. He felt spiritually drained but his scrawny, half-naked body remained poised on the square plinth. From high in the green Himalayan Mountains he could see, through his box of light, all the struggles of mankind.

The sun began to lower in the sky and he anticipated the gift of nourishment. A young monk entered the temple carrying a small tray. His movements felt like a gentle breeze and Longchenpa inhaled the aroma of Jasmine flowers. He could sense the sweat on the monk's brow, hear the dust falling from his feet and feel the energy of the outside world. The Samanera bowed and scraped his chin along the floor beneath the Lama as he crawled backwards from the sanctuary.

Longchenpa sighed as he sunk into his renewed isolation. He had lived 100 years this way, seeking absolute enlightenment through the box of light, just as his teacher had and many others before him; all longing for that illuminating void.

As the cup touched his lips the fragrant smell of Jasmine entered each nostril. The delicious liquid slipped down, soothing his throat and energizing his fragile transience. Through his tiny single window, he watched the cloak of dusk falling, creating shadows and swirling mists through the coniferous forests beyond. In the distance, tall firs lined the ridge of the emerald mountains like attentive choir boys.

Soon strands of silver moonlight aligned themselves upon him and night descended in a dark veil. He inhaled deeply and held on to the breath, allowing every morsel of oxygen to be absorbed by brain and body. Closing his eyes to blind himself from the moon he imagined the hours of daylight that he had, once again, deprived himself of. He visualized the innocent dawn, writing its dazzling message across the sky and gradually dimming all the heavenly bodies. He imagined the feel of warm sunshine on his face.

Longchenpa felt lifted above the restrictions of mortality and was awakened to an affinity with the universe. In his mind's eye he walked barefoot upon cooling moss on a path through long grasses and ferns. He entered a field of ripening corn where tiny fluorescent damsel flies darted in and out of flowing wheat like small fish; he could sense the gentle murmur of their invisible wings.

He transformed into a huge bottle green dragonfly, his elegant sapphire tail extending far behind him. He looked left and right to admire his luminescent wings, their transparency allowing only his shadow to reveal his presence against the thickly wooded emerald mountains.

At last he was free!

He maneuvered close beside a young musk deer, frocked in innocence and walking gracefully on stilettoed feet across the fauna. Momentarily her huge lash adorned globes glanced across at him, bowing her long neck in curiosity. His six feet attached to several pink hooded flowers of Himalayan Balsam, draped in heart shape leaves. He sped on, reluctantly leaving the sweet-smelling sticky nectar behind. A white butterfly flurried along erratically next to him, searching for Temple Magnolia; her paper thin wings blinked camaraderie at him.

Longchenpa then took the form of a mighty Himalayan Griffon with a large noble golden beak. His enormous cream feathered wings spread majestically beside him as he soared high above tea plantations neatly cultivated in endless rows along the mountain. Women up to their necks in bushes wore wicker baskets strapped to their hats as they stretched out to pick the delicate new leaves. Some gazed up at him and smiled, their hooded eyes alight with wonder.

He glided over rivers glistening from nearby glaziers, all snaking vibrantly through the lush green pastures. A family of snow leopards knelt cautiously to drink from the effervescent waters, their long spotted tails lifted perpendicular for balance. The bigger of the ghost cats raised its dramatic head to look up at him. He flew on past, not fooled by their endearing looks.

Up and up he ascended until he reached the ice covered mountains, his pale powerful shape barely visible against the snow. He found himself above the mighty Everest, the forehead of the sky. He marvelled at the majestic giant named '*Holy Mother*' by his people.

After a while, Longchenpa was aware that he'd escaped the earth's gravity, leaving the problems of mankind far behind. He was shrouded in lights which thickly dotted the velvet blackness. Stars mingled within his feathers as his wings began to glide without any effort into ethereal silence. A great peace fell upon him.

In the distance he could see an apparition, opaque but almost invisible. He was drawn closer to it. The light caught in every angle of the face like a mirror with many facets. Its hair consisted of rainbow coloured strands, continually changing shape in tiny wafts of light from the atmosphere. It sat at the edge of a great basin-shaped hole where raging fires intermittently released huge white balls of fire out into the atmosphere.

A voice radiated from the strange being. "Do you claim to be a spiritual guide?" it asked.

Longchenpa found he could not speak; but the being understood his inner thoughts.

"You must help the world before it is too late. Time is short for you, but you choose to distance yourself from these things. The human race will soon destroy itself with war and conflict."

With these words a strange sadness haunted the spectre and tears glistened in its eyes. Feeling no fear, Longchenpa plead for knowledge as to what he should do.

"Perhaps you have to be weakened in order to understand the human condition and to appreciate humility," it responded. "It is your duty to empower the innocent with your wisdom … to give them a voice."

Suddenly Longchenpa was plunged into complete darkness. A stark coldness crept right through him, invading every part of his body. Asphyxiated and paralysed, no breath went in or out of his lungs. He was suspended in a bottomless blackness, a deep empty void. At any moment he thought he might lose consciousness, but instead he remained frozen and his thoughts plummeted into pool of great sadness. It was a terrifying place filled with negativity and great emptiness, where nothing, least of all hope, existed. He knew then that he must be dead.

-o0o-

After what seemed like an eternity, Longchenpa's eyes opened. He was back in his sanctuary … back in his chosen place of isolation from the world. "As every flower fades, there is the knowledge that the plant will bloom again," a voice echoed around him.

He knew no matter how temporary life was, there would always be a constant … a creator watching over mankind and the equilibrium of the universe. "Only love is real," he muttered under his breath. Longchenpa then slept like he had never slept before in his whole life.

When Longchenpa awoke, things felt very different. He did not have all the answers, but tomorrow he, the Lama, would take his place once again as Guru and gather his villagers around him. He would stare into the children's beautiful upturned faces and choose his protégés to pass on the wisdom he had learned. From now on he would move amongst the people of the world to guide and teach them to love one another and live in peace.

Longchenpa would live this way until the end of his days … no longer waiting for the light.

TRANSFORMATION

CLAIRE DAVON

You approach the glade with caution. It is darker than you thought possible, even on a moonless night, as if a blanket has descended over the horizon. Clouds cover the sky as far as you can see, obliterating light.

You don't know what has called you here, only that you have been summoned. Your dreams have been filled with the vision of this night for weeks. The pull grew stronger with every passing turn of the earth. Tonight you knew without question this was the time you were expecting. You went when summoned, to this uncertain destiny that awaits you. There is no thought of refusal.

You pick through the trees surrounding the area, moving branches out of the way as silently as you can. You wince at every snap of twig, every rustle of leaves. Silence seems imperative. In the darkness you can't see more than a few feet in front of you. The gloom surrounds you like a black cloak.

You pause, breath sounding loud in your ears. It does not seem possible that there could be other beings on this strange night. Tonight it is only you and this place. All else is stillness.

There is a form lying supine in the middle of the opening. What you can see resembles the outline of a person. The night crowds around the being, blurring its silhouette.

With the mincing steps of prey, you edge into the clearing. Your attention is focused on the outline twenty feet away. The figure is motionless, lying on its side as if sleeping. You take another step, poised to run. But there is nothing else around, and no sound but the thump of your heart.

You don't know if you are still in a dream or have woken from it. This is like the images you have had night after night, each appearing more vivid until you found yourself here. This place seems unreal, but the sweat on your arms and the clouding of your eyes tell you that this could not be slumber.

There is neither sound nor horizon once you step into the clearing. It's as if a hush has fallen over everything. The only reality is the small semi-circle surrounded by a stand of tall trees. Thinking back, you have no memory of walking or the path you took to arrive. You remember doing the actions, but not the steps you performed to accomplish them. You look at your clothing. You recognize the pajamas as the ones you donned before going to bed last night. Their floral patterned flannel should not have been enough to keep you warm, but your body feels no chill.

You are where you need to be. You know that with a compulsion so strong that it overwhelms everything else. You, and no other, were intended for this glade, this night. This fate is for you alone.

You set your feet carefully, looking down at your bare toes. You make as little noise as possible as you approach the still, silent figure. At ten feet away you pause and listen again. Nothing. You look up, but the tops of the trees have vanished into the blackness of night. Blinking, you see a new trail of stars, arcing down over the skyline toward the figure in the glade. They gleam, but shed no light to guide your way. Branches rustle, as if guided by wind. Nothing else stirs.

You debate calling out, but stay silent. You are not even sure if you could form words. It seems wrong to do so, as if speaking would defile this sanctuary.

Sanctuary? You are startled by the word. You would not have thought of this space as somewhere safe. Still, the image refuses to leave your thoughts. It spins there, as if on a thread. Sanctuary.

All is dark, the deepest night, but you can see. The opening, the person, the trees, that was what you came for. You are sure with the knowledge. With a few steps you are in front of the form. It is still and unmoving, but you can see the faint rise and fall of its chest in the slight flutter of its bed of leaves and twigs. Alive, you think, for now.

You are close enough to see the person. Its hair is waist length, a lustrous black as dark as the surrounding night. It is a female, unlike any other. Her skin is as pale as milk. She would be tall and thin if she were standing up, with slight curves identifying her as a woman.

Her dress is the same color as her hair, black and ankle length with no sleeves and a generous v neck. It glimmers in the night as if lit by the stars that curve toward the glade. You want to feel the cloth of that dress under your fingers. The pads of your fingertips pulse with the desire.

You bend, put your hand in front of her face and feel a slight breath. You crouch, resting your weight on your flannel clad legs and study her. Something about her is timeless, like a statue whose beauty would be admired from a distance.

She stirs, opens her eyes, and looks at you with eyes as black as coal. You can see no white in those eyes, nothing to break the unremitting blackness.

"You have come," she said, and her voice is rough and broken, like shards of glass have pierced her throat. "You are here."

You do not understand these words, but find that you are nodding. She is wearing a necklace of onyx stones. They gleam in front of your eyes. You want to pull the chain from her body and place it around your neck.

"It is time," she says, remaining supine. She seems insubstantial, the leaves visible through her body. She takes your hand and places it on the stones. Electric power surges through your fingers. It does not hurt, but it makes your hair stand on end. Your body heaves, your bones shifting. You should be frightened and yet you are not. The woman continues to fade. Within moments, she is gone and only the slight indentation on her bed of leaves tell that she had ever been there at all.

You get to your feet. The ground moves away from you and you are confused for a moment and then you understand that it is you who is moving away. You are lengthening, adding height you have never possessed.

You understand that this is how it was always supposed to be. It was what you had been born for. It was the meaning of the dreams. Not dreams, but prophecy. This was, and had always been, your fate.

Air blows across your body and you look down. The flannel has dissolved from your arms and chest and your skin now glows the same color as the vanished woman's. You look down and see black cloth forming. You continue to grow and shift until you are standing six feet tall, wrapped in night and stars. If you could see your eyes you know they would now be black as the woman's had been. You are not frightened. This has been inevitable since you found yourself here.

"Nyx," a voice says. You do not recognize it, but it is familiar. It roars through you with the strength of a command, rippling and knife sharp. "There is much to be done."

You nod, straightening to your new height. Your floor length gown gleams of the stars that glide around you and arc up. Tendrils of long black hair wave over your hipbones. The pressure of jewelry at your neck makes you reach up and touch the onyx stones. You graze them as if they are talismans, whispering thanks to their darkness.

You see a deep black chariot and understand that it is yours. It is a hand span away, close enough to touch. It had not been in the glade before now. You enter the half circle, stand at the front, and then gesture upwards. The chariot moves at your motion. With it comes the stars and the shadows, surrounding you like a cloak. The evening is a living thing that pulses with your breathing. It is inky black all around you, your pale skin the only color in the darkness.

You move up into the sky, night flowing with you. You have work to do.

TODAY NEXT YEAR

WAYNE DEAN-RICHARDS

He woke before dawn, chest tight, lungs screaming. *Lie still*, he told himself. When that proved impossible, pushed his tongue around inside his mouth as if something was hidden in there. It didn't help, but then today it was always this way.

Making no noise, he dressed quickly. His urine reeked of panic and he brushed his teeth too hard, bloodying his gums.

He took the old tea tin from under the stairs, chose randomly before replacing it, and though there was time to eat he chose not to, swallowing the blood in his mouth on his way to the car.

His sister always ushered him in and made him tea. When it was no longer possible for her to avoid saying something, she would tell him she didn't see the point of what he did, didn't understand what he hoped to achieve by it. Always then, he'd try to show her the photo he had with him and always she'd refuse to look. This is why he decided not to go and see her today.

The moon, low and to his left, urged him to go back to bed, back to sleep. He'd feel better if he did, but knew he couldn't, not today.

The roads were empty yet he drove as if he were in heavy traffic as the moon paled and dipped, the ribbon of light below it thickened.

It didn't take him long to get back here. He could have walked. Maybe next year he'd try that. Now though, he brought the car to a halt, saw that the house had been recently renovated and the front lawn replaced by a driveway, but was sure a friend used to live here. If he knocked would Paul's parents answer, at first feeling irritated to be disturbed so early, then pleased to see him? Was that how it would be? He and Paul used to cycle to the nearby park. There they climbed trees, his hands hoisting him high into the penetrating blue, when today it was all they could do to hold the steering wheel.

Pulling away from the curb he drove along narrow roads, dug at the brake when he saw Paul step out of the newsagent's by their old school. The car slewed to a halt. Never mind that it'd sound stupid or sentimental, he'd tell Paul that just a few minutes ago he'd stopped outside his old house, would ask him if he remembered their ascents into the blue. But there was no one outside the shop. How could Paul have disappeared so quickly; a question he'd have dwelt on if a car hadn't drawn up behind him. Over-revving, he drove quickly away.

When he reached the church he parked and shut off the engine. A truck passed by, closely followed by a motorbike, after which the silence lengthened and grew weighty. Though tinged with grey the light seemed to bring out the red of the bricks, seemed to sharpen the spire. At last he studied the photo he'd taken from the tea tin. Black and white, as most photos taken in 1955 would have been, it showed his mother and father arm in arm, smiling for their posterity, impossibly young, impossibly distant. He was sure this was the church where they were married, yet once again there was no sense of communion, no re-connection and therefore no point trying to speak of things left unspoken.

Never mind, he told himself. On the anniversary of their death today next year he'd choose another photo from the tea tin, maybe the photo of his father outside the steelworks. Though the steelworks was long gone, perhaps it would help that he'd witnessed red hot billets disgorged from a furnace then shaped by men whose faces were smeared with sweat. Perhaps, he told himself, perhaps...

OPEN AND SHUT

CLAY DRYSDALE

The front door slammed with a bang. Sighing, he braced himself for the certain onslaught.

Chelsea marched into the living room and threw her overcoat on the worn, tan sofa. "I can't believe you! How many times have I told you to bring up the garbage can on trash day? We don't need the city fining us again!"

Marital discord had become the norm for them over the years. "Sorry. Some of us aren't perfect like Your Majesty."

"You know, you're a real piece of work. Every day I come home and find you sitting in that ratty chair. I should have listened to my sister. She tried to warn me about you."

He was unfazed. "I'm sitting in this chair to relax after a long day at the plant. Maybe if you didn't stay at the office so late you'd get home before I do, every once in a while." He lifted his chin and stroked his stubble with his fingertips. "And speaking of your sister, why do you always have to bring her into our arguments?"

"What kind of a question is that?" Chelsea asked. "She only came up because she was forever cautioning me against marrying you -- all the way up until the day I walked down the aisle."

"Oh...I know she did," He said, barely above a whisper. A note of confidence lingered in his words.

"What do you mean, you know?"

"I just mean that I know." He lifted his head and his eyes gleamed as he met her gaze. "Anyway, marrying me must have been quite a letdown for you, considering the wonderful upbringing you had. Let's see now... drunk father, crazy mother, pedophile brother. Hmmm." He paused for effect. "But look on the bright side. At least you inherited your mother's hips." He looked down at Chelsea's frame and widened his eyes in mock disbelief. "Childbirth should be a breeze for you."

"That's IT!" She grabbed a nearby vase and sailed it toward him. It shattered against the wall, a foot to the left of his head.

He glanced down at the pale blue pieces of clay littering the hardwood floor. "Your aim never was any good." He remained calm and composed. Her eyes glared in fury.

After a few seconds he said, "Well, I'm outta here." He stood and walked toward the door, his back to her.

"Oh no you don't!" Chelsea lunged at him, knocking him squarely in the back and sending them both crashing to the floor. She grabbed a fistful of his thick, dark hair and pulled hard on it, as if it were a tug-of-war rope. "How's this for aim, you jerk?" she screamed at him.

He remained calm even though his head was cocked backward at an awkward angle. "Let me ask you something, Dear. Why do you think your sister kept warning you about me? What reason would she have for trying to change your mind about getting married?"

Chelsea quit pulling, but did not relax her grip on his hair. Her eyes narrowed. "Just what are you saying?"

"Perhaps she was trying to make things easy for you. Maybe -- just maybe -- she was trying to let it be your decision to call off the wedding. Yours instead of mine...and hers."

He paused, letting the truth take root. Chelsea's brows furrowed in thought. "In case you're wondering, yes, I loved you. I wanted to marry you. The problem was I loved her also, and she loved me back."

Then he drove home the dagger. "Or should I say 'loves'. At least that's what she told me 45 minutes ago." His eyes glanced over to a light pink scarf lying in a rocking chair across the room. Her eyes followed his. Neither one said anything more.

Chelsea was still sitting on his back, frozen and lost in thought. Her mind traveled back across a dozen years. Fragments of conversations, knowing glances, and too-warm smiles began to coalesce in her mind's eye. With resolve she let go of her husband's hair and took a deep breath to regain her composure.

Chelsea arose and retrieved her overcoat from the sofa. She walked across the living room and out the front door, never looking back. The latch clicked softly behind her as her fingertips slid from the knob.

NIGHT HAG

JESSE DUROVEY

The middle of the night is always the worst, Connor thinks. That's when, if he doesn't keep his guard up, his past comes back to haunt him.

He thought it would be safe to stop taking his medication, if only just for the day. The meds make him feel foggy and bland, even if they do keep the nightmares at bay. He just wanted one day free from the fatigue and apathy which hangs on his shoulder like a vulture. Now, he sees the shadows slipping closer and he can hear the old, familiar droning in his skull.

The darkness can still hurt him.

The bedroom is dim and shadowy. Connor tries to move closer to Dana, but none of his muscles obey his commands. Only his eyes rove back and forth like tiny, blue searchlights. A small band of light taunts him from under the bathroom door. *The pills are in your medicine cabinet, dumbass,* Connor thinks.

Connor replays a memory of going to the park with Dana that afternoon and reclining on the verdant blanket of grass. Connor had tucked a flower that looked as vibrant as a lion's mane into Dana's dark hair. Her laughter made him forget about the worries which lurk in the darkened corners of his memory. When she got up and walked to the public restroom, she left Connor lying among the grasshoppers and ladybugs, staring up at a blue sky full of gossamer clouds.

102

He must have dozed for a few minutes but when he woke up, Dana had not returned.

Connor felt exposed on the grass and stood up. The birds had stopped singing and even the cicadas ceased their rattling timbre. The air felt charged with electricity, a violent hue of green which reminded him of an impending storm. His mouth watered. He fought the urge to vomit. *Where was Dana?* Connor thought.

A deep, vicious growl sent a tremor through Connor. He turned to face a large dog, its fur shaggy and filled with tangled whorls of tan and black. It looked like one of the mutts that he used to see wandering the Afghan tribal lands. A couple of guys in his unit had even adopted a pup, but sadly they saw most of the mongrels eating dead bodies in the streets or being trained to kill each other by Taliban warlords.

This dog's shoulders reached to Connor's waist.Iit raised its hackles and lifted a foamy upper lip to reveal thick, yellow teeth. Its crimson eyes horrified Connor—he had seen those eyes before. It was the same mutt from the night of the botched raid—the raid when Connor had accidentally shot an Afghan mother and child. He was sure of it. Connor remembered when the raid was over and he sat with a cigarette between his trembling fingers. The dog ran by with the child's hand in its mouth. Connor shot the dog's retreating form with his M4 carbine.

In the park now, Connor stared into the dog's red eyes, a bead of cold sweat trickled down his armpit—the smell of his own fear sour in his nostrils. He prayed he wouldn't piss himself.

"Hey, get away from him!"

The dog turned its great head toward the sound of Dana's hoarse yell and barked twice, strings of saliva flying. Connor was sure it would lunge at her but Dana kept walking forward, waving her arms until the mongrel gave a reluctant snarl and lumbered off. Connor collapsed on the lawn, his heart hammering in his chest.

He wanted to rush home to take a cocktail of antidepressants and Ambien and then chase the pills with a mouthful of vodka. Dana convinced him a stray dog wasn't worth getting so agitated about and urged him to take her to dinner. By the time they got home, he forgot about the incident at the park and collapsed on the bed, sleep taking him in a dim and sightless embrace.

* * *

Now, in the darkness of the bedroom, Connor realizes the truth. *I screwed up*, he thinks. *It's that mutt from the raid in Aliabad, and now it's here for me. It must have led that Afghan kid's mother to me.* He doesn't understand it, but he feels like the pills must have protected him—masked his scent and kept the monsters at bay. Now, he feels he is at their mercy.

He struggles to look at Dana, but he can't turn his head. He can feel her breath as soft as velvet on his cheek. *How can she just lay there? Doesn't she hear them? They're creeping just outside the bedroom door*, he thinks.

Connor wants to hide under the blankets like a little boy—but his arms are heavy and impotent at his sides. He tries to shake his body back and forth, but he feels like he's being crushed by the mass of some unseen and vengeful force.

The bedroom door creaks open. Connor's heart pounds like a prize-fighter's. He tries to speak, to cry out or make some sound that will wake his sleeping lover—but his voice sounds foreign and primitive in his own ears.

Connor blinks, and three dark, shadowy figures stand at the side of his bed. Their features are smoky and indistinct, but he makes out the shapes of a woman, a child, and a gigantic dog. Their faces are masked in shadow—all but their red eyes. A roaring sound surges against Connor's eardrums—an ocean crashing with impossible force—blocking out all other noise.

The night covers him like a burial shroud.

SHAKEN, UNDETERRED

SHARON ECKMAN

He spent his last £30 on a plate of oysters and a glass of champagne.

"You are such a delusional prick," she said before throwing him and his Bond DVDs out the door.

What would James do, he wondered as he stood outside in the incongruously warm air, looking up at the window of their – her – flat? Such a momentous event, surely there should be a storm, or at least a drizzle. Her face appeared, a pale blur, and his heart lifted in an instant of hope until she raised her middle finger and turned away.

What would James do, if James were an actor who made most of his laughable income from Bond-impersonator stripograms? A passing resemblance to Daniel Craig was no longer enough, even if you came with your own swimwear. There was a time when people had stopped dead on the street or peered in at restaurant windows at him.

"Are you? Oh wow, are you him?"

A couple of times he'd said yes, just because and signed Daniel's name with a flourish on a serviette or the back of a chequebook.

"God, what are you like?" she'd said once with a laugh still denoting affection.

"He's my nemesis," he told her. "All actors have one and Daniel Craig is mine. So I'm sure he wouldn't begrudge me the occasional signature and free pint."

When he began posing for selfies with random members of the public, her laughter became less affectionate. "You're not Daniel fricking Craig, are you? You can't even get a job in rep."

"There is no rep anymore ," he said, the voice of thespian doom.

"Fringe then," she replied, undeterred. "When was the last time you ever brought any sodding money into this house?"

"That video..."

"They paid your travel. And gave you a Pret sandwich. Which you ate. Get a bloody job, you lazy arse."

He looked on the MI5 website to see if they were recruiting. If he couldn't be Daniel Craig, perhaps he could be a spy. He'd been in an episode of Spooks, hadn't he? OK, it was a walk-on – or walk-by, if he were honest – but still. He understood the genre.

In what he termed an ironic twist of fate, he got a counter job at Pret until they let him go for not being happy enough. Calls to his agent went unreturned. He'd only ever wanted to act. If he couldn't do that, then what was he? Who was he? Did he even exist?

He sat at Searcy's bar at St Pancras station, plastic carrier bag full of DVDs under his stool. He watched the Eurostar doors swish open, travellers with pull-along cases met and hugged, or resolutely stepping away into the unforgiving swirl of London. What would James do, apart from stealing a Bugatti, and shagging a beautiful woman with a shady past and unfeasibly sharp cheekbones?

He checked his pockets. Fluff, a semi-shredded tissue and his phone, out of credit.

He looked up as the barman cleared his throat. For one so metrosexually cool (gelled hair, eyeliner), the barman exuded a puppy-like excitement.

"Go on, you're him, aren't you? I've been dying to ask... can I get you a martini? On me?"

He drained the dregs of his champagne, never losing eye contact with the barman. He smiled; mystery, danger and invulnerability in one flawless package. "Shaken, not stirred," he said, easing the carrier bag further under the stool with a delicate movement of his foot.

HELL IS A HOLIDAY

BILL ENGLESON

Velma had begged me to take a run up country to look for Hedda Gobbler, a friend's wild chick. I could never say no to her. Hedda had apparently hooked up with Dom Fricker, a rogue domestic who'd absconded from some horrendous bird factory in the southern foothills. I'd heard about such places, huge factory farms where the inmates were cloistered in stacks and force fed god knows what to puff them up enough to be succulent tasting after death. If I ever caught up with Dom Fricker, I hoped he'd share some of his stories. You had to keep learning about life's waiting horrors or you were toast. Or maybe stuffing!

Even though Christmas wasn't the best of times to be a main course in plain sight, I was resigned to leave the city behind and bring in the New Year on the road.

Before I could take off in search of Hedda, however, I needed to get my facts straight. Velma told me that her friend, Lana Gobbler, lived on the outskirts of town in an abandoned chicken coop. Lana had fallen on hard times a few months earlier and was squatting in the Semi-Rurals. "She doesn't have a phone, Turk. You'll just have to take your chances that she's home."

"Don't worry, babe," I reassured her. "My whole shtick is taking chances."

With that bubble of bravado still stretching believability, I headed out to question Lana.

Lana hadn't done herself any favours by moving to her new location. The whole area was a snafu shantytown of abandoned sheds and dilapidated shacks. It wasn't as decrepit as I'd heard Detroit had become, but it was in a *serious* state of decay.

Velma once told me that she met Lana, who had been her manicurist, at Nails and Feathers, a hoity-toity hair boutique. "A chick's got to baste herself, Turk, if she's going to stay in the game," was something Velma often said.

She'd been going to Nails and Feathers about a year after her previous salon turned into an abattoir.

Snake Tucker owned Nails and Feathers. As head honcho, he had run through all of the girls in his shop in the year Velma had been frequenting his establishment, but finally met his match when he hit on Lana. She was tough as toenails at that point and beat Snake back with a hair dryer. He sacked her and put the word out that she was toxic.

Though her loyalty was torn, Velma returned to Snake's magic hands. She figured that, while Lana was a pretty good friend, Snake was a master stylist and, once you snagged a good one, you hung on to him like a wishbone. At the same time, she felt guilty and wanted to do Lana a favour to make up for returning to Snake. *I* was the penance. "I'll owe ya big time, Turk. It'd break my heart if I couldn't make it up to her."

She had me. She had pulled my heartstrings so tight, my neck was strangling from love.

I set out after dark on Dec 22. It was feather-freezing cold but, happily, dry. I made my way through the shadowy dark side streets and back lanes. Almost from the get-go, I sensed I had a fiendish feline on my tail. Even with my tazer, I knew I was a sitting duck for any of the sly, deadly and grotesque urban vampire tabbies who hunted with abandon wherever they wanted to. They were especially known to ride on the roofs of cars, waiting for just the right moment when a weak motorist, wrapped up in the hubbub of driving and living, forgot to be on his guard.

I continued steering into the night, easing out of the city and slowly, gradually, heading for the Inner-Rurals.

The residents of the Inner-Rurals felt they had the best of both worlds, poised as they were between country, the Outer-Rurals and city, the Inner-Urban. I thought they had the worst of both, but try telling them that. Not only did they have people all around them, forceful zoning bylaws demanded their giant turfs of sod must be kept cleaved at all times. Those same bylaws demanded that their crew-cut foliage always look as green as emeralds. To achieve this, they often had to accent the colour with chemicals.

Don't get me wrong! I liked green rolling hills, trimmed, neat, look-ing like a real *proper* lawn; it all appealed to me. Raised as a backyard pet on a decent size city lot, surrounded by concrete and high-rises where my kind was not permitted to go, my life had been tolerable. Within the relatively large yard where I was raised by my people, I was more or less content with my lot. They showed me a lot of love, as much as this turkey could handle, anyways. Which was quite a lot, really. They accepted me for who I was. They were vegetarians. I discovered this after eavesdrop-ping one summer afternoon on an eye-opening culinary discussion they had with our barbecuing neighbours. Well, once I realized that my kind were considered eatable by the majority of humankind, I thanked my lucky stars for *my* non flesh ingesting humans. I reciprocated their love and dietary inclinations by any means that would make me loveable. In hindsight, I must admit they were a little odd. He taught Sociology at the University and she was a peace activist. Gentle folk, they were. Rare to find in humans.

I don't really weep much, a few turkey tears at most, but I could feel some droplets of drizzly dribble down my face. It happens when I get wistful about my humans. I pulled myself together and focussed on the road. As I was driving by a mirrored building, one of those glass towers that careless fowl occasionally splat into from time to time, I used the opportunity to take a glimpse. THERE IT WAS!!! A massive Urban Vampire Tabby was clutching the top of my roof. It was a huge sucker; maybe 3 turkeys tall, and was gazing into the reflecting high rise, its ap-palling red eyes staring straight back at me. Worse still, its carnivorous claws had pieced my roof. It wasn't going anywhere unless I could shake it loose. I started pumping the brakes hard, trying to dislodge it. It wasn't moving. Then one of its claws slashed my forehead. I was one swipe away from cashing out.

I was in a tight spot, so I slammed down on the gas. In ten minutes I hit the Sprawl, an Inner Rural anomaly of low flat buildings which housed fly-by-night services humans assumed they could not do with-out.

Up ahead, I caught a gander of possible salvation. It was a sight you don't see often; an old couple, him looking like Albert E, that iconic scientist and his missus, also looking like Albert E, albeit with a bun on her head rather than a frizzy mop, were out there, bold as brass, walking some dumb pet turkey like it was daylight. But it wasn't daylight. It was dark as ink. No one *lived* in the Sprawl. All it was good for was com-merce. You *went* there to purchase goods and then you got the heck out.

No dawdling, except maybe for some fast food or java. And even if you did spend more time than recommended in the Sprawl, you never took your dumb cluck pet turkey with you. That was just asking for trouble.

The Urban Vampire Tabby on my roof was having the same thoughts. Just as I was ruminating on Sprawl decorum, the creature pounced onto the pavement and, in two jiggles of a turkey's jowl, sprung on the doomed domestic. The old couple dropped the leash and cowered backwards. The UVT chomped into the soft thin neck of their precious pet. Blood spurted like a waterspout from an open, heat wavy fire hydrant. The old woman shrieked. Her hubby, the old Albert E. look-alike, stood there frozen in arthritic alarm. I wondered for a moment if he was thinking what was crossing *my* mind, that there had been stories of old folks being dragged into alleys by packs of UVT`s and eaten up like the barely nutritious appetizers they were.

Quick as a wink, the pet turkey, pretty and ribbon pink, was a lifeless and bleeding bag of bones. I stayed where I was, in the relative safety of my vehicle. The UVT was smacking its lips uncontrollably. It had been easy pickings for the Feline creature. I wondered if it was still famished. It might not matter. Bloodlust was in its eyes. It looked up at the old Albert E couple. I could see we were on the same page. And the same cookbook! They turned, started to skedaddle. The UVT held his position. He had read the situation precisely. The old folks could run, but they couldn't hide.

THE MAGIC THAT SHE WROTE

KAIN FAIRBROOKS

She died that day.

The woman from the cottage house across the field from our farm. I could see the medical people, dressed head to toe in a white uniform, carrying out her body on a stretcher. On top of her body was a white blanket that draped over her corpse.

My father explained to me that she was a very old and lonely lady, who carried many burdens on her shoulders. But no one knew exactly what she was, how she lived, or where she came from. Speculations from the other gossiping neighbors filled the air, but no one knew for sure. The only thing I knew about her was the exotic garden that grew in the back of her cottage, where the forest was said to begin. It was barricaded by a grass wall that stretched for miles through the trees and plants that grew back there, although some were overflowing above the wall. I would stroll by it every day to and from school, pondering, "What was she keeping in there?" Sooner or later she would catch me with my hand against the cold grass that breezed with mystery.

"Get off that wall!" her old shriveled voice would shriek harder than a banshee.

I was scared of her. That frown she gave me was worse than the one Mama had towards me. Her old saggy skin frightened me out of my wits. She barely had any eyebrows. Her gray hair was placed in a bun sitting on top of her head. And those eyes, there was something in her chestnut eyes that caused her to scream in great anger. But what was it?

That day she died, in the middle of the night, I decided for the first time that I should go inside her house. I put on my knee high boots, grabbed my father's flashlight, and left the house without disturbing anyone.

I tromped across the fields towards her home, my heart racing with excitement. I wondered what would be inside her home and what would happen to her garden that she kept locked away? When I came to the cottage house, I knew her front door wouldn't be opened but I tried anyway. My small childlike hand gripped the doorknob and turned it. To my surprised, the door opened. Why would the door be open?

Nonetheless, I still entered the house. I clicked on the flashlight to see what was inside. It was clean to a certain extent. No dirty carpets, no cats, which Mrs. Marcy claimed, gossiping she was just some cranky old cat lady, but there were papers. Papers filled the coffee table beside the salmon sofa which had quilts covering one of the cushions. Papers scattered across the carpet, next to the bookcase. It was a sea of papers inside that house. Across from the couch was a fireplace mantel. Sitting in between two golden candle holders was an envelope.

I moved cautiously towards this envelope, making sure I didn't step on any papers that were thrown about. My hand reached out to grab it, but a sudden noise disturbed me. It was the sound of a violin playing. Its beautiful sound led me out of the living room, through the dining room and toward the backdoor. My hand opened the door to reveal a beautiful colored garden containing almost every flower, vine, earth imaginable. I had stumbled upon a secret garden that basked in the moon's light. I set my flashlight down on the small steps before strolling down them into the soft grass.

"This place is incredible!" I awed, smiling one of the biggest smiles I ever had.

I traveled through this garden of wonders that was much bigger than I assumed it was. Like a hand, the strings of the violin led me to the very center of this garden. Standing there was an alluring young boy with dark blonde hair, wearing a tux without the jacket.

His eyes were closed as he played the song that lead me. Surrounding him were dancing female statues, all wearing different types of dresses that seemed to have frozen in time. The air around him swarmed like a dream, one from which I could never wake and didn't want to. Soft and calm, it was something I had never felt.

"Do you like the music?" His voice questioned as his red colored eyes opened, piercing right at me. I nodded my head, and he stopped playing.

"Who are you?" He asked. I opened my mouth to answer but he gave out a chuckle.

"It's alright. The most important part is that you're in time for the masquerade."

"Masquerade?"

"Yes!" he nodded his head, before lifting up his arm. The bow slid across the violin and as it slid golden dust began twirling out from his playing.

He played the song '*Waltz from Masquerade*' by Khachaturian which I knew from a movie. The golden dust flew towards the female statues that were frozen. It engulfed them in a sparkling glow, and they transformed into real women who began dancing. As they danced around the young man, the grass beneath them turned into an elegant floor and soon everything around me became as if I stood in the grand ballroom with a chandelier hanging above me. People wearing colorful masquerade costumes began to appear out of this magic dust. Some were dancing on the ballroom floor, others stood along the walls drinking from the pretty colored glasses, and some gawked as the talented young man continued to play. Chatter from the uncanny people filled the ballroom with life.

An orchestra appeared beside me, played along with the young man. Once the song was over, everyone applauded, and he took a bow.

"Ladies and gentlemen!" He spoke to everyone in the room, "It is an honor to have you all here with me tonight. A very special occasion has arisen.. I will be having the first dance with this young lady."

He held his hand out towards me. Everyone's eyes gazed at me, waiting for me to respond. My heart pounded against my chest. I had never danced before, let alone a formal dance! Still, I smiled shyly as I approached him. When I did, the golden magic in the air slowly turned my pajama dress into a beautiful red ballroom gown. Black gloves appeared on my arms as I reached out and grabbed his hand.

The violin in his other hand vanished, disappearing into the same golden dust that created everything. We started to dance, but I felt nervous and unsure. "I don't think I can dance." I whispered to him.

"Just follow my footsteps." He reassured.

"Am I dreaming?" I asked.

"No." he smiled. After the dance, he said, "You must leave this place." When I asked him why, he wouldn't tell me. He then kissed my forehead, "I will see you again."

The golden world around me began to vanish, and I was left standing alone in the middle of the garden I had once entered. I gazed around. The beautiful red dress changed back into my pajama dress. The statues weren't there anymore, nor were the traces of the young boy. Was he telling the truth? Will I get to see him and his golden world once again?

Through the large garden, I found my way back into the cottage. Walking up the steps, I swooped down and grabbed the flashlight. I turned it on as I strolled back through the dark cottage house, but this time I stopped at the fireplace. I reached out and grabbed the letter. I hopped over to the couch and softly sat down on the quilt. I opened the envelope which contained a letter that was folded in three crisp folds. I held the flashlight over the letter's words. It read;

'My dearest Rose Minuet

    It is time for you to live the life I have written for you. I knew you would come when I died because that is what I wrote. My story has ended and now yours will begin. Because I am the author of your life, the creator of your world, and now you will embark on an adventure of which I have always dreamed, the adventure of traveling beside a prince and his masqueraded dreams. However, the papers that are scattered aroundare about you and your tale. I will give you two choices now. The first is to read your own tale, your future, till the very end of your last breath. The second is to walk out the door and live it. Choose wisely, for the world is in your hands, because you have become God.

    Sincerely, Elizabeth Words

What? I have become...God? My eyes examined the sea of papers surrounding me. It felt like I was going to be consumed by life and death. My body trembled and the letter slipped out of my hand. Fear of what the future held set inside me. I stood up, leaving the quilt on the sofa. I would choose. The papers beaconed. The door beaconed too. In that instant, I knew what I would do.

FROZEN

PETER FANNING

I hung up the phone and held my head in my hands. The dark walls of my apartment felt like a tomb as my mom's voice rattled around in my head.

"Your father's frozen."

Sounds dramatic, but I had a hunch about what had happened. I'd dumped the brunette for a blonde, only the brunette turned out to be quite vengeful. I shut off the Nintendo 64 and picked up the phone.

"Natasha, you've got to undo this thing."

"What thing?"

"Look, I know you hate me, but…"

Click.

She stopped answering the phone. Then she changed her number. A restraining order followed. Then she vanished. To this day I tell anyone who will listen, never date a witch.

Out of guilt I moved home and we tried make things work. And yes, Dad was frozen solid but he wasn't dead. When the weather turned hot we carted him out to the front lawn in hopes that he'd thaw. The neighbors stared. I felt terrible. Worse than terrible. I'd brought Natasha over for dinner a few times and she and Dad had butted heads. This was all my fault.

But Mom wouldn't hear it, she made the best of things. In typical

Mom fashion she sat with him every night watching Jeopardy, her vodka and cranberry resting in his lap to keep chilled.

Five years passed. Mom carried on conversations with my father as though he were a few degrees away from responding. I worried she was losing it. We all were. My dad was frozen.

Mom swore she could see a smile on his hardened blue lips when the Cubs were on. I nodded along. By then I'd hired an investigator but it seemed Natasha had dropped off the planet. Life went on. Somehow I got engaged to a sweet girl. I waited to tell her about my dad. Maybe he'd come around.

By year ten, Mom was still going strong. Both of us were excited about the whole global warming thing. Iintroduced Julie, who after fainting, stuck it out with me, even when we bought the house next door. There was no progress on the Natasha front. She'd taken her broom and bolted.

Twenty years. I was 42 and had a nine year old son. My poor dad's mug still frozen in time, which was weird because time and worry had crinkled my mom's pretty face. But she still held hope, making more than one inappropriate joke about his stiffness.

A local news station caught wind of a frozen man and I thought the lid was going to blow. A neighbor came over, screamed bloody murder and ran off telling anyone who'd listen. Mom fended them off, but the sharks were swarming. So when my phone rang I braced myself for another journalist sniffing around.

"Hello David."

A husky voice prickled my ear. "Natasha?"

"Long time."

My blood charged, rippled through my veins and I fell against the wall. Julie watched with a hand clinging to her mouth.

"I'm getting married and I feel it's time I let you off the hook."

Then she was gone again. I dropped the phone and Julie dove to my side. We heard a shriek. I bolted out of the house, ran next door, rushing inside to find my father on the floor shivering, his t-shirt and pants soaking wet and clinging to his sides. I glanced at Mom, her face ashen and her breathing heavy.

"It's....so....cold...."

We got Dad changed and covered him with blankets and towels. I gave Mom a tearful account of Natasha and what happened. Julie stood in the doorway with our son, her mouth hanging open.

"I can hardly tell you two apart."

My Mom turned to me and then to my dad, her cloudy eyes filling with the horror and shock of losing a husband and at the same time gaining a son. Trembling, Dad looked over to me.

"Twenty years, huh? Well, did the Cubs win a pennant?"

ELLA MAR

JASON FEINGOLD

I walk upon the beach tracing the patterns of the waves, feeling the sand pulled from beneath my feet in the constant ebb and flow and the undertow that gnaws. I look seaward. The ocean is supposed to be blue. It should be blue. If the world were willing to meet my expectations, it would be blue as blueness itself.

Walking on this beach does nothing to mend me. There is nothing here, nothing at all. The vastness and power of the ocean make me insignificant. I am not free. I am not wise. I just don't understand, like a rat in a cage.

I need nothing more complicated than a Freytag triangle to explain my life. It is an ardor, a specter, a long, slow dissipating. I turn the page to read another chapter, but the story is over. The flyleaves are as blank as night.

There is no lesson to be learned from *el mar*. Or is it *la mar*? There is only vastness, emptiness, and the wait for the hand from above that will one day come to squash me flat. This beach is not profound; for all its noise, it is silent. There are only lines that divide one colored vapor from another. There are only the places that *she* will never go, the sand upon which *she* will never walk, and the water that would not be blue enough for *her* either.

This is my destiny and final purpose, spoken by the design of the tide: to wear away the earth until all is ground into dust.

HOLDING HANDS
WITH IVAN

DAVID FORD

All that greeted Abigail when she awoke, was her pillow. She was a girl far too young to be lonely, yet there she lay in a void of despair, holding the sheets close to her for comfort and safety. Another day alone and afraid was just beginning.

That Saturday began the same way every Saturday did, with breakfast at her favourite diner. Abigail had lived in the city since she was twenty, and every weekend for the last four years she came into Louis' and ordered bacon and eggs with a strong coffee. She always sat by herself in every single chair in the joint and heard all the golden hits on the radio while she watched friends become lovers, and lovers become wed on the other tables. The year was now 1957, and the world was not liberal enough to see a twenty-four-year-old woman sit alone and not think there was something wrong with her.

Today she couldn't take it, and watched the door instead. Abigail once believed in fate, till fate forgot about her. Then the red double door swung open and in stepped the most handsome man she ever set eyes upon. His jaw was chiseled, hair as brown as the sweetest chocolate, his bright blue eyes immediately fixed on her.

Abigail began to blush. He was coming towards her. Why?

"Excuse me," he said, forcing her to look up through her shame, "It looks like this place is a bit crowded. Do you mind if I sit with you?"

"With me?" Abigail replied, looking around at the hordes of empty tables around the diner. "Yes, if you don't mind,"

"Sure, I'm Abigail."

"Ivan," he introduced. As he sat a strange sense of familiarity came over Abigail, she felt like she'd met him before, but from where?

"Do I already know you?"

"No, I think I'd remember meeting such a pretty girl," "I just feel like I know you,"

"Maybe it's just fate,"

"You believe in fate?" she asked, reinvigorated.

"Of course, I only came in to check the time. Who'd have known you'd be sitting there?"

"It's half ten," she said, looking at her watch to avoid looking stupid.

"Perfect. Abigail, would you like to go for a stroll?" "Really?"

"Yeah, then the cinema, and dancing?" "I love the cinema and dancing!"

"Who doesn't?"

"Well come on then, let's leave while the radio is playing rubbish. I don't recognize any of these songs."

"They must be new," Ivan declared as they stood up and left together.

The sun was warm on their backs as they walked through the park. The smells of fresh cut grass and cool summer breezes surrounded them in their own little bubble.

"So, what do you do?" Ivan asked.

"I'm a book keeper for an accountant. What about you?" "Shipyards, but I'm more interested in you. Your job sounds great. "

"Just a lot of numbers really," she said, bowing her head. "You need to be clever though."

"You build ships for the country, that's much more important than number crunching." Abigail instantly wished she'd not come on too strong. She was terrified of scaring him off.

"Can I ask you something?" "Ok," she braced herself for humiliation.

"Can I hold your hand?" That's not what she expected.

"Oh, of course you can," Abigail hand was taken by the softest and warmest hand she'd ever experienced. She felt safe and comfortable right there. This was all she'd ever wanted, someone who thought she was special and was proud to be seen with her. She never wanted their stroll to end.

"The park feels smaller than I remember," she sighed.

"Yeah, it does. Let's go see a film. *An Affair To Remember* is on."

"I've wanted to see that for ages. How did you know?" she said, squeezing his hand.

"Hunch," Ivan lead her to the picture house.

They sat together at the back of the theater. Abigail imagined herself as Deborah Kerr and Ivan as Cary Grant aboard that ocean liner, forgetting the rest of the world existed. Halfway through, she heard Ivan yawn, then felt his arm around her shoulders. It was difficult not to laugh like a schoolgirl when he did it. She couldn't wait to tell her friends. She snuggled into his arm. He was cheesy, but if this affection was for her, she didn't give a damn.

"That was a great film," he said outside.

"Magical, I loved it,"

"I bet it'll still be your favorite in fifty years." "You'll have to stick around and find out."

"I'll hold you to that," he said, hugging her tight into him like it would be the last time. "Do you want to get dinner?"

Before she knew it, they were sitting in a restaurant she'd never seen before, and Ivan was bringing over two portions of fish and chips.

"This is my favorite, how did you know?" Abigail said, tucking in.

"To be honest, it's been my lucky day. Starting when I met you," he said, putting a chip in his mouth.

Abigail's cheeks were beginning to hurt from all the smiling. "How do you know how to make me feel so special?"

"It's quite easy when you're already so special anyway," Agony in her cheeks now from smiling, but she didn't care. This was wonderful. After dinner, Ivan walked her home. Abigail began to feel the pit in her stomach deepen with every step, until finally they were at her door.

"I don't want today to end," she said as he held her tight. "Well, I did promise you a dance,"

"I've got a record player inside," she offered, hoping he'd kick etiquette into the curb.

"Perfect," he said, as etiquette fell onto the road.

Inside, Abigail went to get them both a drink as Ivan picked a record. She entered the room just as Nat King Cole began to sing *Unforgettable*.

"You really are lucky. This is my favorite song. I'm not even surprised by now,"

"I suppose I'll have to try harder then," he said, taking her hand and holding her waist, they began to spin slowly on the spot to the lush vocals and huge piano sound.

"Ivan, you could leave for Timbuktu in the morning and I'd never forget you as long as I live," Abigail said as the song wound down.

"I know you won't, Abigail," he replied as his eyes welled up. But Abigail began to yawn, such a big day.

"Sorry," she said, "I'm not usually up so late,"

"You should get some rest," Ivan said, looking deep into her sparkling emerald eyes. "You'll never lose your beauty as long as you live." he promised. "I hate going to sleep alone. Will you stay with me till I'm asleep?" she took Ivan's hand in hers, hoping he'd have one last correct answer today.

"Of course, I'll sit with you and not leave till you drift off,"

He put her to bed and lay beside her, hearing her breathing soften every second. "I'm so glad I met you, Ivan," she said, in a dream like state.

"You're the best thing that's ever happened to me, Abigail,"

"Ivan, I love you," she said, he put his arm over her and whispered into her ear, "I love you forever," Abigail never stopped smiling as she fell asleep that night.

As soon as he was sure she was sleeping, Ivan rose and picked his jacket off the chair. Reaching into the pocket, he pulled out a yellow envelope with *Abigail* written beautifully on the front. He put the card on the window and glanced down at the tarnished wedding ring on his wrinkled old hand.

"Happy anniversary, my darling,"

The varicose veins showed his age as he swept the white hair off her forehead to kiss it.

He took *An Affair To Remember* out of the DVD player, put it on the shelf next to Nat King Cole, and

left.

"Ivan?" a gentle voice called from down the corridor, "Ivan, how is she?" a nurse asked, rubbing

something on her blue uniform.

"She had a good day, today," he forced a smile. "We met fifty-nine years ago today, you know, got married exactly two years later. Now I have to introduce myself every morning,"

"Alzheimer's is a horrible disease. My dad was the same," she empathized as only a nurse can.

"I'm just glad that even though she wakes up in a world where she's never met me, she still chooses to fall in love with me every day. That's what keeps me going you know. That I can still make her happy even though she doesn't know me anymore,"

"It's weird how everyday she falls completely in love with you all over again. Do you think there's a reason, like soulmates or something?" she asked. Ivan put his hat back on and began leaving.

"You don't forget love, Susan. That's all it is."

Ivan pulled out his car keys and headed home.

ALBERT

JOHN GRAMLING

My name is Albert. Every morning around six AM I grab a coffee, a copy of the The New Yorker and head to the Grand Central Station for no observable reason. I'm neither coming nor going. I sit amid the early morning rush throughout the day, usually until 1 PM. I'm eighty-six years old and am constantly asked, "Why?" "Why do you do this every morning without missing a beat?" "How long have you been doing this?" "Is there something or someone you're searching for within this sea of strange faces?"

I'm not a young man. I don't find pleasure in dancey hoopty-hoops or whatever popular culture has evolved to at this point. That chapter of my life ended decades ago. At eighty-six, I day dream about what could have been, what could be and how I used to fit into it all. I see my face in the suits boarding the trains in such a hurry. This was once me, hustling about, trying to outpace everyone else. These days I just like to relax and look at this life from a distance. I can live ten thousand vicarious lives a day.

Unbeknownst to me, I've probably seen thousands of wedding an- niversaries, birthdays, job interviews, hurried marriage proposals, you know name it. Take this gentleman beside me here, for instance. He's a young man, maybe in his early twenties, greased hair to the side, shoes untied, stains on his khakis. I could barely get a whisper from him. How could I? The world was new to him, it was intimidating, it was competitive and frightening. This was a caricature of me in 1938. As a young man I sat in this very station waiting for my train to pull in. Only back then, it was used to take me back and forth from interview to interview. It took years of busting my ass like this to land a worthwhile job at an accounting firm in lower Manhattan. I can see it in this young man's face that he was no different from myself. Time is the great equalizer, and one day perhaps he'll be sitting here in Grand Central people watching as I do.

Fifteen years ago, my wife as diagnosed with stage 4 liver cancer. We lost her several months later. The grief one feels while holding the hand of your long-life partner cannot be described in words, so I won't even delve into the details. Needless to say, this left me with lots of spare time, lots of Earthly questions and lots of reflection.

Eleven years ago I began visiting the station. It was by the advice of no shrink or therapist, it was a simple impulse. So I grabbed a coffee, a copy of the New Yorker and went down the Grand Central. What I had begun to notice, is that despite my grief, despite my loss in the world, people were still doing what people do. They were going to work; they were arguing in public, they were subsequently very openly making up in public. Life had gone on. The same will be true of me when I decide to cast myself from this Earthly rock. Individuality is an important virtue in life, but in death; we're all egalitarian in death. For whatever reason, this gave me great hope. Like watching the men and women hustle from train to train trying not to miss their meeting, watching the janitor wield his mop, seeing a couple in love or watching a good brawl or two. These are transient interactions between transient beings. The sharp mind of a pressed steel knife may be necessary to cut through business deals and to succeed in today's highly competitive environment, but it isn't the key to neither happiness nor universal peace. This is dictated by experience, by white knuckled rides that you think you'll never live through. Wisdom and serenity are highly underrated features of the human psyche. To ask an old geezer who had served in France during the Second World War (apparently the first one wasn't "great" enough and another was needed), greed, power, influence. These are all nice things to hold on to, wouldn't you say? I'd certainly enjoy a bit of wealth and influence, wouldn't you?

Point being, happiness cannot be found in power and influence. The world is a shark tank and the dolphins are but along for the ride. This strikes me a bit backwards, as sharks are not wise. Sharks are not serene. They are certainly not intelligent enough to be rulers of the sea. Their instinct is to seek, destroy and devour. The dolphins on the other hand, have developed complex language. They're just as much thinking animals as they are instinctual. But alas, the sharks have the teeth, the tenacity and the willingness to risk themselves for their next meal.

I come to Grand Central in order to witness this in human society. The meek are devoured by the aggressive, unless the meek adapt and become bloodthirsty themselves.

My, has everyday life has changed here. If you look closely enough, you can still see glimmers of chivalry, politeness and modesty, and the occasional good deed. This was once common courtesy, believe it or not. Before everyone went and got themselves in a big selfish rush, people took the time to stop, look around and notice the beautiful city in which they were encapsulated. Men wore hats, women wore dresses, even during the busiest time of rush hour, and it wasn't out of the ordinary to take several minutes to aid a fellow stranger. This sense of community has been long eroded. What will become of the future? I'm afraid it's far too late for me to answer this riddle. This responsibility rests upon your shoulders.

CLOSER

PETER HALL

The collision had made time wheel in frozen circles full of pain and darkness until the voice brought him back.

'Co… in Ben, answer…if…hear me.'

The mechanic had sounded drowned, the hiss of static rattling through his ear drums soaking her every word like waves hitting a beach. He punched the pad in his arm, ignoring the tiny scarlet meteors as the suits mitt slid off the buttons.

'You still there?'

Golden's voice emerged from the depths.

'Ben? You alright?'

The droplets floating past his eyes were getting thicker; never a good sign.

'I don't know.'

He'd no way of telling where the damage was either. The suit had pumped him so full of endorphins when he was hit he was finding it difficult to think. Besides, what was left of its readouts were invisible under the stain of shattered electronics.

'Ben, I'm on my way just hang tough. I know you can do it you've been here before remember?'

He waited for a moment, enjoying the slow play of light as gravity tore stars towards the hole eating this corner of the mapped zone.

126

'Yeah, what was that?'

'I don't know, some bit of space crap. The place is full of it.'

That didn't come as a surprise. The planet had been core nuked long ago, although the snapped hulks of its orbiting relays still tumbled aimlessly around its axis.

'What happened to the launch?'

'Vaporised chum, it jettisoned you when the damage went critical.'

'And the others?'

The silence was a heartbeat longer than it should have been.'

'Dead.'

Ben and the rest of the crew had been strip mining the hulks hole 38523/B hadn't already swallowed for weeks now. He supposed they'd been lucky to get away with it so long, ore work was one of the most lethal jobs humans did on civ edge. There weren't many reckless enough to be interested in its charms. It still beat the alternatives.

'The cargo?'

'Got it, decompression doesn't dent metal. Apart from a few scratches it's Ok.'

'And the planet?'

This time the pause was longer.

'Tell me.'

The Shards remains sat on a knife edge; the black hole it guarded nibbled at its edges a little more every solar day. They'd taken a gamblers chance on the odds staying in their favour, and they had, until now.

'It's gone active.'

'Damn.'

Ben craned his neck to get a look and wished he hadn't. Down below the first amber tint of continental rupture was blooming across the shattered land masses like daisy chains strung together from fire and rock.

'Can you see that?'

'Yes, the planet's dying. What you're looking at will have spread across three of its last continents in thirty minutes. The remaining two will follow not long after that.'

Bill drifted above the raped fields of a forgotten world, and thought about home and his family.

'You're not going to be here in time are you?'

Their ship was a relic, a misbegotten cast off from the endless civil wars ravaging the sector. Whatever scavenged parts it contained weren't up to a rescue conducted at the speed that might save his life.

'Just keep calm, breath slow, and deep, conserve your oxygen. I'll be there as soon as I can.'

'You haven't answered the question.'

'Probably not, but I've hit various things with a big hammer. We might drag a few more grades out of the engine.'

Ben closed his eyes. He was bleeding out, the slow creep of numbness like a tranquilizer crushing him in a silk fist. Only the suits sheath was keeping him alive.

'Golden?'

He could feel something clammy under his ribs pressing against his skin; he didn't want to think too hard about what that might be. Another string of detonations crisped across the alien topography below.

'It's beautiful.'

'I know, hang in there. I'm coming.'

Bill closed his eyes, when he opened them again it was to the blink of flashing neon. There was still an icon working on his HUD after all.

'System failure in three minutes.'

The suits voice sounded like his old landlady's, dry and cultured, with no room for pity. Not that he wanted it: it had been a good life.

'Can't wait. Look, tell my family nice things, Ok? I'm going to make this quick. It's going to hurt a hell of a lot less if I go now.'

It was a trick he'd picked up in the last failed campaign to dismember the alliances men. The tired remnants of the meagre colonial forces had all learnt it. Better to know a quick way out than to be taken prisoner by the things they'd been sent to fight, and the scrap code sequence had been easy to remember. It began with his birth date.

'See you in the next life Golden.'

'Don't do this Ben, please.'

'We'll see each other again. You know that's how it works; death, rebirth, destruction, creation. You can't stop them, nothing can.'

'Your oxy's running out. It's making you sound like the last time you got drunk. I don't need to know the mysteries of the cosmos Ben. I just need to get to you in time.'

Ben laughed.

'Don't you see? You will, nothing can change that, energy doesn't stop with breath, and it doesn't listen to the void. Part of me will live in you when I die. I'll see with your eyes, and speak from your heart?'

'I don't want you to go.'

'I'm not Golden; I'm just going a little deeper.'

Ben, ex sergeant at arms, thief, and ex con lights up like a diode. High voltage electric lines his body, twitching limbs in a dance no one else can see. It really is beautiful he has time to think as power spreads his teeth in a rictus. The planet is dying and it's taking him and the last of its murdered dream with it.

Golden wiped her eyes, and smiled. There was nothing else to do as the tiny speck on the screen went nova, and something settled behind her eyes.

'Hallo Ben, make yourself at home.'

THE GIRL BELONGS TO SONG

AARON DAVID HARRIS

The air from your nostrils blows against my fingers like a warm fan on its lowest setting. It takes too long for your chest to rise and fall. You are getting weaker. Your skin is cold, and much softer than the first time we met. Remember that day?

Mrs. Lee's mansion. The warm, graceful sunlight reflected off the waves of the lake in the backyard. She was a good teacher. All the other voice instructors lied to their students, stroked their egos for the paycheck, used cheap software to enhance their voices. Mrs. Lee was different. "Skill is only achieved through the brutality of practice," she always preached.

Her lessons were brutal. I hated her so much for that. Although, I regret hating her now. I owe my life to that woman. Without her, I wouldn't have my skill. And without my skill, I wouldn't have you.

I was singing my scales when you came for me. I hated those scales. They made my throat hurt, made me sound like the ugly little beast I often saw in the mirror.

But you listened to my scales, didn't you? That's why, out of the blue-green murk of the lake surface, you rose, approaching me with slow, heavy footsteps. I remember your glowing orange eyes and teeth, and your tough, sandy gray skin.

Remember when they tried to take you? Mrs. Lee didn't know they'd been spying on the mansion, that a soldier had been perched on the roof for months, not until we heard the missile wailing and whistling in the sky. Courtesy of the people who wanted to capture and study you.

But the missile failed. My scales made you stronger than they anticipated. When the smoke cleared, the troopers marched in with their guns and knives and fists. You pick them apart. Your long tail coiled around them like fleas hopping onto your back. I watched that tail crush them like cardboard, and toss them into the sky as their arms flailed without life. They couldn't hurt you. And you were so fast. Your movements were a blur in my eyes.

It wasn't until Mrs. Lee's tight grip around my hand slipped loose that I realized something was wrong. She clutched at her chest, then fell over, sprawled awkwardly on the ground and coughed violently, blood spewing from her mouth and nose, wetting my cheek and mixing with my tears. The bullet in her left ventricle was meant for you.

I felt your fingers crawl under my armpits. Suddenly, my feet were off the ground. I cried and I struggled. I thought it was your fault she died. I was wrong. The soldiers kept shooting. You had me in your arms and they kept on shooting anyway. But you didn't attack them back. Was it because you got what you came for? Was it too much to manage my awkward little body and fight them at the same time?

You walked us back into the lake. I thought you were going to drown me. Why couldn't I feel the water engulfing me? Why didn't it soak my hair and my clothes? Why didn't it fill my lungs and kill me? You did something. You protected me somehow.

They say you come from another dimension. At least they were right about that. I woke up to strange glowing lights. The air smelled like stale cotton candy. But I couldn't hear anything. It was so silent I could hear the sweat rolling down my face. This place was your home. And it was dead.

I hollered for help. I begged, demanded even, to go home. You sat with your legs crossed and did not speak. What did you think of me when I punched you in the jaw? Did it feel like an insect landing on your face? Were you laughing inside when I hurt my toes kicking you in the back? It would have only taken seconds for you to tear me to shreds.

Instead, I heard a voice. My own voice, though my mouth had not opened. It was weak and distant. Fading and breaking. Then I looked at your eyes. It was you doing my scales. Your eyes flickered to the tempo like a bad light bulb in the basement. You wanted me to sing. And I did.

This time, though, my voice didn't hurt. It echoed pleasantly around your home. When I sang, you stood to your feet. When I sang, I didn't feel ugly. When I sang, the glimmer in your eyes grew from a weak flicker into a strong, constant orange glow that illuminated your home and fed your tense muscles.

Then your hand caressed my face until you found my ear. It was my turn to listen. I closed my eyes. And through your whispering fingers, you showed me your history. Your species has lived in silent dimensions for centuries. You come to our world for sound. Sound is food. Your name is Song, because that's the sound you eat.

You came for me because you needed the strength to defeat your enemy, another sound eater like you. This one didn't feed on songs, but on terror. Its name is Scream.

You showed me those men who came for you, the men who shot at me and killed my teacher. They thought they captured Scream years ago. But they don't know everything. Scream wanted to be captured. Scream pretended to be under their control, pretended to give them knowledge. Let them think they were advancing science. In return, they kept its belly full, feeding it with the cries of the kidnapped and the torture of the innocent.

You showed me the history between the Song and the Scream, a blood feud that spans generations. You two are the last of your namesakes. And you need my help in the final chapter of your war.

I opened my eyes. And I sang for you. For hours. For days. Forever.

You took us back to my world. We rose out of the water by the bay, where Scream waited for you; a bigger, chalky white doppelganger of you with spikes around its shoulders and knuckles. Its face was locked into a permanent smile. The men were waiting there, too. Scientists. Soldiers. Fools. Fleas among kings.

My shoes squished the warm sand when you put me down. I remember the long gaze between Song and Scream, a silent exchange that spoke about a hundred lifetimes of hatred and pain. Moments later, the final battle began. Scream moved and fought like you. Its spikes cut at your flesh, spilling my voice out of your opened veins. Why was it so much stronger? How long had those fools been feeding it? How many voices were shouting out in agony to fuelit now?

When Scream delivered his final blow, the fools swarmed in and surrounded you, hoping to put you behind a cage and study you for science. I almost smiled when Scream turned on them, when it cut them all down like a wild machete in a field of tall grass, leaving the scientists and soldiers in a dark red heap of blood and confusion. Your war was so very far beyond their understanding. Scream wasn't going to share its kill with the fleas.

But I refused to let you die. So I sang. I sang whatever words came to my mind. I sang them in the scales you love so much. As I did, your eyes flashed with life. You could hear me, but so could Scream. I barely blinked and the creature stood over me, leering down with that evil grin. It picked me up and made a terrifying noise. It was trying to make me cry out. But I would not feed it. This girl belongs to Song. I didn't scream. I'll never scream. I just kept singing.

And then you stood up one more time, covered in wounds, but re-energized. A strike to Scream's back and it dropped me. It threw a fist at you, shattering its spikes against your hard palms. For the first time, Scream cried out. I remember you paused to look at me, fascinated by the irony of that.

Then you jumped high into the air, flipping, turning, then stopping mid-flight. Your hands glowed like a pair of burning stars. Your palms pointed at Scream as a searing beam of light poured down on the creature from the sky. Your enemy was no more.

You collapsed in the sky, dropping to the ground, dead weighted. I took you into my arms and here we are right now.

I hope you've been listening to this song. I hope you're chewing every note. I hope that every word pleases your palate. I prepared it special for you, like grandma's mac and cheese on a Sunday afternoon. Like a bushel of juicy apples from the orchards in the fall. To you, my words matter. My voice matters. My song matters.

I'll sing it until you wake up. I'll sing it until we are home. Until I see the glow in your eyes.

THE HARBOR CROSSING

MARTY HIAT

Splash and waves echo off the ferryboat prow into the depths. Surface chop marks the daily distance between worlds while harbor waters slip uncontained out to sea. Mid-harbor, ferry and travelers merge. A natural symphony set to the steadfast tempo of the sea plays out in private minds from stem to stern. Bow-spray bears scattered witness to the tender perpetuity of finite lives.

The lady at the rail is wrapped in high collared faux fur. Positioned at the bow, a child grasps her black-gloved hand, standing too close to the rail. The wind whips the boy's hatless head. Her lipstick is too thick. "Daddy will follow us out tomorrow," she lies. "Tonight he has lots of work to do."

Below decks a pale young man smokes a cigarette alone. His seaman's coat is unbuttoned. He's never been to sea. In the fluorescent chill of the compartment his reflection in the window shimmers as the ferry shifts. He draws on the Lucky Strike, wraps himself in his own arms and leans into his body against the glass. The cigarette burns down in the tray. He closes his eyes.

Across the galley, the Colonel reads the evening paper. His black civilian overcoat is buttoned to the neck, wrapped tight to hide dress blues. His close-cropped head is also hatless, hardened by myriad winds of culture and calendar. He doesn't suffer the cold. The thick lenses of his glasses reflect the subtle details of the room while his eyes take in the headline news.

At the bow rail, the lady's thoughts are on the island with the man she'll meet. She has followed him here as another in a long line she's trailed into premeditated seduction; seeking to launch herself to the other side of the nameless void of a chosen life as the banker's wife. Her son will go to sleep upstairs. As she drifts away with the bow spray, she barely feels the child leave her hand.

The young man in the galley wraps the cold around him like a deep sleep. The woman and the kid at the rail stirred the past, like an "amen" to his plans. For his mother, deep seduction was a way of life that simply paid for things. Her affairs, for him, became a cascade of nightly shadows from behind the closet door. For years he couldn't remember when he'd seen her last. Her image had become a dream of her fading smile and island rocks. Tonight, he wandered from another job layoff onto the ferry, stumbling almost blind into the deep eyes of the hatless child. Breakers on the high rocks of his memory crashed. He knew where she was. He would follow her there.

The Colonel loses focus on the news and put his paper down. His last harbor crossing was as a Captain at the end of a second tour in Vietnam. "Leave," they called it, but he learned long ago that one never gets away. Hot desert dust or jungle bugs, diesel, distant darkening skies and endless demands of events beyond his control bore the same impact on the young, able lives in his command. Their earnest desire to survive became his private crusade against the cascade of disaster that unfolds in war. "In the starlit darkness" he'd once read in a book he'd found on a park bench titled *The Shepard's Cannon*, "*…you fear everything. You yearn to fight but the enemy is beyond the firelight in the black, unseen under the same bright stars. You feel it surround you driving deep within your cloak, wiping all warmth of flickering fire until you are small and lost and cold, too frail to protect your flock. At that instant, your greatest enemy becomes your deepest ally. You see yourself as all the stars see you. And you are undeniably awakened.*" His own fragility, never exposed but undeniably accepted, had become an untraceable thread to the delicate breadth of his own humanity and a link to deeper awareness. "Grand Wolf Eyes," he called it, a privacy of his own mind which supplied him a mystical sensitivity to the subtleties of approaching death, blending milliseconds of courage into a timeless ability to respond when the inevitable arrived before its time. Strangely now, in the shallow hull of an island ferry, half way across to a home he had forgotten, his grand wolf eyes stir him, signally softly that death is near.

The marked corpse he sees is not bloody, but pale. A civilian son of no one, as lost and stripped as any soldier in peril he's ever seen, is seated before him. Splash and waves on metal mix with the galley's fluorescent shadows. In the fragility of his own, knowing the Colonel feels the young man's decision to die. Although he knows not why he can plainly see that this man's enemy is deceptively within, as inherently deadly as any terror of war, shrouded by cigarette smoke, wrapped in the past. As the ferryboat ferries on through the chop and harbor waters slip by, a private civilian suffering becomes a warrior's professional concern.

The Colonel leans forward and puts his head in his hands. He closes his eyes and feels his own fragile self curled deep within. He feels his too clean military dress shirt wrapped neatly beneath his civilian coat. He hears words of hate mongering from homecoming troops. He sees lists of wounded. He hears politics and policy. He sees his own young wife, older now, in someone else's arms walk off languidly with flowers in her hair. He sees himself from a distance, in a chopper over desert sands.

Orderly lines of lives he's saved march into an infinite unnatural sea of lives lost on his soul. Measure and balance of fate, circumstance and error spin into a tunnel of light that leads silently forth to a young man in the grip of his own private war. Surrounded by whistling wind and harbor swells the Colonel absorbs the full weight of yearning for his own innocence lost. The desperate desire to understand the unthinkable burdens every nerve. He weeps within while waves crash. Engines reverse and the ferryboat slows down. Compartment lights flicker and in the minds' eye of a warrior's waking dream, the young man in the seaman's coat opens his eyes.

Across the compartment, the young man sees an older man, head in his hands. In the window glass reflection they are side by side, with a child between them. The older man leans back. His distant eyes meet the young man's gaze in silence. Engine sounds, diesel smells, chamber lights and the approaching chaos of the dock bring the harbor symphony to a close as the ferry nears the shore. The young man blinks and shivers, coughs and snubs out his cigarette. The warrior returns to his paper. The little boy on the bench entreats the young man gently, "Your coat is unbuttoned, aren't you kinda cold?"

Through the clutter of the docking ferry the young lady from the bow rail rushes unsteadily down the galley steps breathless, shock pale. "Have you seen my son?" She demands of the Colonel. "He's right there," he tells her, indicating with a glance across the galley. "No, no," she insists, "A little boy! I think he went over the side." The Colonel is certain. "He's there," he says flatly, "Nobody drowned tonight." In a fury, she looks again. The warrior's grand wolf eyes sweep the room. Her hatless son is there. The child smiles at her pleasantly. "I gave him some gum," he tells her, misreading her shock as concern for his companion. "And I told him to button up." Waves fill the silence between them all. "He feels much better now."

THE CHEER SQUAD

CHRISTINE HILLINGDON

The CD shop named *Merlin's Music* was situated at the top of a narrow winding staircase. It was about the sixth I had visited that ardent summer morning. The fact that this one's walls were adorned with sixties memorabilia, together with recent chart topping artists, did nothing to alleviate my hot blistered feet and grumbling empty stomach.

Ordinarily I would have gazed enraptured while nodding my head in time to the nostalgic beat of the late, great *Billy Thorpe* CD they were playing, but today I was hot, thirsty, tired and fed up with my search that so far had proved to be in vain.

I propped up my head in my hands with my arms resting on the counter and yawned widely as the tall, black bearded young man came over to me.

"Hi. What can I do for you?" He asked cheerily. I looked into his large blue eyes that seemed to search my face appreciatively and thought of quite a few things that he could have obliged me with.

"I am desperately trying to find a copy of the *Buckingham & Nicks* album," I said, drawing on my last bit of energy to appear like I was still alive and kicking.

"You mean *the Buckingham & Nicks*, as in *Fleetwood Mac?*"

"You've got it." The man blinked with surprise.

"You must be older than you look!" I smiled a thank you and watched him lift a huge, black leather music catalogue onto the counter. "Sorry, my computer's down," he apologised.

138

"Mine died altogether. That's why I'm here." I confessed.

As he began thumbing through the pages I glanced around at the shop. I noticed I was its sole customer. This could mean one of two things. One; it was fairly new and not many people in Adelaide knew of its existence as yet. Two; it was a poorly stacked CD shop.

"It's been deleted," the shop assistant informed me, drawing my tired mind back to the problem at hand.

"Yes, I know, but I was wondering if you knew of anywhere overseas that would be worth trying to obtain it from?"

"You really want it that bad?"

"I do," I smiled and he shook his head in mock disbelief.

"OK. I have a friend in this line of work in the States. I'll see what I can do for you."

"Great. How about if I drop in or call you in a few days time and see how it's going?" I suggested, picking up my shoulder bag.

"I have a better idea. What are you doing on Sunday afternoon?" I looked at him incredulously.

Was he asking me for a date? Here in the shop, amidst the line of business! It was my turn to blink with surprise.

"Don't get me wrong," he held up his hands defensively. "It's all above board. You see, our new chain of CD shops is competing in a football match against one of the radio stations. Get ourselves some publicity and well, we need a cheer squad. I was wondering if you would be interested?"

"But, I don't know the first thing about football!"

"You don't have to. You just need to look good and give us players lots of loud and attentive support."

He picked up a plastic card and held it out to me. Taking it from him I noticed it had the name and telephone number of the CD shop on it as well as his name, Craig Simmons.

"Look, think about it and give me a ring, but make it before Friday if you can."

Our eyes met and held, full of unspoken words.

"OK. Thanks." I slipped the card inside my bag and headed for the stairs.

*

I rang the CD shop on Friday morning and as luck would have it Craig was busy with a customer. I spoke to another man with a very husky voice who appeared to know the reason for my calling even before receiving much of an explanation.

"So, are you a yes or a no?" He interrupted rudely. "If you *are* coming just give me your name and number and be at the *Claremont Oval* at ten thirty on the day," he said hurriedly.

I wondered how many acceptances and cancellations there had been already?

"Umm, well...," *yes*, I thought to myself. I did want to see Craig again but *no*, I wasn't sure about being in the cheer squad. It was forecasted to be a stinking hot day, after all. Besides, I really couldn't stand football.

"Well what, lady? Come on, I've got customers waiting." He was becoming quite impatient now, which was understandable.

"Well...OK." I quickly gave him my name and telephone number.

"Right. Thanks. Bye!" He slammed the telephone down leaving me with a loud dial tone in my ear and uncertainty in my heart.

It was then I remembered I hadn't asked about the *Buckingham & Nicks* CD.

I decided that could now wait until Monday.

*

All day Saturday I mulled over the situation. It really wasn't like me to be so undecided and it was annoying the hell out of me. On the negative side was the weather, the football match and every chance of being swamped by gorgeous looking, unattached, man-hunting females. At least half of them would have to think that Craig is as cute as I do, which didn't leave me feeling a whole lot lucky.

On the positive side it would give me a chance to see and hopefully talk with him again. Maybe find out if those blue eyes of his do hold the key to thoughts, other than me being in the cheer squad. And besides, it could all be rather fun.

I listened to the weather man again that evening and Sunday was now going to be even *hotter* than first expected. I grimaced and filed the temperature away in the negative box in my mind.

Was it really worth it? Do I really *need* to get a sunburnt nose? How did I know he wasn't bringing along his girlfriend, fiancée or heaven forbid – wife!

He could even be gay.

But, intuition told me that Craig was as unattached as I am. If I didn't turn up to the football match I doubt very much if I would be missed. I would be ringing him in a few more days to see if my album had come in

Stuff it. I won't go.

The telephone rang just as I was thinking about going to bed.

"Hullo. Is that Amanda Stevens?" A deep voice asked hesitantly.

"Yes." The voice sounded a little familiar, yet I couldn't place its owner.

"Great! Well this is Craig Simmons from *Merlin's* CD shop. Was it by any chance you who spoke to me regarding a *Buckingham & Nicks* album?"

My heart skipped a beat.

"Yes. That's right. I'm also down for your cheer squad tomorrow but I was thinking…"

"Well actually, that's why I'm ringing. I've gone and sprained my wrist."

"Oh, that's a shame," I said, puzzled. "I guess you won't be in the game tomorrow then?"

"Exactly. I was wondering, well…seeing you aren't into football…"

"Yes?"

"Well I was rather hoping you would come out with me for a drive up in the hills and maybe a picnic instead?"

I mentally cart wheeled around the lounge room. I could not believe my luck.

"I would love to, Craig," I told him, using his name for the first time and wallowing in the sound of it.

"You would? Wonderful!"

"But, seeing it's going to be so hot, what say we skip the picnic and find a nice pub instead?"

"Good idea. I'll pick you up at ten thirty?"

"Fine. Goodnight."

"Night."

I replaced the receiver grinning at the blank television screen like a schizophrenic.

Fate certainly worked in mysterious ways.

And I was still none the wiser about the *Buckingham & Nicks* CD!

LIFE STORIES

CHRISTINA HOAG

"Whachoo got there, ol' man?"

He raised his head and met the bloodshot eyes of the skinny guy on the neighboring cot who had just spoken. Another junkie. Or tweaker. Or crackhead. Same difference. Like all the young ones in the shelter. He looked back down at the tattered newspaper clippings he had spilled from an envelope onto the cot.

"Hey. Didnchoo hear me, ol' man?"

He kept his head down this time and concentrated on sifting through the pieces of paper, brittle and jaundiced with age.

"Donchoo got no manners?"

He peered at the newsprint. The headlines and the masthead were easy to read: "*The News, Paterson, N.J.*" "*Arson blaze kills three.*" "*Mayor faces corruption scandal.*"

But the smaller font of the text was fuzzy. He strained to discern the byline that he knew was there, that was him before his hair and his whiskers turned into feathers of snow. No matter. He knew what it said anyway. Of course, he did. *By Mario O' Grady.* Puckering his bristled brow, he reached into his memory for the who, what, when, where of the stories, but those details were far out of his grasp.

A hand dove into the pile of paper and closed long fingers around it like crab legs. He reached out to stop it but was too slow. The hand shot into the air, out of his reach. Needle tracks and bruises peppered the ropy forearm like fruit gone bad.

"Gotta learn some manners, ol' man. Gotta learn it's polite to speak when spoken to." The junkie's voice curdled the air.

"Give me that!" He lunged at the junkie's fist, but his muscles were rusted, and the younger man edged back smartly. "Give them back!"

The old man's stomach turned to hamburger meat.

"Okay, ol' man." The junkie's face cracked into a smile-less grin. "Heeere they come!"

In a deft move, the junkie ripped the papers and hurled the pieces up. The old man watched his life arc up and flutter down. For a moment he was still, accepting the mock honor of the confetti, but as the pieces fell lower, it became urgent that he save them.

He moved as fast as his thick limbs allowed, swiping the air with wild scrapes. He caught a few pieces and as others plummeted, he whirled and snatched until his lungs burned. He grabbed them from the beds, the windowsill, the floor, so no one could get them and hold them beyond his reach again.

In the windowpane, he caught the reflection of the other men observing him and he saw what they saw – an old man chasing his life like a kid catching snow. He shuffled back to his cot, stuffed the torn articles into the envelope and packed his rucksack.

***

Dusk was falling. Fatigue weighed his legs. The banshee wind flapped the corner of his woolen coat and coiled itself around his waist like a rope, compelling him toward a stretch of abandoned rowhouses ahead.

His feet crunched on glass shards as he poked a path through the knee-high weeds. He spotted a loose board on a back window and mustering some strength, pried it off. Rats scuttled. An unhinged plank protested. But no humans, no junkies.

His eyes adapted to the dark and he hunted around for trash to make a fire. When the flames unknotted his fingers, he foraged in his bag for the extra apple he had sneaked out from the shelter that morning when Mrs. Bruce had turned her back.

He had told her he wasn't coming back. She wished him luck and went on to the next in line. He had wanted to tell her why, to give her an explanation. More than that, a justification. He hadn't justified his actions to anyone in years. But she didn't demand one and he swallowed the urge. He scuffed his way into the sunshine and shivered in its deception. He spent the rest of the day wandering about the streets, panhandling, invisible as always.

He rummaged in his bag again. His hand clamped onto the welcoming cold of a glass bottle - the *Thunderbird* he had bought that afternoon with pandhandled change, enough for a pint. He raised the bottle to his mouth and gulped a good draught. The liquor raced through his veins, making him smooth and warm again. The wind yelped outside like a guard dog.

He took the manila envelope from his sack and shook out the torn stories of his life. By firelight he tried to fit the pieces together like a jigsaw, managing only to join the pieces of his byline by the size of the words. "*Mario*" with "*O'Grady.*"

He had kept everything he wrote that bore his byline and over the years, the envelopes grew into stacks in a closet. He would stagger home after last call at the *Shamrock & Shillelagh*, open the closet and stare at them. They proved that he never let himself be defeated, despite his drunken father's fists.

After he was booted by a new editor who didn't put up with fifths of bourbon stashed in desk drawers, the pile of envelopes diminished, lost in moves from place to place. Only this envelope remained. After all these years, all that it took to destroy it was a childish tantrum.

"Goddamn that sonofabitch!" he said aloud. The wind showed its sympathy with a gust that buffeted the building. He shook a handful of torn pieces in the air to show the wind. It sighed in commiseration and fell silent as if it could find no more to say.

Crone's fingers of cold burrowed into his flesh. He shook the last drops of *Thunderbird* onto his tongue and chucked the bottle. It clattered onto the floorboards.

The fire ebbed. He nourished it with the rest of the rubbish he had collected. In a while he would have to gather more. He leaned back, hoping to lose himself in the coziness of remembrance. But all he could see was the derision in the junkie's eyes and mouth, the baleful stares of the other men, and himself performing like a street corner clown.

"You took all I had, you robbed me!" The wind took up his refrain with a whistle that bent the walls.

He'd have to return to the rescue mission soon. It was getting too cold to sleep rough. But that junkie would be there. Or another one. The wind gusted. A door banged, but the old man didn't startle.

The flames ebbed to a smolder. He tried to shift his legs, but they had
stiffened into leaden stilts. His eyes settled on his torn life in his lap.

He took a scrap of paper and fed it to the embers. The flame flared barely enough to warm his fingers. One by one, he burned the pieces, leaning over the fire to inhale the smell of charred paper. He saved pieces with his byline 'til last. When the last had melted into a cinder, his eyelids slid shut.

****

Transient Found Dead, The News, Paterson, N.J., page B14.

A homeless man was found yesterday frozen to death in an abandoned rowhouse in Paterson, police said. The man, in his late 60s, died approximately 10 days ago. Police request anyone with information that may lead to his identification to come forward.

NO ANSWER IN THE DARK

DAVID HOENIG

"Is that you, Sal?" the old man asked as he looked abruptly over his left shoulder down the hallway. He squinted against the dim light. "Sally?"

He waited a moment but heard no reply, so turned back and shuffled forward into the library. The rich smell of his pipe tobacco lingered in the air and he took a deep, appreciative breath. He gaveup the habit years ago, but the scent recalled memories of younger days, like when he and Sally had been at that seaside restaurant in Bar Harbor, and…

He turned suddenly back towards the doorway and leaned his head out into the darkened hall. "Sally? Darling?"

A quizzical expression appeared on his face when there was no reply. He sighed and returned to the library. He went to the crystal decanter on the sideboard and poured himself a lowball glass, mostly full, of eighteen-year-old *Lagavulin*. He carried the scotch to the padded, burgundy leather chair in front of the hearth and sat.

He took a sip and held it in his mouth for a moment before he swallowed. He let out a sigh of contentment as the smoky warmth spread through his chest, and then leaned his head back, eyes closed. The glass sat precariously on the wide arm of the chair as he listened to the stillness of the library, its heavy appointments seeming to absorb sound. Outside a nor'easter raged, rattling windows as cold gusts of soot-laden air swirled in through the chain curtain over the fireplace, but the noise seemed lost in the poised silence around him.

When he spoke, his voice sounded odd, even to him. "I know you could never stand the stuff, Sally, but you always let me indulge myself. I always appreciated that kindness, you know."

His eyes opened all at once and he glanced over at the door to the hallway. Some scotch sloshed onto the burgundy leather with the suddenness of his move, turning it black in the dim light of the library. "What was that?" he said loudly. With an effort, he pushed himself to his feet, and put his glass down on the sideboard. He shuffled to the doorway, this time going through it and turning to look down the length of the hall. "Sally?"

He moved into darkness, away from the small island of light which spilled hesitantly from the library, with uncertain steps, hands stretched toward both walls as he inched forward. "Sal, is that you?" he said, peering over the edge of his glasses to better penetrate the gloom.

"What... Aaaaugh!" he screamed as a black four-legged creature launched itself from the floor at him. Backpedaling and turning desperately, he slammed back against the wall even as the thing dug claws into him. He half stumbled, half slid along the hallway wall toward the light escaping from the library.

"Dagnabit! Agnes, you mangy mouse-stalker, you nearly killed me!" he swore, though he quickly put both hands under the cat to take the strain off where its claws had dug through his clothes and into his skin.

She purred in answer, retracting the sharp points, and he lifted Agnes to cradle her against his chest. Heart thumping and breath rasping, he returned to the library and made his careful way into his chair. Once he sat down again, Agnes turned in his lap twice before settling down. His labored breathing slowed as he stroked her soft fur and she purred, neither of them paying attention to the storm flailing futilely outside. When the cat rolled over on her back to look up at him, his hand drifted absently to scratch her neck and chin and her eyes closed blissfully.

Sitting in the cold library with the warm cat in his arms, the rest of the house seemed cold and empty, and very forcefully reminded him that Sally was gone these last few weeks. Abrupt tears turned the dimly lit room into a blurry watercolor as he remembered anew that she would never answer him again.

GREEN AND ORANGE

JESS HUCKINS

Her green half hides in the recesses of her memory, sad and longing for the girl who spent summers hiking and kayaking in the mountains of Vermont. It misses the frenetic energy of her straw-hued hair, how it frizzed up as she rescued earthworms that would otherwise dry into tacky paste on the driveway. She misses how she built woodland nests that squirrels and other critters would never use. As they say, it's the thought that counts. Her green half, which feels closest to home when she reclines in the grass and peers up at the sky, doesn't like this new woman, this resource-waster who takes long showers and heats her home with oil and always forgets to water houseplants.

But her orange half understands. This half is the color of the brick walls around her home and the dry leaves of the plants she kills. It reflects the flame of her lighter and cheers when she throws a plastic bottle into the trash because it's too much effort to carry it from city street to city street in search of a blue bin. She knows this hurts the planet, but her orange half keeps her too busy to care. It doesn't remember how to make a wet-wood fire or where to find each constellation in the night sky, but it knows painkillers and insomnia and smoke-filled bedrooms. This half is displeased when something makes her green half smile, like when a wading egret kicks off and takes flight or when the golden colors of sunrise slant through the green leaves as she jogs loops through the city park.

Her orange half claims she has plenty of time to find her way back to the mountains, and that she needs to focus on not focusing on it while she lives where she lives. This half will reign unless she forces a change. Then, and only then, can her green half return.

IN-FLIGHT MUSIC

ANNE E. JOHNSON

"Please put carry-ons in the overhead compartments first."

The flight attendant was squeezed close to Rachel, who could smell fumes of the bologna sandwich he had for lunch.

"I need to put my coat up there," Rachel said, irritated that a healthy youth would eat bologna.

"Ma'am, we'll fit the coats in later."

Sitting down hopelessly, Rachel wadded up her spring coat in her lap. It had been that kind of morning. Snarled traffic on the Thruway. No seat upgrade despite having paid a kidney for a last-minute ticket to LAX.

"You okay, Ma'am?"

The girl in the next seat had a pale face that was half hidden behind jet-black Goth bangs. Rachel thought of her own rebellious hair choices from four decades earlier. "I'm fine," she snapped defensively.

The girl pointed to her own eyes. "Sorry. I didn't mean ... It's just that you were..."

Rachel realized that her cheeks were wet. "I'm fine," she repeated more gently, rifling through her purse for a tissue. "Thanks for asking."

"I've got one." The friendly Goth girl pulled a tissue from her handbag. A black handbag, of course, stamped with a large silver cross.

Somehow the small kindness made everything worse. Rachel battled back the waterworks, determined not to fall apart before they even left the tarmac.

"I'm Brittany," Goth-girl volunteered.

"Oh, of course you are," Rachel longed to say to this impossibly young thing. Aloud she said, "Hi. I'm Rachel."

"You from LA?" Brittany asked.

"Yes. My mother still lives there." Suddenly homesick, Rachel hugged her bunched-up jacket. "Haven't been back in a while."

"Oh, sweet. You're visiting your mom, then?" Brittany was applying a mud-colored lipstick without using a mirror.

"Yeah." Rachel hated being sentimental. She stuffed her coat under the seat in front of her.

"Oh, that's so nice."

Done with the pleasantries, Rachel hid behind a paperback novel. She didn't absorb a single sentence, but kept the book open as her mind dragged over the past ten years' worth of non-communication with her mother. Now Mom was in the hospital. Heart trouble.

"I'll be fine," Mom had assured on the phone. Their first conversation in three years. Rachel had felt an urgent twinge of guilt, and booked a flight immediately.

And here she was en route, no turning back.

She couldn't remember exactly why her relationship with her mom had soured. Maybe from an unacceptable man, bound to ruin her life, *blah blah blah.* Not talking to each other had become a dull habit. It was easier to continue the silence than to figure it out and fix whatever was wrong.

Despite the paperback wall, the Goth-girl chirped at her again. "Whereabouts does your mom live? Valley? Santa Monica?"

Rachel couldn't face any chit chat. "How does this work?" She asked loudly, avoiding the personal question by pointing to the screen in front of her. She knew from her years as a middle school nurse that the best way to control an unruly kid was to dangle a technological question. Brittany chomped on the bait.

"The in-flight music? You need headphones. They passed them out earlier. You didn't take any?" When Rachel shook her head, Brittany pulled a pair of ear buds from the silver cross purse. "Here."

"You don't need these?"

"I have tons. Just borrow 'em."

It didn't seem too sanitary, but Rachel couldn't find a graceful way out. "Okay, so where do I plug them…Oh."

Brittany pushed the plug into the end of Rachel's armrest and her fingers danced nimbly across the touch screen. She scrutinized Rachel. "You like country? Oldies?"

"No," Rachel nearly yelled over the noise in her ears. "I see how it works. Thanks."

"Volume's right there." Brittany pointed to an icon on the screen's lower right corner. She wedged her skateboard sneaker heels up against her rear end and pulled her head down into her charcoal hoodie. She seemed to fall asleep immediately.

"Ah, youth," Rachel murmured.

She clicked on a random selection. The reedy sounds of *REO Speedwagon* launched into the song "I *Can't Fight This Feeling.*"

Rachel's emotions were thrown several ways at once. The cheesy piano chords made her skin crawl. She also felt old, since the song came out around 1980, when she was about to start college.

She loved that song when it was new. It expressed things she couldn't. Hearing it now for the first time in ages, she was surprised how well she remembered it. She mouthed the lyric about not being strong enough to show love. With each line, the protective shield around her heart melted away.

The band sang the chorus and Rachel scoffed at the line about throwing away the oars of a ship. "Ships don't have oars," she laughed to herself. But she was hooked by the song, up to her chin in the sentimental swamp. Nostalgia flooded in and carried her away.

Suddenly Rachel recalled being eighteen again, sitting at the old kitchen table. She wore headphones, listening to an *REO Speedwagon* cassette that was so worn its sound wobbled. Her mom mixed pancake batter and smiled at her.

Rachel hadn't pictured that smile in many years.

Her mom asked, "How many pancakes?" Rachel, tapping the song's slow beat with her left-hand nails against the placemat, held up her right index finger. Slowly she raised the middle finger next to it. She laughed and shrugged. Two pancakes. Why not? Her mom laughed, too, wagging her spatula.

The song ended with a final chord, not a fade-out, jolting Rachel back to the present. For a few seconds she listened to her pulsing blood and the jet engine.

Next to her, Brittany whimpered, troubled by whatever Goths dream about. Rachel draped a blanket over Brittany's shoulders and ran a hand along her upper back. "Shhh," she breathed, feeling peaceful enough to calm someone else for a change. "Thanks for the memories," she added, unplugging the ear buds and tucking them into the pocket of Brittany's bag.

When they landed at LAX, Rachel was so eager to see her mom's smile that she left her jacket behind.

THE RICHEST MAN IN THE WORLD

JOHN KANIECKI

"Do you trust the wizard?"

"He's not a wizard; rather the man is a sci-en-tist, whatever that means?"

Surman stood upon the side of King Nebuchadnezzar. The advisor had a very precarious job. On the one hand he was responsible for giving sound advice to the grand monarch. On the other, he could not be presumptuous or in the slightest manner be condescending. One slip of his tongue and he might follow his predecessor into jail or worse.

"Then do you trust this scientist?" There Surman had not only repeated himself, but in a roundabout way had challenged the king of kings. After all it was clear by his actions that King Nebuchadnezzar had faith in this stranger.

"He does have most convincing proof of wonderful things does he not?" The monarch had a grand smile. "You saw his flashlight haven't you?"

"Indeed I have," Surman spoke in awe. "As I have also seen his pistol."

"Truly they are great magic are they not?"

"No, they are from science," corrected Surman. Afraid he had ruffled the hair of the monarch he quickly added, "as you have so distinctly pointed out already."

"And this time machine," Nebuchadnezzar's eyes flashed open wide in wonder. "Oh the marvel of it all."

"But you are not certain that this man can travel in time are you?" Surman knew that the direct approach was sometimes necessary. Nebuchadnezzar could get talking on a subject and spend hours babbling.

"Sometimes in life we must take chances," the grand monarch replied.

"And what are you paying for this trip in time?" The chief advisor knew the answer already. He just wanted Nebuchadnezzar to think very hard on the matter.

"Oh, half of my kingdom," replied the king with a casual wave of his hand. As if he was offering a fellow half of his lunch.

"You are the richest man in the world!" Surman retorted.

"And what of it?" hissed the king. "Yes I have palaces grand filled with harems of delightful ladies for my pleasure. Sure I have more gold and silver then any man could dream of or desire. I have horses for a hundred thousand riders, doesn't that make it all so clear?"

"In what way, oh Great One?"

"I have everything a man could desire," Nebuchadnezzar said with a sigh. "There are no more worlds for me to conquer," the king paused his eyes staring vacantly at nothing. "What this man offers me is more than I could dream of." Again the king paused. "No, it is more than any man could dream of."

Surman held his tongue, contemplating the words of his sovereign. Personally he thought the mission foolhardy and perilous. Still, it was his job only to advise. He was to support the king in all matters, irregardless of his own personal opinion.

"Think of it man," King Nebuchadnezzar spoke with the excitement of a boy on his birthday. "To see all those wonders. Flying ships that travel through the air. Tall buildings that reach up into the sky. Chariots without horses. Why you heard the sci-en-tist talk as well as I. Doesn't it fill you with a sense of wonder all those marvelous things that he describes? Wouldn't you give half your kingdom, but half your life just to spend one day there? Why society must be grand beyond belief!"

"It is your decision, oh wise King Nebuchadnezzar," Surman acquiesced with a reluctant sigh. He knew that there was no way he could sway his sovereign from traveling to the future.

"So he walks into the box, you set the instruments and you pull the switch?" Surman wanted to make sure he knew all the details.

"That's right," replied Doctor Goodman with a smile grand. "Nebuchadnezzar will arrive in the future, in the greatest city that ever existed on the face of the Earth. He will arrive at the pinnacle of civilization."

"Yes," said King Nebuchadnezzar, "I will be going to New Yawk City." The monarch was smiling grandly. "Where buildings stand a third of a mile tall and huge horseless carriages travel underneath the streets."

Surman gritted his teeth. His liege was acting like the perfect fool. This Doctor Goodman reeked like a total fraud. However, his wonders from the future not only had the advisor baffled, but confounded all the experts of Babylonia. "And he can bring nothing with him?" asked the advisor.

"No," Doctor Goodman said softly. "Only with transference with the time machine itself can physical objects be transported."

"So he will arrive in this New Yawk City totally naked?" Surman asked bitterly.

"Come now," objected King Nebuchadnezzar, "what I need surely I will attain. Why I'll be in the lap of luxury will I not?"

"Yes indeed you shall!" eagerly agreed Doctor Goodman with a smile, "indeed you shall."

"Then it is all settled," the king of kings said as he entered into the chamber. Doctor Goodman shut the door behind him. He examined the controls and dials making sure they were exactly set. Then he pulled the lever. The machine started vibrating and then suddenly stopped. The door then was opened up revealing a vacant chamber. All the Babylonians were overwhelmed with awe.

"Okay mister, I'm sure you got some good reason why you're wearing your birthday suit in Times Square?"

"Yes," replied King Nebuchadnezzar, "I have just traveled through time to witness the greatest city of Earth." The monarch looked upwards at the tremendous towers seemingly touching the sky. In the air he saw an immense bird. He contemplated that the awe inspiring sight was a machine carrying people. The King let out a long delightful laugh.

"Okay, okay and just who might you be then?" asked the cop.

"Why I am King Nebuchadnezzar of Babylon, the king of kings!"

"O'Malley, this is Lewis, send the transport to Times Square, we got ourselves a real winner here."

King Nebuchadnezzar continued to take in the sights overcome with awe.

"You'll be coming with me, Your Majesty," the police officer said gruffly.

"And where shall you be taking me?"

"Oh we got a great place for all visiting royalty who show up naked, it's called Bellevue Psychiatric Hospital."

"Splendid," cried out King Nebuchadnezzar, "will there be a harem of wenches awaiting me there?"

CLOSEST

KILMO

Ben felt like the minute hand of a clock whose gears had sprung. The collision had left him spinning through frozen circles full of dust and darkness for long enough, he couldn't tell what was up and what was down.

'Co... in... answer...if...hear me.'

The mechanic sounded like she was underwater, the drowned hiss of static rattling through his ear drums soaking her every word like waves hitting a beach. He punched the pad in his arm, ignoring the scarlet meteors as the suit split wider.

'You still there?'

Golden's voice emerged from the depths again.

'Ben?...are....y....alright?'

The droplets floating past his eyes were getting thicker.

'I don't know; I think something hurts.'

He'd no way of telling where the damage was either. The suit had pumped him so full of endorphins he was finding it difficult to remember where he was, let alone start the right rescue protocols.

'Ben, I'm on my way just hang tough. I know you can do it.'

He waited a moment watching the slow play of light as gravity tore stars towards the hole eating this corner of the zone.

'Yeah...what was that?'

'I don't know, mining spill? Junk from one of the orbitals? Their peri-helions are decaying so fast there's not much of them left that's stable.'

The Shard had been core nuked long ago, only the snapped remnants tumbling aimlessly round its axis told you it had been inhabited at all.

'What happened to the others?'

The silence was a heartbeat longer than it should have been.'

'Dead.'

Ben and the rest of the crew had been stripping the hulks hole 38523/B hadn't got to yet for weeks now. He supposed they'd been lucky to get away with it so long.

'The cargo?'

'Got it, decompression doesn't dent metal. Apart from a few scratch-es it's Ok.'

'And the planet?'

This time, the pause was longer.

'Tell me.'

The Shards remains sat on a knife edge; the hole nibbled at its edges a little more every solar day. They'd taken a gamblers chance on the odds staying in their favour, and they had, until now.

'It's gone active.'

'Damn, get out of here and do it fast.'

Ben craned his neck to get a look and wished he hadn't. Down below the first amber tint of continental rupture bloomed across the rock like daisy chains.

'Can you see that?'

'Yes, the planet's dying. What you're looking at will have spread across thirty percent of its land mass in minutes. The remainder will follow not long after that.'

Ben drifted above the fields of a forgotten world and thought of home.

'You're not going to be here in time are you?'

Their ship was a relic, a cast off from old wars. Whatever scavenged parts it contained weren't up to a rescue conducted at the speed that might save his life.

'Just keep calm, breath slow, and deep, conserve your oxygen. I'll be there as soon as I can.'

'You haven't answered the question.'

'Probably not, but I might be able to drag a few more grades out of the engine if we're lucky.'

Ben closed his eyes. He was bleeding out, the slow creep of numb-ness like a tranquillizer crushing him in its fist. Only the helmet's air was keeping him alive.

'Golden?'

Something that would have been better off staying under his ribs pressed against the suits skin as detonations crisped across the topography below.

'It's beautiful.'

'I know, hang in there. I'm coming.'

Ben closed his eyes when he opened them again he winced. There was still an icon working on his HUD after all.

'System failure in three minutes.'

The voice sounded like his old landlady's, dry, cultured, and very uninterested.

'Can't, tell my family nice things. I'm going to make this quick. It's going to hurt a hell of a lot less if I go now.'

The last failed campaign Ben had been a part of had taught its survivor's hard lessons. Better to know a quick way out than be taken prisoner by the things they'd been sent to fight, and the code had been easy to remember. It began with his birth date.

'See you in the next life Golden.'

'Don't do this Ben, please.'

'You know that's how it works; death, rebirth, destruction, creation. You can't stop them; nothing can. I'll breathe through you when I'm gone.'

'Your oxy's running out. It's making you sound like the last time you got drunk. I don't need to know the mysteries of the cosmos Ben. I need to get to you in time.'

Ben laughed.

'Don't you see? You already have, nothing can change that. Energy doesn't stop with breath, and it doesn't listen to the void.'

'I don't want you to go.'

'I'm not; I'm just going a little deeper.'

Ben, ex-serjeant, thief, and murderer, lights up like a diode. High-voltage electric lines his body, twitching limbs in a dance no one can see. It really is beautiful he has time to think as power spreads his teeth in a rictus. The planet is dying, and it's taking him and the last of its dreams with it.

Golden wiped her eyes and smiled. There was nothing else to do as the tiny speck on the screen went nova, and something settled behind her eyes.

'Make yourself at home.'

THE CAT LADY'S LAMENT

E.E. KING

I never thought I would end up like this, practically a tabloid horror story. Why, someday I bet I'll be discovered dead in my tiny, piss-scented apartment, being devoured by my seventy or so cats.

Thing is, I never even liked cats. They're too sleek and indifferent, too snotty and superior. I started out just like you. I had a job, an apartment in the city, and a goldfish. It wasn't a bad life, not exciting or anything, but still. It was all I expected. All I needed.

I'm a plain woman and I know it. I was suited to being what I was, an insignificant secretary for County Animal Control. I wore tweet skirts, wool stockings, sensible shoes and thick, thick glasses. I had long ago given up trying to be pretty. I gave up longing for romance or spice. Every day I walked to work, answered phone calls, scheduled appointments and fielded complaints from the crazies who seem to think that cats and dogs are just the same, or even better, than people.

And then along came Max, handsome as a movie star. His hair was black and sleek as dreams. His eyes were the vivid green of new peas. He was more charming and unexpected than roses in winter.

I was walking home when he stopped me - right in the street - and asked if I had the time. I was wearing a watch, so he knew I did. So few people do these days, relying on phones for just about everything. Well, I told him what time it was - 6:00 PM - without stuttering, or even flushing. I hadd no expectations. He was too handsome, graceful, and suave for the likes of me. But instead of thanking me and hurrying away he began walking beside me, talking to me as naturally as breathing, just as if he had nothing better to do.

By the time we reached my door he knew my name, where I worked, what I liked and had asked me out to dinner. I accepted.

He showed up at 7:30, right on time. He brought me red roses, opened doors for me, and held my hand. He told me I was special, even beautiful, though I'm not and I know it. He courted me for three weeks. It was just like a romance novel without any of the nasty sexual stuff. Max was a gentleman through and through.

On the twenty- fifth day that we had known each other, not that I was keeping count or anything, I'm just naturally organized. He showed up at my door with chocolates and a large box.

He told me he was going away on a business trip for two months. He hated to leave me, but there it was, he had no choice. He said he would get a big raise and when he came back he had something very important to ask me. He hoped I would say yes.

Well you didn't need to be an Einstein to figure out what he had planned. I couldn't believe how lucky I was. I started to dream of white gowns and diamonds.

He said he had a favor to ask me. He'd been caring for his aunt's cat, Sofia, he said. He didn't like cats either, it was something we had in common. But he was so kind he could never say no to anyone. So he asked me please, please could I look after it, just while he was away. Then he would return, give it back to his aunt, and we would be together forever.

Of course I said yes. I was going to be his bride!

While I was away at work, Sofia had ten kittens in my closet, right on top of my best shoes. It was disgusting.

I took them to the County Animal Shelter. I'd never actually been inside the shelter before. I worked in the office.

The head of the shelter begged me to keep the kittens till they were old enough to adopt out, eight weeks, she said, otherwise they'd be put down. I never would have, but Max would be back by then, and maybe his aunt would want them. Maybe he'd be upset if they'd been killed. So I said took them home.

Max didn't come back. He didn't call. He didn't write. I thought about taking the cats to the shelter, but by then I had come to know them. They ran to meet me when I opened the door. They purred and rubbed up against me when I stroked their soft, soft fur. They slept next to me, soothing me with the steady sound of their breathing.

Then my neighbor moved out, abandoning three cats. I took them to shelter and discovered that the county killed animals left there over five days. Five days. And it wasn't a pretty death. I saw the ovens.

So I began taking home the lost and the doomed. Suddenly they were everywhere, cats; left at my doorstep, dumped on my desk, abandoned in my hallway.

I thought I was unique, exceptional in the way I had become a cat lady, if in no other. Then, I met Rochelle. We bumped into each other in a back alley, stuffing plastic bags of cat turds into any available garbage cans. We had too much for our own bins. It happens when you have more than twenty cats.

We became friends, or I should say friends in the way the cat ladies are. We never went to lunch, on walks, to movies, or did any of the things that normal people do. But we met occasionally in back alleys disposing of used litter. We exchanged eye drops when the cats got conjunctivitis, and loaned each other amoxicillin.

I don't even know how we started talking about men. Rochelle was like me, dowdy and plain. Born to be an old maid. No man had paid her attention, even when she was young. Then, long after hope had died, the most handsome and charming man she'd ever seen had asked her out. He was amusing, respectful and oddest of all, fell totally in love with her. But then his mother died. She lived in England and he was her only son and heir. He had to go back for the funeral.

Before he left, vowed eternal love and hinting he might return with a diamond ring, he asked Rochelle for a favor. He begged her to look after his aunt's cat. He didn't like cats himself, but had promised his aunt, and it was only for three week. Well, he never came back, and you know the rest.

The other night, when I was in the back alley disposing of used litter I felt someone staring at me. Looking up, I saw a large, black cat with fur as sleek as dreams. Its eyes were horribly familiar, the green of new peas. It scrutinized me with those bright, bright eyes, watching me furtively stuffing sacks of feces into stranger's trashcans. Its whiskers twitched upward as if grinning. Then, blinking slowly, it disappeared into the darkness, tail waving in farewell.

TROMPE L'OEIL

ROBERT KIRVEL

As a courtesy to folks unfamiliar with the expression (let's assume a 90% probability of non-affluence in French pronunciation) the phonation is trump LOY, and the phrase means fool the eye, the way those sidewalk drawings entice people into thinking there's a bottomless pit ahead, when it's just a neat trick of drawing in chalk on a slab of cement. Or maybe painted in pastels 15% of the time. I'm no expert, so 15% is ballpark.

About drawing—or art, you decide—she hires a designer who's supposed to come with a "fabulous pedigree"—whatever that means in the non-canine world of interior design—and the woman comes storming in through the main rooms of our house with her nose up in the air as if our furniture has a flatulence problem. Immediately I know from her altitude this will cost me far more than the gopher damages. A good 5-will-get-you-10, it runs into 5 figures.

What I don't expect is how she comes up to me out of the blue, one afternoon when my wife is off playing cards. This person measures a good 6 by 2 wide, so that's 12 square feet of woman coming at you, ready or not. Waltzes right up about 1 inch from my face with her breath running over me like a rip tide. Whoa there! On a stink scale of 0 to 10, this designer person warrants a 7-plus. Putrescene, they call it. I heard about putrescene from my dentist., It stuck with me ever since; the name of the chemical that causes uber-foul breath. It's the kind of thing you don't forget, the kind of person I am. Putrescene: super descriptive, although cadaverine is even better at sounding how it means.

Anyway, inside a week flat there's her artwork on my wall. A done deal you couldn't avoid, but really: art? I wouldn't give 2 cents.

So I ask her, expecting a viscous comeback, but no. She's super slick. "It's subliminal." That's all she argued after I asked; no other justification for a floor-to-ceiling painting of a walk-in closet on our dining room wall. Her "creation" she calls it, measuring 8 by 5 feet wide, is of a double door standing two-thirds open into which a person can just see clutter inside, because it's dark in there. Six shelves full of closet stuff, only painted on the wall, a dozen shirts on painted hangers, lazy underthings sprawling around. On the messy side.

"Really? A bunch of clothes painted on the wall of our dining room?" I ask her that.

"It's subliminal." That's what the artist tells me. Maybe she means subtle. Some people confuse the two.

"The difference is greater than the similarity." That's how my wife reacts. "As with people," she adds.

Is it me, or am I the only one who doesn't know what my wife is talking about, half the time? Am I so bats by now that it's time to blow my brains out? Then I remember a bumper sticker I read someplace. Wag more. Bark less. So I keep my mouth zipped and write a check for 11 grand for a drawing—well, painting—of a walk-in closet measuring 5 by 8 feet by about 1/16th of an inch of paint, however thick a coat of paint is. Some closet. Some dining room wall, courtesy of Ms. Subliminal and my wife.

Sometimes my better half thinks the way a Beach Boys melody wanders all over. Everything goes along great for 8 or 10 beats, and you think you know what's what, then—wham!—the unexpected. The tune she's singing shoots way up high a couple octaves and switches key 2 or 3 times, the way an old Beach Boys song does. On the surface it's all even-steven, until her thoughts go into terra incognita and you realize not only that it makes cartographic sense—in an alternative universe way—but that what she's got in mind is interesting. Unexpected. Beauty of an unexpected flavor from my wife I mean. That's when our gopher shows up again.

The love of my life swears the gopher tunneling through 65 feet of our side yard waits for her to step outside every morning to "stick its tongue out" at her. Her exact four words. The gopher pokes its head out and taunts her like some teenager, she says. I tell her the idea is loony, a gopher is too busy taking care of gopher business to pay attention to her and make some human gesture with a tongue. How would a gopher know that tongue sticking is a human insult? But no, she's convinced the gopher's ill will is aimed at her and is deliberately making fun when she gets angry at the loss of another exotic plant, enjoyed by the gopher gullet. Fourteen plants so far. Fourteen tongue opportunities. "As if a gopher cares about my wife," I say to my wife in exaggerated irony to get the point across. Or is that sarcasm? Six to one or a half dozen of the other. As if a gopher gives two hoots about her, but that's the beauty of the thing, you see. In her mind, which runs 80 miles an hour, my wife is the centerpiece of the universe and garden and gopher mentality, of the dining room and that trompe l'oeil closet I've come to accept. Well, accept 50%.

So now when I think something is wacko about what she does, like hiring a pedigreedy decorator to slap a fake closet on our wall, I bite my lip. I can ignore the closet on the dining room wall by scooting my butt over 2 feet to face a picture window instead and look out at our view, gopher or no gopher. I give my odds for happiness 95%, and if the gopher tries anything smart, I'll just turn the other cheek.

HOSPICE

NORMAN KLEIN

I got out of my car reminding myself not to let my ex, Lorna, get to me. It was just like her, a snail-mailed request for a visit written in bold black ink, and the reason printed in larger gold letters. '*We must set things straight with the children,*' it said. My first thought was that the children were in their forties, old enough to muddle through, then I realized it had to be something serious that I didn't know about.

The day after the black and gold mail came, an email from Lorna warned me that the front door had been nailed shut. I was to come to the back door, give a shout, and let myself in, which I did.

"Sorry, Greg, it sticks a bit doesn't it?" Lorna said. "I'll put that on my '*to do*' list."

"I love the new window. Nice view of the gardens," I said.

"Remember this recliner?" she asked, pushing the hand pedal to raise herself upright.

"Was it your father's?" I asked.

"No, it was yours. I gave it to you for your birthday and you threw it in the garage and covered it with a tarp.

I didn't remember the recliner or tarp, but it sounded like me. So I smiled and she moved on to say how pale and pudgy I was. I countered with describing my weight lifting routine, and she let it go at that.

"That's right, I haven't seen you in ten years, have I?" she said.

"Maybe more," I said.

"Well, anyway, thanks for coming. And don't worry I'm not going to ask you for money."

"Good, but I will take you to lunch if you're up to it."

"I'm not. That's why I asked you to come. I'm dying. Did Andrea tell you? She wasn't supposed to, but I knew she would, now that she's livingwith you."

"She told me two years ago."

"That was just a close call. How is she doing, by the way? I'm worried about her."

"So am I. She has two jobs, and she can't sleep at night. She worries about you, and by the way, she wants you to call her."

"Tell her I will when I know more."

"More about what?"

"Finding a hospice."

I waited for her to tell me how long she had left, but she wouldn't say. There had been several false alarms in the last five years. The last one began with a twelve-hour operation and ended with two setbacks and a week in London with her lawyer friend.

"So what's going on with the children, Lorna? What's this about?"

"It's about the will. Rick says I'm under water, but Andrea says if she sells the house I would get enough for the hospice and the rest would pay for the work she's done on the house for the past ten years."

"Sounds good. So what's the problem?"

"When I last spoke with Rick I told him a will had been written, and he asked if his children would be provided for. I didn't take it seriously. You know how he is. I thought it was his way of telling me he didn't believe I was dying."

"I talked to Rick on his birthday. He and Bob were thinking of adopting a child. Maybe two."

"But not right away. They can't afford it," she said.

She went on to explain how she told Rick she had only weeks to live, and that Andrea had her power of Attorney and would also serve as the executor of the will.

"Okay," Rick had said, "I know it's complicated, because I'm asking for money to be put aside. Now that I think of it, I'd feel better if Dad was the executor of the will."

"Hmm, funny you should suggest that. That's what my lawyer said as well," Lorna had told Rick.

"Rick called to say the lawyer wanted to set up a trust that would have me owning the house and paying the mortgage until the house was sold," I said.

"It's fine with me. I don't care. I know nothing about it," she said.

"Sounds like the same lawyer who represented you when we split."

"So, what's wrong with that?" she asked.

"Never mind, that's water under the bridge. The will is signed. Andrea is your executor."

"True, Andrea needs to be executor to protect her interests," she said.

"I agree. Andrea has to come first, because she's dead broke." I said.

"But that reminds me, Greg. There is one thing you can do for me. It's the *Delft Blue*. I want you take it away and hide it, because some day she'll want it. I know she will."

"Will do," I said, glad there was something I could do for her.

"Greg, do you remember our little talk twelve years ago, just before you announced your engagement to what's-her-face?"

"I think so. You told me you had become a Christian Scientist."

"Well, I'm not sure any more. Lately I've been more a Unitarian Universalist. If I die tomorrow, tell Andrea that."

"Will do," I said, hoping that was the end of her list.

"Thanks, Greg, and here's one final thing. The most important thing of all, really. I would like you to deliver my eulogy."

"No, Lorna, the kids should do that," I said.

"I've already asked. Neither of them will do it. I have some notes here, things to say and not say."

"Could I see them?" I asked.

"No, not until you promise me."

"Why not let your lawyer do it?"

"He can't. His wife would kill him."

"Okay, here's a suggestion. I'll pay Andrea to do it, but the funeral will be by invitation only."

"If that's the case, I'll ask her not to invite you or my lawyer," Lorna said looking out her window.

"That's kind of you," I said, admitting for the first time she truly was dying.

HOW TO FREE
AN ELEPHANT

GREGORY KOOP

It was the moment between parking the car and spreading Dad's ashes that Mom became old. It wasn't when streaks of grey began to sneak in amongst the auburn about her temples. It was that moment. A pragmatic woman, a high school principal, she had starched her skirt, steamed her blouse last night before calling to remind me to: *Meet at the house at 8:30, park around back—we'll take my car. I'll drive. We'll spread the ashes; then we'll have breakfast, the Husky Diner, Dad's favourite. Oh, and I packed his ashes already...* We were there at Avery Park. I could see the memorial. But there she sat, looking at nothing and staring off was never something I could recall her doing.

I remember holding my breath during her moment. I also took in Avery Park for the first time in ages. It was a flat swath of manicured lawn, annexed from aureolin prairie and framed by Black Gully Lake's opal waters, a stretch of brush, mostly poplars, and a gravel range road. It wasn't really a park. There were no playgrounds, gardens, or picnic tables. It didn't even have signage. It was a lawn with a cairn commemorating RCAF Alberta, a WWII airfield training school. The monument itself, a twisted spire of fieldstones, sat atop a sandstone base adorned by carvings of elephant tusks.

This was where Dad brought me every Sunday when he would mow the grounds and wipe the bird shit from the obelisk.

170

Mom muttered something as she gazed beyond her hands and wrung the steering wheel, "He never did know how to make an exit, did he?" She didn't look up, but I felt her voice point to me. "At parties he was always that guy. You were usually asleep on the bed with all the coats. Sometimes I would curl up beside you, my feet tucked inside my dress. Remember?"

"You always wore a petticoat—it made your lap all pillowy." I scraped away at nothing under my thumbnail. She was watching my hands now, so I stopped.

She continued. "He never knew the right time to leave. The light over the kitchen sink was on for goodness sakes. We'd have to be at the door, my hand on the knob and they'd have to take his glass. I can see that nod of his, his shuffle to the door," she clutched her keychain, "and his keys in my other hand." Mom turned off the ignition.

"It wasn't so late two hours ago." The words leapt from both our mouths.

Mom smiled. "And punched his duckbill."

"Well maybe we'd better head home before we run out of moonlight..." My voice trailed when Mom didn't say it along with me.

"Well....are we doing this?" Mom popped the trunk and got out.

I followed the lawn towards the cairn. I froze halfway and marched in place, letting my feet feel the turf again. "This grass doesn't feel right."

"You sound like your dad."

I dragged my feet, pushed my heel downwards. "It feels different."

"It's the same." Mom clutched my forearm and knelt, her hands drawn to the curve of a sandstone tusk.

"What's with the elephant tusks, anyway?"

"Oh. Your dad never told you?"

"No."

Mom palmed some ash and massaged a tusk white. "It's for the elephant."

I shrugged as she massaged another beige tusk ashen.

"Avery, the Asian elephant."

I shook my head.

"I always wanted him to tell you about Avery." She sighed and let a long breath swell inside her. "When we were children this spot used to be a military flight school. Granddad was an instructor. And in '44 some shoddy circus went bankrupt when it stopped here. The ringmaster cut town leaving everything, including an Asian elephant named Avery. Fuel was at a premium because of the war, and to make a long story short, the military took her. She pulled planes out of hangers and lugged heavy equipment around. Oh, and did she cast a spell on your dad. Most little boys had a dog growing up. Can you imagine? It's funny—he used to wrap a length of manila around himself, letting it dangle behind him. And that elephant, she would hold it, his little tail right there in her trunk." She looked off over the lake as she rubbed another tusk. Her voice laboured as she stained the carvings with Dad's memory. "He calls this place Avery Park for her. It's actually named something like *Princess Louise Battalion Memorial Park*."

"I don't understand. What am I supposed to do with that story? Is all that true?" The spire of the monument wrung itself through my eyes. It didn't look like a statue. It became sharpened.

"True story: he also designed and built this monument."

"Are you kidding me?"

"Well, that's what you do with a sensitive heart. He never sold much but this piece here." She removed a can of spray lacquer from her purse, held it back a couple feet before letting a mist rest upon the tusks. "The only thing he didn't like about it was the tusks."

"What?"

"Avery was female, she didn't have tusks, but how was he to honour her without depleting the fact that this monument was for RCAF Alberta." She tapped the commemorative inscription loaded with names of dead soldiers.

"He wanted to name you Avery."

"Oh my gawd. Are you kidding me? Why didn't he tell me? I came here every week with him. I think I even asked him once about the tusks. He told me he didn't know. Why didn't he tell me the truth of how important it was to him?"

"It was too much pain for him. When he quit his art he quit. He wouldn't even doodle on a napkin. I begged him when you were a child to tell you about Avery. He said, 'I can't.' And when your father says he can't, he can't. So we let it be."

"I don't get it." I stomped my feet against the lawn again. I needed something to feel familiar. "What's wrong with this grass?"

Mom reached into her purse.

"Here." She held out a rolled up cloth tape measure

"What else are you hiding in there?"

"It's bentgrass. How tall is it supposed to be?"

"Dad always cut it half an inch."

"That's right—to keep the ryegrass at bay." She shook the tape measure. "Measure it."

I bent over and draped the tape amongst the blades.

"It's an inch." Mom held out her purse. I dropped the tape measure back inside. "How did you know?"

"He felt everything. He was like a radio tower for energy and emotions. His sensitive heart affected his entire world. And you're sensitive, too. It's not weakness. It's awareness, vigilance, empathy. Every Sunday, Dear. It's muscle memory."

I nodded and held out my hand. Mom pulled herself to her feet. "Why, Mom? Why didn't he say anything?"

"Oh, Honey..." she squeezed my hand. "I can tell you this. I don't know if it will make sense. But here it is. That elephant was such a sweet part of his life. And you deserved to hear about her."

"That's not—"

Mom reached up and placed her hand upon my cheek.

"The day your father and the military got the elephant, the animal wept. So vividly he used to tell this story. Your father stood with his dad, who was supposed to figure out how to use her. They looked her over, walked around her. Your dad noticed that all about Avery's cheeks, forehead, neck, ears, and shoulders where scars. I guess the circus handlers would use a sharp metal stick to control her." Mom cleared her throat. "He stepped to the elephant. That brave little boy stepped right up to that giant beast and reached up a hand, letting his palm rest where he thought her heart was. And he found it. Do you know what that elephant did?"

I shook my head.

"Avery gently wrapped her trunk around his back and up under his armpit to his chest where his heart was pounding. She gave him a squeeze. Then she wept. She held that sensitive boy and he held her. She cried for hours. Your dad stayed with her for the rest of her days. He slept with her, he ate with her, he gave her all the kindness she deserved. He gave her a home inside his heart."

"But, Mom, why did he do it?"

"He loved that Elephant and needed to hold her inside. I think if he shared her, it would let her out."

"No. I mean, is that why he...umm..." It felt like my throat had turned to stone. My words sank back into my oesophagus. I stared at the tusks of the monument, Mom's hand still gracing my cheek. "Is that why he...umm...to... to himself?"

There was a nod. I saw it. Mom's chin tipped down with a long blink from her eyes. A tear slipped down her cheek.

"Let's go to Husky. This old woman needs to eat," She said.

WELCOME TO SPACE

ELENA KRAUSE

In the mountains that line the BC/Alberta border the sky is something you can ignore, just an open door at the end of a long, tree-lined hallway. I like it and that's why I live there. I like the comfort of knowing there are things between me and infinity. Things with roots.

Here, the sky is more like a mouth. The mouth is open; the throat is black. The stars flash like glistening teeth. The monster doesn't come toward me; it just waits in silence. It knows I'm going to fall in.

This yawning abysm is the perfect real-life metaphor for my future. Not in a hokey, melodramatic sense, but in the most literal, visceral way I can think of.

I remember this sky from years ago, when I came here for summer camp; it's impossible to forget. As a young child, I thought it was something solid, like black cement, something you'd run into if you went high enough. I thought rocket ships had to break through a ceiling to get into outer space, that the stars were stuck in this dome like light bulbs. I don't remember how old I was when I found out the only thing between me and the moon was about 385,000 kilometres. I was too young to fathom that kind of vastness.

Now, I'm starting to, but only in a vague, tip-of-my-tongue kind of way.

I could fall in there, I think, staring up into it from where I'm perched, cross-legged, on the hood of my car. *What a lonely way to die.* I wish I was holding someone's hand right now, just in case, but I came alone.

I stretch out my legs and lay back on the windshield, using slow, deliberate movements, the way a person does at the edge of a cliff. At any moment, I could plummet into space at a speed that would kill me before I ever left Earth's atmosphere. I brace myself. The windshield wiper digs into the small of my back but I don't readjust. Pain is a silly thing to worry about in the face of the universe's open mouth.

At a moment like this, the knowledge of gravity does nothing for me; I'd prefer a tether, a rope, roots, something physical to hold onto. The idea that this unseen force has held me down for my whole life and is, therefore, reliable, is awful logic. There are a lot of things in my life that have held me for a long time, only to let go suddenly and inexplicably. People, obviously, but also concepts, ideas, places, tire swings.

Just this morning it happened again.

I sat in a plastic chair beside an ugly plastic houseplant. The chair looked more alive than the plant. I was about to hear terrible news. I knew it because the specialist came and sat beside me instead of at his desk across from me where he'd begun our meeting. This, I thought, was probably meant to be comforting. I can see how it would have been, if I didn't have trouble seeing anything not directly in front of me. That was why I was there in the first place. Maybe he would realize his gaffe later on and feel stupid. I didn't say anything at the time, though, just stared vacantly ahead, acutely aware of the ever-increasing vignette around the edges of my vision. He said these words, in this order: *Retinitis. Pigmentosa. Degenerative. Disease. Eventual. Complete. Blindness.* Also: "You shouldn't drive anymore." The words floated, one by one, out of my blackened peripheral.

I decided to stuff them back in and leave them there, where I couldn't see them.

I nodded along until he stopped talking. Then I marched out to my car, a rust-colored Chevette in deplorable condition. I hoped he was watching from the window of his office. My vision had been bad for so long, disintegrating so gradually, that I didn't find driving difficult yet. I thought it was a little extreme of him to say that I couldn't drive at all anymore. I would show him.

I meant to go home then and make myself something to eat in front of the TV, but on the way there I heard a song on the radio that felt like a scene from a movie where a person is brave. I thought about my diagnosis and the words from the doctor. I drove past my exit. I decided I wouldn't stop until I absolutely had to. I wasn't blind yet.

It didn't take me long to realize the specialist had been right after all.

This would be my love letter to road trips, but also my breakup note, my it's-not-you-it's-me. *Road Trips*, I would say in swirling cursive on tear-stained paper, *I love you, I always have, but we can't see each other anymore.*

As my eyes grew tired and blurred with tears, I tried not to think about how selfish and reckless I was being. I drove all day with the music loud, stopping only for gas and granola bars, until I found the actual middle of nowhere and the sun started setting and I couldn't see the lines on the road at all anymore. My eyesight was always the worst in the evening – a telltale sign, I'd been told this morning, of my new disease.

By the time I pulled over, I felt dizzy and sick. I retched out the open door, then drove ahead a little so I wouldn't forget and step in it. I was in a wheat field. The clock on my dash was broken, so I could only guess at where I'd ended up, how far I'd gone, how long I'd been driving. I'd veered off the highway onto a gravel road some time back, feeling like it would be safer, but now I realized how foolish I'd been. I would have to spend the night out here. Instead of laying my seat back and falling asleep, I crawled onto the hood of my car, and this is where I've been since.

I'd forgotten how much longer the sunsets last out here, how much longer the shadows hang around and how strange everything looks in the last few minutes before you can't see it at all anymore. I wonder if this is how it'll feel to go blind once and for all, like watching the sun set, watching the colors around me get muddy and dark and blend into one another. Or maybe it'll happen suddenly, like a light switch flipped off.

However it happens, this is it, right here; above me and around me, here's my future. Darkness so thick you could drink it and so unfathomably deep you can't understand it.

I can't see farm lights or stars; I can't tell where the fields end or the sky begins. I hear crickets, wind, an occasional vehicle.

I close my eyes, open them, there's no difference. *This is what it's going to be like.* I'm grateful that this darkness will lift when morning comes, that I'll have a few more months before it becomes my permanent reality – if the specialist knows what he's talking about. I close them again; I pretend the windshield wiper in my back is someone's elbow. It's not comfortable, but it's comforting.

I'm startled out of my thoughts by the sound of a large vehicle approaching from behind me. I hear it rumble to a stop. A door opens and slams shut. I sit up and spin around but I see no headlights. I hear soft footsteps in the wheat and stiffen; someone is trying to slip, unseen, through this property. Have they already seen me? Suddenly, I'm thankful for the night and the cover it provides.

A voice comes to me through the darkness. "Car troubles?" I jump, but I'm relieved; the voice is friendly. I smile slightly, shake my head, and immediately feel ridiculous using physical gestures the man would not be able to see. Before I can answer aloud, he speaks again.

"Oh, good. Listen, I'm sorry to ask you to move, but we've still got some work to do here this evening."

I feel cold all over, prickly, like the blood inside me has frozen solid. "This evening?" I ask, my voice scratchy. "What time is it?"

"Oh, I know what you're thinking," says the friendly voice out of the blackness, "we sure do work late around here." He lets out a soft laugh. He's probably shaking his head, lifting his wrist to check his watch, scratching his neck, smiling. I can picture it all but I can't see it. "That's the life of a farmer, I guess. Uh…let's see – it's 8:15. We're actually doing well today though – we might even finish before the sun goes down!"

Gravity lets me go – but just me, not anyone else, and I shoot into the sky and it swallows me up.

OMA

ANDREW LARIMER

Oma's house throbs like childhood and breathing units that push you past birthday cards, ticking cat clocks and her salt-soaked dentures. The wheelchair wheels click on aged jasper floors and dilute any nostalgic echoes that once ricocheted down this hall, while her crinkled face clings to what familiarity it can. Oma's veins glow blue, bruised by time and I fight the urge to look away. But I can't because someone must feed her now that mother is gone.

"Hey Oma. It's me, Alexei."

This house is filled with chapped walls and doctors' expectations, surrounded by a willingness to stay and dead cacti.

"95 today. Can you believe that, Oma?"

I try to picture the woman she was when she once glittered in the morning light and smiled with crooked grace. I try to remember when her birthdays consisted of exchanging obnoxious saggy grannie pictures on birthday cards. A time when age didn't force half-hearted obligations and when icing wasn't smudged on these pity-me-pink cakes.

"It's Strawberry-Banana, your favorite."

No one ever believes their independency escaped after that tumble in the shower or during that stroke while they are spooning green peas or that it came from the dementia that yawns during 10 a.m. service. They think independence is in an untouchable future that aches on the end of fingertips. That it's constantly tomorrow. Oma's tomorrow was years ago.

"Full yet?"

I exhale with arms folded over my chest to try to blanket any pity from surfacing. So I just sit alongside and feed this precious prey of borrowed time and wonder why she is still wrestling with existence. I'll be gone before she finishes tomorrow morning's cup of coffee and after my sympathy becomes degrading.

"Ready to go back to your room, Oma?"

She nods at me and I realize what isn't said is actually a scream that never stops. She knows her voice is two seconds from hushed, so she says nothing. And so do I. I simply pile the quilts over her frailty and kiss her forehead.

I turn off the lights and my mind dodges the truth with the shadows and holds hope for an easy moment. Blowing out candles does the same.

Oma's nurse walks into the kitchen and I look up from cradling my face in the creases in my palms.

"Can you handle it from here?"

"Mmhmm. I'll take good care of her."

I suppose there's nothing left to do. Because we are weak and it's easier this way. So we wait between her meals, between her dainty bites and the silence separating her sips of water. Between night's deathly hands and the persistent pattern of early morning rain. We wait with unwieldy hearts for next year's birthday cards and for the rest of the cake to be eaten. For tomorrow's cup of coffee to be halfway drunk. For next week's last small steps across cold jasper floors. Then, after the cat clock is bundled in her wool quilts and stored in folded cardboard boxes, we wish we wouldn't have waited at all.

FREEDOM IS A HEARTBEAT

ROBERT LINDBERG

Hadi was told by the supervisor to transport all the empty crates of vegetables to the basement. Hadi's stomach churned at the thought of dark quarters again. After two months of work he was still the only one appointed with that task.

He flung the crates haphazardly, one after one, and marveled at the idea of stacking empty crates all the way up to the eternal blue. If anyone could do it, it would be him.

A thin beam of sunlight pushed through the mountain of crates blocking the window. The fourteenth crate flung in the air made him think about the long river that flowed through his old home town. However, the river was a long poem away from him now. As were the humble winds of evening. The birds that once soared above him were a fading memory.

The fifteenth crate flung in the air made him think about his published articles. Those that made him a stowaway within the dark deep of a freighter.

In these dark quarters he felt something sear and sting in his body. Something sharp and feathery pointed out from his back. The sting disappeared each time he managed to sneak up on deck. He inhaled so much nippy sea air that he almost fainted.

The sixteenth crate made him think about all the empty paper beside his mattress. For months his ardent pen had been waiting for his direction.

As he flung the seventeenth crate the searing sting returned. It felt like long fingernails clawing his back. Hadi let go of the crates, ran up to the groundfloor and that's when the pain stopped.

LunchBreak on the balcony. Chicken salad. The park opposite in a thick green color. In the distance he saw the bridge stretching over from Malmo to Copenhagen. Hadi closed his eyes and heard the seagulls squeak and soar above him. He smiled to the very last chew.

He went to collect his paycheck. Looked at it and hollered, "300 euros for a month's work! The agreement was 700 euros!" A fellow worker tugged at Hadi's jacket sleeve,

"Not so loud! Just take it for now. It might change with time. It did for me." Hadi nodded without eye contact and stuffed the envelope in his pocket.

The following morning, he got placed in the basement again. Another mountain of crates were in progress, another stomach being churned. That's when the searing pain ripped through his body. The bones in his back started to rearrange. A cracking sound made him fall to his knees screaming with a thunderous might. Salty tears fell on his tongue. He was sure the walls were closing in on him.

He crawled over to the crates and tore them down. The tiny stream of light now shone so bright he had to cover his eyes. Sharp downy bones started to sprout from his back. He managed to stand up, then cracked the window with his elbow and climbed out.

He started running as fast as he could. Jumped up in the air , he took off. Huge whitefeathered wings lifted Hadi higher towards the sky. One flap catapulted him forward at a tremendous speed.

He soared on the wind currents, witnessing parts of town he had only heard mention from colleagues. Shiny cars parked along the marina. Women with colorful dresses walked their tiny dogs in a district for shopping with strange architecture.

Hadi continued his flight and the majestic feathers became blindingly white as the sun reflected upon them.

He shifted his wings and swirled around in a loop. He climbed higher and dove faster, laughed and hollered. And then steered towards the seaside. He inched closer to the bridge and settled softly on the highest point. Sat down and swayed his legs to and fro.

He grabbed empty sheets of paper from his pocket. Once again his ardent pen flowed with a direction that detailed long roads traveled, oceans sailed and those dark quarters.

THE DRUNKEN GUNFIGHTER'S GHOST

MARC LITTMAN

Ned tried to rouse his drunken body from being sprawled on the dusty street of a desert ghost town that had turned tourist trap, but quickly gave up the ghost.

Early morning dew collected on Ned's forehead and dripped into his bloodshot eyes. He blinked, then squinted up at a broken railing on the balcony of a faux hotel that he had crashed through countless times after the peeved sheriff blasted him with a blank after Ned missed his shot, much to the delight of sadistic tourists enjoying an Old West gunfight.

"Hell of a way to make a living," Ned muttered as he rummaged in his long waxed cotton duster for his secret bottle, a mirror image of the one filled with water he used in the stunt show; only this one was filled with *Wild Turkey*.

No one witnessed his epic struggle to take a snort. It would be hours before staff arrived to unlock the mystery house, rev up the silver mine train and open the general store stocked with overpriced sarsaparilla, toy gun six shooters and geodes.

Ned spied his Stetson hat lounging by the town jail. He tried again to shake his lethargy and retrieve it, along with his cocked pistol that took aim at his swollen head from its discarded place on the nearby wooden sidewalk.

"Bang!" Ned's cracked lips smiled. He drained the bottle of booze and released his ghost to meander through the empty old Western town that saw its heyday in the 1880s during the silver mining boom.

The glint of sunlight on the jail drew Ned's spirit like a lodestone. He floated over and gripped the iron bars and peered inside, communing with the pitiful mannequin, a fellow drunk sleeping off a bender.

"Too smart for your own good, that was the start of your trouble, Ned," the spirit mused. Drawn by raucous young voices, the drunken gunslinger's ghost meandered over to the one room schoolhouse. He studied a teenaged Ned, the only student paying rapt attention to the weary hunched back calculus teacher who was jotting a convoluted equation on the chalkboard. Only Ned was primed to solve the math riddle, eliciting jeers from his peers.

Young Ned blushed crimson, painfully aware that being a nerd isn't cool. He buried his head in his arms and huffed the caustic odors emanating from his desk inkwell. Meanwhile, his keen mind dissipated into the ether and the ghost drifted over to Boot Hill.

His buddy, Sotero, was dragging on a hand rolled cigarette. He lay slumped against a cross with his name crudely scrawled upon the wood and was weighted with the dead soldier's helmet and assault rifle from Afghanistan.

"You were too stoned to shoot him, Hotshot, so I took the hit," Sotero spit in his comrade's translucent face. Ned grimaced and reeled backwards. His hands gripped his gut but couldn't plug the hole of remorse.

The shadow gunslinger scurried from the cemetery and burst through the swinging batwing doors of the rollicking saloon. Sidling up to the gleaming marble bar, the ghost averted the oversized mirrors and focused upon downing glass after glass of liquid fire. Finally, a skimpily dressed coquette ensconced herself on the gunslinger's lap. She teased his ragged hair with her slender fingers. Ned's spirit detected a young woman and toddler son tiptoe into the fray, the woman frantically searching for what she hoped she wouldn't find.

Dejected, the woman angrily retreated through the doors. Ned, in his drunken dream, stumbled after her, but tripped on a knot in the wooden plank outside and fell headlong into the horse watering trough.

Ned's red-rimmed eyes swelled like saucers before he splashed into the foul liquid, but the reflection he saw in the water stuck: a middle-aged drunk who squandered a brain, friendship and family. Ned's ghost surfaced slowly. He leaned back on his rusty spurs and bridled himself for his final gunfight. Fury flamed in his dead eyes.

Hollow boots thudded down the ghost town's wooden walk. Ned turned his drool covered face toward the menacing shadow. The ghost scooped up Ned's gun, moseyed over to the still prone sot and handed it to him, but the wasted stuntman balked. "I ain't afeared," Ned took another swallow. "I've been dead meat for years."

"Draw!" the ghost commanded.

Ned just shook his head and laughed then suddenly lunged for his gun and fired, but this time a bullet hit its mark and it wasn't a blank.

MAX AND THE FAIRY GODMOTHER

PAUL LYNCH

Max was just thirteen years of age and he lived in a poor community on the outskirts of town. His three siblings were younger and didn't understand why they couldn't afford the good things in life such as more clothes, food, and electronic gadgets other children enjoyed. Their mother had two jobs one n a restaurant, and the other as an office attendant, but because of some bad decisions and poor education, she couldn't provide much for her children. Max's father was now in prison facing time for failing to pay some money he owed from a previous business partnership. He couldn't support them from behind bars and although he divorced his children's mother, he too found out he was in the living hell in his mind. Max often wished things were different, only if imaginations could come true. He often recalled his grandma who had succumbed to cancer saying, every cloud has a silver lining. Would things make a dramatic shift in their lives after all? Their mom needed a higher paying job which could support her and the children. It wasn't always like this though. Max could remember when he was at the tender age of five years, his parents were happily married, their house was in a good state and they could afford grocery in abundance. It was ironic how the tables had turned and how quickly they did. The tables had turned for the worst, Max often thought, and not for the better.

Janet, their mother, too remembered when she was happily married, but now she constantly recalls her heartaches and the whiskey bottle that she hid in her drawer so that she could drink her fears away. But the more she drinks is the more the pain is evident and no amount of strong wine could remove the pain of misery and a broken heart. Max knew his mother drank, but he constantly told himself that she would eventually come clean. After all, their father's absence made a difference now because Max was the man of the house. He often imagined being strong and in charge, buthad to endure it ungracefully for now. His younger siblings Abby, Trish, and Michael often played together, but not Max. He was now thirteen and wanted to be sure of his future. With a few more years he would probably be off to college. He wasn't the most brilliant student, but he was one of the most determined for success. Max preferred to be by himself, than with others. Mr. Allen his English teacher called it being anti-social, but he called it meditating on destiny. Max had one friend, Toby. He was from a good home in the finer part of the city and his viewpoint regarding his family was they were the best and happiest there could be. But Max knew his friend's destiny and happy family were not really his own and if he was to be born in the best family it wouldn't be any other way. Toby was really a nerd, but he had a good spirit and mind, often sharing his lunch with Max. Both boys were on the same soccer team and played well, but Janet's job forced Max to go home early after school.Soccer practice must be on hold for a season. This made Max disappointed, but he knew what had to be done. He was the security guard of the house as his siblings needed protection when mother was away.

After school one Friday evening after dinner, Max went to his room that he shared with his brother and fell asleep sitting at a desk. In a dream he saw an ancient looking woman who had wings on her shoulders like an angel and a wand in her hand. A bright light emanated from around her. Max was very puzzled yet afraid and jumped to his knees and said to the woman, "Who are you? And where have you appeared from?"

He wondered if this would be an adventure from the book A Christmas Carol that he read in the school library. The only problem was that this wasn't Christmas and she didn't look as though she was one of those ghost he had read about.

The woman replied, "I'm your fairy godmother and I'm here to help you and grant you one wish. I have been observing you all this time."

Max was a bit confused and and he asked, "But I didn't ask or wish for any fairy godmother. Furthermore, I think this is a bit strange."

"Oh, forgive me Max, my name is Elizabeth," introduced the fairy godmother.

Max thought he was in a strange dream so he just went with the flow of things because eventually he would wake up and realize it was Saturday morning.

Max said, "Where are we going? Can I ask for my one wish now?"

He said this because he never thought his experience was real, but thought it was rather a figment of his imagination.

The fairy godmother replied, "Oh, we are going to your friend Toby's house first. The wish will stay for last. Just close your eyes and imagine you're at the house and we'll be there."

Max wondered why Toby's house was important in this encounter, but he obeyed and before he could blink they were at the house. Max noticed and observed the house was very huge with a large swimming pool. His entire family apartment could fit in this mansion, ten times. Toby never mentions his house being this huge. Why didn't he ever invite me over? I guess this house has plenty of food and comfort.

But the fairy godmother read his thoughts. "Look closer. Haven't you seen anything different, from just the physical things?"

Now Max saw Toby's parents were quarreling and it appeared they did this every day. Even Toby's father was clearly an alcoholic, but Toby never spoke of this darker side of his family. Max observed an ongoing argument and abuse that must happen every day. He realized his friend's life and family were not better than his own, although they were very rich. The fairy godmother then showed Max other families revealing similar patterns of distress, hopelessness, poverty, and even despair. He thought, I'm not from the best family or the worst. I'm not from the very best neighborhood or the worst. I'm not the most brilliant kid, but I'm one of the best in terms of character and heart. The young boy had a happy heart for the longest time. The fairy asked, "How about that one wish?"

Max considered this an opportunity of a lifetime and he made his choice carefully. He wondered if he were to wish for his dad to get out of prison, or for his family to be rich, or for his mom to have a good job so she could support them in everything. But from this experience tonight he simply asked the fairy, "Ensure that my family at home will always stick together, no matter what."

The young boy learned that a good family is always the best. The next morning, he awoke from sleep. He realized his house was different. It was comfortable and there seemed to be enough food. His family seemed happy. His encounter with the fairy godmother proved to be a great lesson and blessing.

A GOOD GRANDDAUGHTER

JOHN MATSUI

June glanced at the clock by the Golden Ages logo: 5:59 p.m.

"Ready, set . . ." she said to nursing station partner, Audrey.

A single musical note preceded the swish of an elevator door.

"Good evening June, Audrey."

The perky voice belonged to a pretty, young woman.

"Good evening, Kerry."

Kerry dressed simply – blue jeans, a loose-fitting, off-white shirt, and sneakers. She carried a backpack slung over her shoulder.

"Your Grandpa will be happy to see you."

"I hope so. Sometimes, he's . . . you know, forgetful."

June watched the young woman walk along the hall.

"Ah, to be so young, beautiful and caring."

"Not to mention, rich. Bet these visits keep her in his good books. And his will," Audrey said.

"Mr. Gambini wouldn't remember if Kerry visited 10 times a day, or never."

Kerry entered the lavish suite where a frail, old man in a silk robe sat motionless, "Hi Gramps! It's Kerry, your granddaughter."

Two cloudy brown irises shifted slowly toward the visitor. Something triggered a parroted response.

"Ah . . . Kerry."

"You don't have to pretend. I'm the daughter of your son, Bobby."

"I have a son, Bobby?"

The young woman withdrew a much-handled print of a tall, man in his 30s.

"Dad worked hard even as a kid. As new immigrants, the family didn't have much."

The old man puzzled over the concept, but how the pieces came together eluded him.

"You and grandma Rosa worked day and night to put food on the table and a roof over everyone's head."

The old man felt the weight of his gold Rolex on his wrist. His gaze shifted back to Kerry.

"Grandma Rosa?"

"Yes Rosa, your wife and the love of your life."

The imagery kindled a deep longing within the old man. This love so precious, yet now unremembered.

"She's in her 20s in this photo. The print's not in good shape."

Several cracks marred the varnished surface. The top right corner had been torn away.

"I'm afraid you're not in the picture. You were but at some point, you lost your head."

The old man didn't get the joke but he brightened when he saw the image.

"Beautiful, was she not?" the old man said.

Kerry flipped the page.

"Here's my mom, Celia, and dad on their wedding day. They married right after high school. Dad took a job as a mall cop. That's when mom got pregnant with Martin, my older brother and your first grandchild."

Kerry flipped to a photo of a boy in a cowboy hat with a guitar on his hip.

"Martin loved Country music. You gave him the guitar on his eighth birthday. He loved that guitar and the grandfather who gave it to him."

Mists shrouded the old man's memories but he understood what this boy meant to him.

"A year after Martin's birth, a cop who dad had befriended in the neighborhood helped him get a job on the force."

Kerry retrieved a photograph of her father in a policeman's uniform shaking hands and receiving a diploma from the Chief of Police.

"To dad it meant a chance to do something good, to make a difference. Plus, a real cop's paycheque brought in double that of a mall cop."

"The whole neighbourhood celebrated. When the guests left, mom and dad carried on their own celebration. Nine months later I was born."

The old man clutched the young woman's wrist lovingly.

"Dad worked hard to get on the organized crime unit and after several years he was put in charge."

His expression changed. The old man clearly wanted to add to the conversation but the details still eluded him.

"With more money, we moved into a big house. You and grandma took a big bedroom on the first floor. Our bedrooms were upstairs."

"One day, dad came home at 5:30 – early for him – wearing a huge smile. He switched on the Channel 6 news. Police arrested Toronto's top crime boss Giuseppe Condello, on racketeering, drug smuggling, and murder charges.

The old man went pale. "You have to hide Bobby, take the whole family somewhere safe."

"Grandpa, these events happened sixteen years ago."

The old man sensed a dark doorway in his brain but his mind refused to enter.

"Was Don Condello convicted?"

The young woman dealt the words like cards, one at a time. "Giuseppe Condello did not get convicted."

The old man made sputtering noises but no words.

"The case disappeared after a firebomb destroyed the police evidence room. Two days later, both witnesses were found dead with their tongues cut out. Police believed an assassin known as the Shadow set the bomb and committed the murders."

"Dad went to see a third witness who had refused to testify. Two days later, they found dad's body with his throat slashed and his body mutilated."

The enormity of the words struck the young woman. Teardrops patterned her shirt.

The old man's heart bled for Kerry and for his own loss of a forgotten son.

Kerry took a slow drink and blinked away her tears.

"My father's funeral had all the ceremony that police bestow on a comrade killed in action. The thousands of cops that converged on Toronto talked tough about Condello's days being numbered."

The old man started to shake.

"I hadn't been sleeping much. I woke Martin when . He grabbed a baseball bat and went downstairs to investigate.

"Martin looked where I stood at the upstairs railing and placed a finger to his lips. He woke you and Grandma Rosa.

"A figure - the Shadow - moved in the darkness. Three soundless flashes flew from his weapon. Grandma Rosa flopped hard on the coffee table.""You crawled toward her. The gunman leveled his machinegun. Martin leaped at him with the bat. Three streaks of fire hit him in the chest."

The old man's head slumped into his hands.

"He aimed the weapon at you. I screamed. Mom ran to me, used her body as a shield. The assassin directed his machinegun at us."

"The coroner pronounced mom, Grandma Rosa and Martin dead at the scene. You had gunshot wounds. I had not been hit."

"The police gave us new identities and moved us to other cities. I came back to Toronto last year when I heard Condello had been murdered."

"What became of the assassin, this Shadow?" the old man asked."I saw his face clearly in the flash of gun fire. It took years, but I found him."

"We cannot allow this evil man to continue to breathe."

"Death is too easy."

"You are only a girl. I don't think you have it in you to torture anyone."

"I have no issues torturing the man who killed my family."

"If I were a younger man, I would do it."

"You are helping."

"I am? How?"

"Let me ask you this. How much do you hate the man who shot and killed my mother, mutilated and murdered my father, who killed Martin and grandma Rosa in cold blood?"

"I curse him. I would kill him a thousand times, in a thousand ways. He killed these gentle people, these good people for money. What lower form of life can there be?"

"I agree. Let's take revenge on the Shadow right now."

"Now? I don't understand."

"It will help to see the face of the killer."

Kerry opened the photo album, removed an object and held it up. It was a mirror.

The old man looked bewildered at his reflected image.

"What is this? I'm confused."

"You have to look closer."

The old man fixed on the mirror. Again, he saw only himself.

"Can you see the murderer known as the Shadow?" Kerry said.

The old man's mind rocked back and forth between confusion and panic.

"The Shadow is Lou Gambini," Kerry said coldly.

An icicle jabbed the old man in the heart.

"My name is Lou Gambini. How can the assassin have my name?"

"Because you killed my grandmother, my mother, my brother, my father and my grandfather,"

"My heart aches for them. I cannot be their killer."

"You murdered my family for money and for the pleasure of killing innocent people."

Lou Gambini clutched his throat. The room spun. His head pounded out the words: evil, assassin, murderer. Every breath became a struggle, every thought a dagger to the brain. He reached toward his granddaughter for help.

Kerry watched the outstretched hand without emotion.

The world went black.

§

"Good afternoon Mr. Gambini," said June.

The thick cobwebs fell away.

"You've slept away most of the day. I'll get you a snack and I'll hold your dinner till later. Maybe you can eat it with your granddaughter."

"My granddaughter?"

"Yes, Kerry. She'll be here in a couple of hours."

The nurse plumped the old man's pillows and helped him sit up.

"Let's cross our fingers and hope she brings her photo album."

DEAD BUT WATCHING

MARK MCCONVILLE

It was gruesome. It was so terrible that it would curdle anyone's blood, if witnessed. And that night, that darkness, the knife through the heart and the light was taking me further than I've ever been before.

But suddenly I was back in the room. Observing my killer stealing my possessions, my prized watches and expensive cigars. I couldn't do a thing, everything I touched fell through my hands.

I couldn't attack, I couldn't put up a resistance, I became worthless. And his sniggering made me angry as he counted the money. He was in a perfect situation, cleaning the knife and placing it back into his black rucksack.

And I looked on. My fists clenched, my blood boiling, but he went his own way, leaving the carnage behind him.

And the house felt cold, colder than normal.

As the days passed. I was still standing staring at my dead self. My pulverised body, laying there attracting flies. And then it happened, the door swung open and a few voices rattled against the stench.

"Wow"'What do you mean wow?'

'That's a lot of blood'

'Yeah, but you're a professional right?'

'Of course'

'Okay, let's get this checked out then'

They checked everywhere and examined my limp, pale, body.

'Right through the heart'

'Damn, what a way to go'

'It was quick, so quick'

I felt tampered with. But they had to do it, it was their job, their way of paying the bills.

As they left, I let out a bellow, a scream, a whimper, but there was no acknowledgement.

That was that. I was dead to them and the world. A pathetic ghost, screaming for hope.

Hope? I never screamed for it when I was alive. But now I craved it, I needed it, I mourned my existence. I was an arrogant fool, damaged and broken, emotionally disengaged.

I just wanted to feel alive again. I wanted to drink coffee in the morning and behave like a noble human being.

And it struck me that I could leave this bloody mess. Explore, unravel, venture out. I did so with haste.

And the outside world seemed the same. The bustle, the car smoke, the coffee drinkers, the homeless, drained and crying for some of that same hope that I craved. And in this moment, I feel for them. Since my murder, I have become a sympathetic man. The blockage that kept my emotions inside had been blown wide open. In death, now I could feel fully.

I kept walking through the town. I saw people barely alive, drugged up and fighting sleep. I saw children with dirty faces, things I couldn't see when I was a superficial, narcissistic asshole.

My life was under so much weight. My dreams flickering and then shut off. And those streets, that smell of stale smoke, the alleyways crammed with heroin users. I looked at them, cried for them, emotionally entangled, bursting with empathy. But their grubby hands and punctured arms were a sign of a drug pandemic.

I stood for a little while and then disbanded from watching on. My eyes were sore; I could still feel discomfort. As a ghost, I felt, I really felt, the rumbling in my stomach, that feeling of anxiousness.

I began to look for my son. It took a while. It seemed like an eternity since the last time I saw him. He must be doing good; he must have a respectable job. He must have it all.

I stepped onto the bus. I felt good that I didn't have to pay. There were some perks for being dead.

As the bus went I felt like I was floating. The passengers were doing their own things, some were talking, some kept quiet, some were on their phones.

And there was me. Looking on at healthy skin, wishing to be drip fed some life.

The bus stopped outside Robert's house. It looked different from before. It looked darker and there were weeds growing everywhere. It seemed like he'd given up, like his life was dragging on instead of being embraced.

And as I walked closer to the house, I could hear people singing and dancing. It was like there was a party going on. It wasn't like Robert to have a party on a weeknight.

As I couldn't knock on the door, I just seeped through the wood like blood on a bandage.

The place was messy and disorganised. There was broken glass strewn on the floor, there were people too drunk to hold a proper conversation. It was chaotic.

Every room was filled with drunks and junkies. There was cocaine on the kitchen table ready to be snorted for a quick thrill. I was disgusted.

I was standing there, watching unsustainable life pass me by. I couldn't halt it. These people chose this path, a path of self-destruction. Their minds were exploding like fireworks, their time on this planet shortened. I was sick.

I had to find Robert amongst the dissolution and denial. I had to see if he was safe.

I looked around…

Until….

I found him in the bathroom looking at old pictures of himself and this girl. I couldn't talk to him, I was invisible, helpless.

He was crying out for someone to hug love into his bones. I looked on, weeping with him.

I placed my hand on his shoulder, but it just sunk through.

My little boy was crying for hope. The hope that I craved for days. He was losing it all, the beacon in his intelligent mind was depleting. And there I was, lacking the power to aid him through the pain.

Then someone began to knock on the door.

'Robert are you ok?'

'Yeah, yeah I'm fine, I'll be out in a minute'

'Okay, there's a couple of lines with your name on them'

I automatically knew what the boy behind the door was talking about. My son was taking drugs. He was killing himself, destroying his life.

And he did it.

He lifted up a needle fuelled with brown liquid. He sat there staring at it, contemplating his decision.

I screamed out, bellowing out until my face turned even more blue. But.

His tears streamed down his young face. He smacked his knuckles against the floor. He screamed out and closed his eyes. He then reopened them, staring yet again at the needle.

His expression disgruntled. His life on a tightrope.

I tried to grab the needle, I really did. I tried to help, I tried, I fucking tried…

And as I screamed out again he injected the needle into a plump vein. His eyes flickered in euphoria.

But.

As the drug sunk in, as its evil took hold. Robert began to shake franticly. He began to foam at the mouth, his body was truly shutting down. And I wept like a child losing the warmth of his Mother and Father.

And it stopped.

He just sat there, dead. And I sat beside him. And I thought to myself, *why couldn't he become a ghost like me. Why was I chosen, a corrupt bastard like me?*

I switched off the bathroom light…

Looking out at those ugly stars…

ONLY CHILD

CATHERINE MEARA

I ride through the park, legs pumping my red Schwinn Beach Cruiser, and their voices get softer and softer, "Cathy gets all her clothes at Pick 'n' Saaavvv ve e e e !   … She's just a dirty wetbaccckkkk …!"

That man is standing in his open garage like he does every day waving for me to come over. I always wonder why. I don't know who he is. Besides, everything inside me tells me not to go over there. Like I get sick to my stomach or something. Oh well, only three blocks to go and then I'm at Grandma's. I count each block, then the two pedals it takes me to get up the drive and into the garage. I jump off my bike and hit the button to close the garage.

As I walk into the house the quiet lays down gently on top of me, blocking out those kids and what they said to me. I hear my Grandma practicing piano at the other end of the house; playing broken tunes that need practice and singing the way old ladies are supposed to sing, in that false soprano voice. I have to take choir this year and we have real sopranos in that class. They don't sound anything like my Grandma. She is wearing a pink dress from the sixties that looks uncomfortable but proper. I say hi and she glances my way while continuing her song. I drop my book bag and go into the kitchen to get a glass of Pepsi. Grandma finishes her piano practice and shuffles purposely toward me.

"Hi Sweet," she says, kissing me on the cheek. "What did you learn in school today?" I never know how to answer this question. Do I tell her that I don't understand math, but that I got a B on my English paper and an A on my art project? Somehow, that answer just doesn't cover what I learned. I want to tell her about how I dropped my gym bag in the locker room and all my sanitary napkins fell all over the floor and everyone laughed at me as I hurried to pick them up. I also want to tell her about how some boys made fun of my Indian friend because of her body odor and made her cry. Or I could tell her about my ride home from school … "I got an A on my art project," I say.

"Oh honey! That's good. Your Mom wants you to do your homework before you turn on the TV. She'll be late tonight. She works very hard, you know."

"I know Grandma," I say, feeling a storm rising inside me. "I'll go upstairs and do my homework."

"Are you hungry?" she asks, the same way she asks every day.

"Not right now." I pick up my books and go upstairs to the spare room I call my own, shut the door and cry for a while. After I cry, the silence feels heavy, like it's all around me and deep inside me. I sit down at the desk and eek out a stupid poem about mean people and then pull out my math, which makes me start to cry again. I tell myself I'm being a baby, those boys and girls are just stupid and mean. I feel bad that they see in me something worth making fun of. What is it? I wonder.

But now I'm safe, here in the house of my grandparents. I don't think any of those stupid people know where I live. I always manage to lose them when I ride through the park; it's like they are vampires who must stay out of the light, they never go past the park.

If I had a sister or even a brother, I wouldn't feel so lonely and I'd have someone to cavort with, someone to play with, someone to share my day with. An older brother or sister would stick up for me, take care of me, and those kids never would even bother me. But I don't have a brother or sister, I am on my own. Nonetheless, I day dream for a while, imagining my sibling.

Mom arrives here about 7 pm -- she looks tired and spent. I can't be-lieve what it's like for her in that office every day. Once she came home crying. I wanted to go beat up her boss; making mom cry, how dare he! She sits down in one of the strange chairs in the living room -- they are like a circle of wood with a pad and they rest on a small bottom. We watch the news. Mom is saying something and I'm looking at her. All of a sudden, the chair falls slowly back, mom yelps as its going down. In a moment she is lying on the floor, her little feet in her sling back shoes sticking up in the air. Mom begins to laugh. So do I, as grandma races over to mom to make sure she is not hurt. The laughing gets louder as grandma starts to crack up. Soon we are practically rolling on the floor holding our sides and mom gets that look on her face like she can't stop laughing. She rolls onto her side and grandma helps her up. We laugh all over again when we leave for home.

I feel much better now. Mom and I giggle for the rest of the night. I really appreciate the fun and I am not in a bad mood anymore.

THE CONSTABLE

EDDIE D. MOORE

"Roan! Get down here on the ground! What do you think you are? A squirrel?"

"Acis, you have been chasing me for days! Surely the bounty is not worth this much effort!" Four silver coins fell from the branches above, landing in front of Acis. "There. I know the bounty is four silver pieces. You have been paid. You can go home now."

"This is not about money. It is about justice. Now, are you going to climb down or am I going to have to chop down this tree?"

Limbs rustled high in the tree as Roan climbed down. The young man dropped from the lowest limb to the ground. After Roan picked up his coins, they began their walk back toward town.

"Fine, I will pay for the chickens. Will that make everything right in the world again?"

"No. I just spent four days chasing you. The judge will make sure you reimburse the town for my salary."

"That's not fair!"

"Fair? The thief wants to cry foul over restitution. That never ceases to amuse me. Don't worry. I have only heard a few people actually died from work. I suggest you walk faster because the judge will hold you accountable until we get back. I have never had to chase anyone this deep in the woods. In fact, I have never heard of anyone going this deep in the woods"

"Is the prize something to eat? I have not eaten since yesterday."

"I'm out of provisions as well. We will just have to hunt this after-noon. I believe the river ahead is the only water source around for miles. We should be able to find a good spot to hunt there."

They climbed a tree that gave them a good view of the area and waited. Acis was about to release an arrow and kill a squirrel when a rustle in the bushes made him freeze. A deer stepped out from among the brush and walked cautiously toward the river. Once the deer began to drink, Acis released his arrow. The deer ran a couple hundred feet then collapsed.

The roasted deer meat was tough but it satisfied their hunger. They allowed the fire to burn low and prepared to get some rest.

"Acis, why do you always come after me?"

"What do you mean? It is my job."

"I know. But if you did not bring me back, I would not cause any more trouble."

"I knew your parents before they died and I promised your dad that I would keep an eye one you. Starting a new life as a criminal would not do your parents justice."

Roan looked away and spoke with frustration in his voice, "You aren't my father."

"No, I am not but I will do all I can to see you grow into an honest man. It doesn't matter to me how many of these camping trips we have to make."

Roan rolled over ending the conversation. He had heard the stories many times over the years, about what honest and wonderful people his parents were. But what good had it done them? A simple sickness had taken them both in the same month, leaving him to live with people he barely knew.

A scream in the woods made them both sit up, awake and alert. Hairy forms ran through the camp grabbing random items and tossing them in the air. Acis and Roan were both knocked down and trampled by heavy thick padded feet. They scrambled away from the campsite while the intruders fought and mauled one another over what was left of the deer.

With wide eyes Roan whispered, "Are those some kind of ape?"

"I believe so. I think we should put some distance between us and them. Let's go."

Roan turned to lead the way but he found himself standing face to face with one of the apelike creatures. It screamed and began to pound the ground and rip limbs from the trees. The other creatures gave an answering scream and came running toward them.

"Roan! Run for the river!"

One of the creatures jumped and kicked Acis in the back knocking him to the ground. Another one jumped on his back and bit his shoulder. Roan grabbed Acis' bow and stuck an arrow in the creature biting Acis. It rolled off him and thrashed about attempting to remove the arrow. The rest of the creatures began to surround them screaming and beating the ground. The largest of the group rushed at them as Acis and Roan dived into the river.

They swam a distance away from the shore and began treading water, while the creatures watched them from the bank.

"Now what?" Asked Roan.

"Let's see if we can swim down river a little ways. Maybe they will not follow."

Roan nodded and then suddenly disappeared from the water's surface. Acis immediately pulled his belt knife and dove blindly into the water. Once he felt a hairy body he stabbed it repeatedly, hoping he would not accidently stab Roan. The creature pushed with its legs against Acis and swam away. When he returned to the surface, he breathed a sigh of relief to find Roan waiting.

They swam until the creatures were out of sight and then waded in the shallows for miles before leaving the water. While resting on the river bank, Acis examined the bite on his shoulder. The bleeding had stopped but he had to clutchhis arm to his chest to keep from reopening the wound.

Roan helped Acis to his feet and they walked toward town. They walked for hours without conversation because Roan appeared to be deep in thought.

"Acis, do you think they would let me work at the mill like my father did?"

"Mr. Collins had great respect for your father. All you would have to do is ask."

"Good. I think I'm done with the woods."

THRESHERS

PHIL MORGAN

I didn't remember the end of the world. I was too young. The Elders told stories of great, gleaming, cities stretching across the horizon. I found that hard to believe. My horizon was a sea of waving stalks, a vast forest of row upon row of sweet, rustling corn.

The Elders spoke of humanity's thirst for oil and how that unquenchable desire led to the creation of a new type of corn. This corn grew everywhere. Insects wouldn't touch it and the coldest winter couldn't wither its green leaves. They told tales how the corn pushed aside all other plants, how it dominated every inch of dirt until there was only corn, miles and miles of corn.

Sometimes, when the hydr'pondicks would be harvested and the entire village gathered around the communal table, the Elders would speak of how humanity had fought against the corn. They described flying machines dropping fire and armies of men hacking the stalks down, of how the greatest minds fought to stop the corn, fought and lost. We heard tales of vast enclaves of mankind slowly dwindling down, dying off, their bellies full and their souls empty.

The day they came I was entertaining my little sister and the other younglings of the village. It started as a low rumble, almost so low you couldn't hear it. You could feel it though, as if the ground itself was trembling in fear.

Jaxon, sweet, kind Jaxon, saw them first. High in the lookout tower, the warning bell began to ring. I didn't understand at first. In my less than twenty years alive, I had never heard its sharp, incessant, peal. I looked up and Jaxon was pointing in the direction of the rising sun. He yelled one word.

"Threshers!"

I heard screaming. It cut across the growling and grumbling of the great beasts the Threshers rode. The Elders had warned us about the Threshers. Warned us they rode metal monsters that ate the corn. I never believed it. Why would I? We had few metal beasts in the village. There was the beast that drew water from deep under the corn and the beast that spoke of the past. There were no beasts who could eat the corn. The corn was god of this world.

I smelled smoke. Not like what came from the cooking fires. It was oily, pungent. I saw it wafting into the village when the wind shifted just right. My sister urgently tugged on my hand but I couldn't looked down. Through the corn, deep in the stalks, I thought I saw something. Black, shiny, terrifying.

I heard the grinding and the whining, the scream of the corn as it died under metal teeth. Strands of corn silk floated through the air, great clouds of it intermingling with thick, blue smoke. More flashes of blackness within the stalks. My sister tugging on my hand. Somebody was screaming, loud and piercing. I looked around but couldn't see who. My throat hurt.

When the first Thresher crashed through the corn, I reacted. I ran, dragging my sister. The great, black, beast must have seen me because it swerved to chase me. I stopped staring at it, put my head down and ran. It was fast. Too fast.

It knocked me flat as it passed. I felt a splash of something hot, wet, and thick. I held my sister's hand in a death grip and struggled to my feet. I glanced at the Thresher. Its shiny, black, skin now generously splattered with a wet crimson. I tugged for my sister to follow me and felt no resistance. I looked down and saw the severed hand in mine. I don't remember if I cried out or not.

The Thresher spun to chase me again and I plunged into the corn. I ran and ran. I have been running ever since, only the corn to keep me company.

ONE INCH TALL TOM

SIMON MORRELL

The trepidation is written all over the boy's face. He clearly feels he is out of his depth, but with an encouraging nudge in his back from his father he takes a step forward. Sonny greets him the same as he does all newcomers; with open arms.

"Hello son. Don't look so nervous and tell me, what brings you to my gym?"

The boy looks to his dad for help and his dad obliges. "He is frightened. Bullies have the better of him, school has the better of him. Hell, life has the better of him." To show he feels no shame about his son's predicament he puts his fatherly arm around the boy's shoulders. "He is just One Inch tall."

Sonny gets it right away despite his assistant looking confused. "One Inch tall. Been there, done that. What's your name kid?" As he asks the question he shoots the dad a look, a friendly look but a look all the same, a look that says, "*Let him answer himself.*"

The boy does so in a quiet voice, "Tom." He stares at the floor, afraid to make eye contact.

Sonny laughs, "One-Inch-tall Tom. It has a fancy ring to it. Tell me your story One Inch." He pats the canvas of the battered boxing ring indicating for Tom to sit with him on the apron.

To his heartbreak, for he had been there himself, Sonny listens as

Tom relays his tale. He tells of a soulless kid who thinks nothing of kicking Tom in the groin for fun. Who thinks even less of endless name calling and lunch stealing. He can't see Tom is sinking, or if he can see, he doesn't care.

Tom clearly chokes back tears as he continues. "It will get easier they say. But it doesn't. It will pass, they say but it never passes. Try and be friends they tell me but who wants to be friends with a guy who inflicts this much misery?" As he tells his story his eyes never leave the floor.

Sonny nods showing empathy. "Happened to me. Happened a lot when I was a kid."

Tom looks up incredulously. "You? But everyone knows you, everyone respects you." He turns to indicate the many accolades that decorate the walls and shelves of the Fight Pit. "All this…"

Sonny laughs. "You know when the bullying stops? When you know you have had enough. You know who needs to put an end to it? You. I can help sure. So can Annie." He nods to his daughter and assistant, a proficient kickboxer herself. "My Annie here will put you through your paces. She is probably one of the better pad holders at my gym. If you can box a few three minute rounds with her holding the pads, then handling a bully is a walk in the park."

Tom reverts his gaze back south but interrupts nervously, "No way. May as well ask me to fly to the moon. I can't hit anyone."

Sonny puts his hands up. "No one is asking you to hit anyone. What did I say? Hit the pads. I didn't mention hitting anyone. What we need to do, One Inch, is make you big. We need to make you big in attitude, big in confidence, big in demeanour. We need to make you big enough to say, *'Not today my man, not today'*. Do you understand?"

Tom suddenly stops staring at the floor and looks up again straight at Sonny. Sonny picks up on it straight away and asks Tom, "Who can stop your bullies?"

With hesitation Tom half replies and half ask, "Me?"

"Correct. You, One Inch tall Tom, you. If you can survive some rounds on the pads with Annie, then you have what it takes to be confident because not many people can. If you can prosper on the mats then you have what it takes to walk tall, to face your fear and take responsibility."

Tom nods and days later returns to the Fight Pit to survive his rounds with Annie, and then prospers through them. Some weeks later, after much soul searching and honesty, he begins to walk upright, make eye contact and becomes big in confidence, not arrogance. Walking into the gym one day it is clear he has something to tell Sonny. "He offered me his hand," he says talking about his bully and beaming with pride. "'No hard feelings?' he asked me."

Sonny laughs. "No hard feelings, and all that jazz. How many times have we heard that Annie?"

"More than once, less than a hundred, Pop," she says laughing as well.

"You know what you became, Tom?" he says dropping the One Inch title. Tom shakes his head.

"Massive Tom. You became massive."

A LITTLE BIRD TOLD ME

WADE NACINOVICH

They're calling in their children for dinner and she's high in a tree, spying on them. She sits perfectly still under the cover of leaves, up in the enveloping air. There's no escaping the calls and hot breezes. Soon a sliver of moon appears on the horizon, the blue falling away behind it and the silhouettes of birds are replaced by the dark spasms of bats feeding in the dusk.

Now she hears her mother and wishes she could stay, but her mother keeps calling out for her. She launches herself down from branch to branch, lands on the sad ground and walks through the stuffy shadow light of her living room into the kitchen. There she eats another meal with her family under the yolky glow of a hanging lamp with the husks of long dead flies melted into the globe. She dabs dinner grease off her lips and chin, waiting to be dismissed.

They put her to bed and she bides her time again, her body charged by some restless energy on the freshly laundered sheets. One by one the lights go off in the house. She tugs up the screen of her bedroom window and crawls outside where she creeps from one tamed bush to another. Hidden behind the hedges, peering out into the night, no one but she knows there are strangers walking by.

The summer night is as hot as it's ever been, the heat crowding into her head and body as she digs up her lawn with a rusted trowel. She excavates fat worms that curl up in her palm. With crickets and fire flies at her side, she plies open the cool soil, letting the worms roll from her hand into a squirming pile on the bottom of a bucket. She carries the bucket back to her bed, earth streaking her forehead and cheeks. She lies down, her eyes wide open. She falls asleep under visions of stars and planets.

She wakes up to find her curtains have blown open to blazing light. A scrumming flock of little brown birds claw at her screen window. Her eyes ache against the light and the birds' wings blow frantic messages towards her. She scratches her head and yawns, cracking open the dried crust of last night's dinner. She passes through the kitchen, grabs a lone piece of toast off a plate, and goes down into the chilly basement where it's still cool and dim like dawn. She slides through an open window and pulls herself to the lawn through a tangle of weeds and briars.

The sun beats down on her itchy head and she flees from lawn to woods, scrambling through thorns of roses, spiny hollies, and boughs of pines. She's pricked open and bloodied, wounds she'll fondly recall days ahead while tracing her finger over pink scars. Along the tranquil street, the telephone wires following the road towards the mountain carry signals through the weeping willows and pines. The wind curls through the trees and houses, slowly brushing away footprints left in the dust.

It's lunchtime. Time for tomato soup, grilled cheese and soda. The itching in her tangled hair is now biting and she reaches up and pulls out a tiny worm. The itching and biting stop, replaced by flapping. The wings move mechanically, the fuzzy bodies attached to them roosting deeper and deeper into her wild curls, crowning her hair in gossamer orange. She enters the house and sits down for lunch. She bows her head and bites into the grilled cheese and a butterfly falls into the soup, struggling in the muck, blending into the quicksand that finally pulls it to the bottom of the bowl. A tiny bird sits on the edge of the window, the butterflies flap, and more cocoons crack open. She chews the crusts of bread and burnt cheese, but the pulp doesn't go away fast enough.

Her mother takes away the bowl. By the end of lunch, a mealy mush sits on her tongue and she cannot bring herself to dispense of it inside her. She stores it away until she can leave. Outside she swipes it out of her mouth as the screen door slams behind her. More orange wings blossom on her head. She squints up into the sky and watches birds dive and rise from tree to tree out of the blue. In the middle of the lawn, a dark lump sits alone in the grass. It's a furry plump bat with delicate wings. She picks it up and shoves it into her pocket.

She strolls around, wayward and invisible, cutting through yards and patches of woods. As she moves, it seems like the bat has risen from the dead and now nibbles and claws at her tender thigh. But then it just stops and she's unsure if the biting ever happened. A lethargy like a blooming contagion drains the spring from her step and then she finds herself in bed. It gets hotter and her skull seems to swell to the size of the room, the wings of brown birds a flapping blur on the window screen. The butterflies slumber in the waves of her hair. She clutches the pail filled with musty dirt and grabs a handful of savory worms to feed her fever. The landscape shifts and tilts out of focus, for it is only delicious worms she sees as she feeds herself more and more, the first as tasty as the last.

She falls asleep and awakens without memory. Her head is ringed in a halo of broken wings and antennae, specks of orange and black scattered around her downy pillow. Someone has stolen the bat from her pocket and a steaming bowl of tomato soup sits on her nightstand. She wipes the worm-dirt from the corner of her lips. Through a little hole torn in her screen window, a delicate pretty bird maneuvers into her room and hops around before sitting on her hand. As it cocks its head back and forth, its talons pinch her pliant skin and blood slowly rises into the punctured flesh. Its head seems to be saying one thing and its feet another.

The hottest of all summer heat squeezes her and turns her inside out. She looks down at the empty bucket and then at the creamy tomato soup and looks back at the bird. She wraps her hand around the bird's shoulder, its wings soft and smooth under her grasp, its heart beating into her palm. She squeezes it harder. Its head locks straight ahead and the little bird stares out at her with hard eyes. She cannot stop herself and stuffs the creature into her mouth.

THE LANGUAGE BARRIER

STEPHEN LEE NAISH

On his way back from the office, Donald Davenport called his wife Martha at home from the phone booth that stood outside The Small Theatre off Franklyn Street. Next Tuesday, there would be a performance of *The Clock in the Sky*, a new play that had recently been written up in a reliable newspaper. After speaking to Martha, Donald hung up and entered though the old revolving doors of the theatre. The familiar rustic interior, the smoke stained walls displaying posters of up-and-coming shows, the gleaming marble floor, and the usual staff whom Donald knew well were inside. Shaking off the dampness from the late evening drizzle, Donald made his way over to the ticket office. Jane the ticket attendant smiled from over her typewriter as Donald approached.

"Good evening Mr. Davenport," Jane said as she finished tapping away.

"Good evening Jane, dreadful weather we're having tonight," Donald said while wiping his forehead with a kerchief.

Jane cocked her head to the left as if she had misheard him. "Excuse me, sir?"

"I said good evening Jane, awful weather. I'm sopping wet."

Jane looked at Donald like he'd just walked in from another planet.

"I'm sorry Mr. Davenport. I have no idea what you're saying to me."

He paused for a moment, deciding small talk was not the order of

211

the day.

"Ok, two tickets for next Tuesday's performance of *Clock in the Sky* please."

Jane again looked baffled.

"Just talk real slow and I might be able to understand you."

Donald had no idea what the hell was going on. He was speaking as plain as he possibly could speak.

"Ok, two tickets please, thank you."

Jane shook her head.

"I'm really sorry; I'll get the manager. Just wait here."

Jane jumped up from her seat and went into the back. Donald stood at the desk confused and slightly annoyed. Just one hour ago he delivered a fascinating proposal to his team at work and knew from their stunned faces that he was an accomplished communicator.

The theatre's manger, Mr. Reed immerged from the back and smiled.

"Mr. Davenport, right?," Mr. Reed said while extending his hand. Donald had met Mr. Reed numerous times at exclusive after-show parties. Donald met his hand halfway and shook it.

"That's right."

Mr. Reed's smile dropped off his face; he looked confused.

"Mr. Davenport, why are you talking like that? We can't understand you."

"Talking like what?"

"Come on stop kidding around; if you're learning a new language that's excellent, but please don't tease us."

"Learning a new language! I'm not learning a new anything. I just want two tickets." Mr. Reed turned to Jane.

"Ok something's not right; get his mailing file up here." Jane rummaged in the top drawer of the ticket desk and pulled out Donald's mailing and membership form.

"Ok Mr. Davenport, game's up. You're from Delaware. They speak perfect English in Delaware—nice try." Mr. Reed laughed.

"I'm speaking perfect English right now!"

"Come on Mr. Davenport, we don't really have time for this game of cards anymore. Our next show is in half an hour. We must get cleaned up and prepared.."

Donald demanded, "Listen to me carefully. I want two tickets for *Clock in the Sky* for next Tuesday."

Mr. Reed sighed and shook his head.

"I don't know what to do."

Donald snatched a pen from Jane and scrawled his request on a fresh membership form. He handed it over to Mr. Reed.

"I don't know what this means." He showed it to Jane, "Any ideas?"

"It's not English."

Davenport snatched the note back from Jane and read it aloud.

"Two tickets for *Clock in the Sky*."

"I'm getting bored of this," Mr. Reed said.

"That makes two of us," Jane replied.

"Yeah I'm pretty fucking bored too," Donald shouted as he slammed his fist down on the desk.

"Ok, go get Nelson; he speaks five languages. Maybe we'll get lucky," Mr. Reed said.

Jane got up and again walked out the back. Neither Davenport nor Mr. Reed spoke whilst Jane was looking for Nelson; they just eyed each other. Jane returned with Nelson a few moments later.

"Hi Mr. Davenport." Donald had met and spoke with Nelson many times after a good show. Nelson was the head bartender and a very well travelled young man.

"So learning a new language then? Ok try me."

Donald sighed and spoke again.

"Nelson, I want two tickets for next Tuesday's showing of *Clock in the Sky*. God help me, that is all I want."

Nelson listened carefully, chewing the words silently in his mouth, but after a few moments, he shook his head.

"I've no idea what he said."

"Fucking hell!!!" Davenport exploded in rage.

"What about this?" Mr. Reed showed Nelson the form with the scrawled note.

"Not a clue, it looks like Russian or Chinese; I think it is gibberish whatever it is."

"I've had enough," Mr. Reed announced abruptly. "Mr. Davenport, you are wasting our time; either you speak in plain English, or we'll have to ask you to leave the premises."

"I'm not leaving without my fucking tickets!"

"Whatever he's saying, he's pretty mad about it," Nelson said.

"Of course I'm mad; I'm talking to complete morons, absolute fuck-wits, no better than apes!"

"It's time to leave, Mr. Davenport," Mr. Reed demanded. He moved from behind the desk and grabbed Donald's arm. Nelson moved around to help. They both grabbed an arm and dragged him towards the old revolving doors.

"This is an outrage. I'm gonna write to the paper about this. You'll be hearing from me. I'll ruin you, you hear me? I'll sue."

"Whatever you're saying Mr. Davenport, I frankly don't care. I'd prefer you keep away from this theatre for at least a month, or I'll call the police next time."

Mr. Reed and Nelson tossed Donald through the doors back out into the rain, which had changed from a light drizzle to a wild downpour.

"You bastards! I'll be writing to the paper about this. See if I don't!"

Nelson threw Donald's briefcase out onto the sidewalk and dusted his hands off.

"Fuckers! You'd have to pay me to come back in there."

Donald picked up the briefcase and rattled around in his coat pockets for some loose change. He found a couple of quarters and took shelter in the nearby phone booth. He potted the coins in the slot and dialed his home number again. The line rang a few times before his wife Martha answered.

"Hello the Davenport residence, Martha Davenport speaking."

"Darling you won't believe what happened to me. I went to get us those tickets for *Clock in the Sky*. The bastards pretended I was speaking another language. They fucking had the God-given nerve to stand there and pretend to not understand me..."

"Excuse me," came the voice on the other end cutting Donald off. "I'm sorry, but I think you've got the wrong number."

Donald wiped his wet face with his sleeve and rubbed his temple; he closed his eyes tightly, tighter than ever. He let out a huge exhaustive breath.

"Martha, it's me honey; it's Donald, Donald Davenport, your husband." There was only a moment's pause on the other end.

"Hello, yes I'm sorry, but you've dialed America. You've come through to the United States of America. You've got the wrong number I'm afraid. I don't speak your language."

Donald Davenport rubbed his eyes, which were filling with tears and took a deep breath. With his throat choked up and taut, he tried to push his meek voice out.

"Martha, it's me; it's Donald...it's..." He began to sob, no longer able to speak.

"I'm sorry, but I can't understand you; I don't speak your language. I'm very sorry. I'm putting the phone down now. Goodbye."

The phone clicked off leaving Donald Davenport alone in the phone booth. He slowly crumbled to the ground. He curled up in a fetal position, the only way to lie down inside the tight confines of a phone booth. He felt his body convulse as he broke down into uncontrollable tears. What did it all mean? Why was he no longer understood? What would become of his life? He let out a whimpering whisper, the noise barely able to break out of his dry and tight throat.

"чому, чомумене."

His tears mixed with the rain.

NIGHT AND FOG

C.H. NEWELL

He still thinks he's over there, ever since she died. But the war ended fifty years ago. He came to America not long after.

As I wheel him up to the house, I think of how badly I want to be somewhere else. In the chair he's permanently hunching, curled like a burning leaf of paper. That's not how I remember him.

Even before we're inside I remember the dreadful decor which hasn't changed since the '60s: shag carpet so dry you couldn't light a candle near it, white stucco ceiling like some modern cave like paint stalactites hanging down in permanent half-drip; as a boy I was foolishly afraid one might wiggle free and find its way directly into my eye, blinding me forever.

Far back as I can remember this house always reminded me of a death trap. Grandma would read me *Hansel and Gretel* nearly every time I was over, right before bed, and I'd have dreams of grandpa – only he was the witch – trying to drag me into the kitchen, shoving me into the oven with flames licking out at the air like a hot, whipping tongue.

Nobody's been back here since the day grandma died, only me. I probably shouldn't have brought him, if I'm being honest with myself.

"Margaret," he mumbles in his watered down accent. "Peg – dahling, I'm home."

Kneeling, I tell him plainly grandma's dead. No sense in being abstract.

"Oh," he says near a whisper, "ja, ja. Did ve cremate her?"

I remind him how natural she looked at the funeral. He doesn't remember, but pretends a little before breaking into a controlled sequence of sniffs and coughs. Looking at his face, now just a cocoon awaiting death to emerge, I'm reminded how much we look alike, and how much this poisons me.

Parking the wheelchair at his office door, I'd rather he went inside on his own. Nobody else except grandma went in there. Until she died, then naturally we all figured it out. Turning against the doorway the big shiny eagle beams a ray of light out into the hall, a spotlight on me calling to come in.

To my surprise he's up on his feet, shuffling into the room. I watch him bump into the tall black boots at the side of his desk. He looks at them, first like they ran into *him*. Then he touches their tops, rubbing a finger or two around the inside of their worn leather and his eyes brighten from their usual murky blue.

Steadying himself with a hand at his desk, the old man moves to the window. It's covered, but strong afternoon light beaming through the cloth drapes him in the flag's colours. The first time I saw the inside of this room it had the same glow falling all over my face; the black in shadows, its red like blood and fire.

Back at the desk again he's trying to wipe smudges off his medals, each a cross with different decoration, running his fingers over their edges. He picks up a thick black crocheted patch, still with brown threading in its back, looking at it, holding it the way others would a rosary; his crooked thumb glides up, down, up, down the pair of solid bolts like two tiny strikes of lightning on its face.

I feel like a memory is perched right beneath his tongue, waiting to fly out.

Only nothing comes.

Then he goes to the closet. Its doors are solid, heavy, his lack of strength shows with the tremble in each arm as he pushes them open. For a fleeting second, I hope he's looking for the old Ruger pistol he stashed there twenty years ago. I hope he sucks the barrel into his gummy mouth and pumps a shot up through his already scrambled brain. Or better yet, that he'd put it to my chest, my temple – anywhere – and take me away from this house, away from him and the family history.

Yet my grandpa, the monster under its time worn shell, keeps rooting around in the closet. Soon enough he pulls out the picture; its edges frayed and soft, but at the centre still stiff, glossy. *That fucking picture.* As

if I hadn't seen it, as if it weren't one of the first of many troubling dis-
coveries I made about dear ole grandpa when I was barely into my teens.

When you first see it there's a distant, cold reaction, almost the way
you might imagine seeing old World War II pictures in a textbook. But
then you really look at it and my grandpa's face – uncannily like my own
– everything begins to come in focus. Then, you see who he's standing
next to, you notice the crowd of arms angled and reaching for the sky,
outstretched towards the man with whom my grandpa is so proud to be
seen.

Only this time, picture in hand, I can tell grandpa has a story I've
not heard.

I would've rather he found the Luger.

I WON'T FLOAT AWAY

SARAH ANN NOEL

Rose was a pink balloon, a seemingly bright and cheery thing. She stuck out upon the sky, whether blue or grey, and was large enough and shiny enough, too, that the moon illuminated her face at night. This was the impression of her, from down below, as far as the humans were concerned.

Rose had plenty of impressions herself, ones that made her delightfully giddy with power. She would float above the neighborhood, studying its goings-on, rather immersed in people's lives—but only from her distance. She knew Mrs. Miller gossiped to Mrs. Little over the fence while watering her lilies; and in turn, Mrs. Little made annoyed expressions every time Mrs. Miller turned her back. She knew the garbage man sometimes didn't empty the dumpster on schedule and everyone accepted its overflowing without question. The Pipers' cat regularly sneaked under the gate to the McGregors' garden and dug up the turnips. And Mr. Mennet returned home briefly each day from 11:17 to 12:09 without anyone else the wiser.

"What a vantage point," Rose would beam, feeling full of important observations and secret knowledge.

"What a luxury," she would tell herself, "Being so close to the warm sun and gently rocked in the breeze."

These incantations were only for her good days, days when the earth below seemed too polluted by drama and negativity. She could rise above all that and remain unscathed, wiser, and warmer for it too. She once lived on the ground, but it began to feel too meaningless to stay. So she filled herself up with reveries and pretentiousness, casting off the weight of obligation and loving sacrifice. With each selfish retreat, she lifted higher and higher, growing rounder and more brilliant, and farther away from reality. "I'm a beacon," she bragged, "Of what self-actualization does to one, with emphasis on the self. This is what I needed to be happy, and look at me now, far and away above the rest."

"It is freedom!" she declared, waving against the sky as a flag for the case of the self-serving.

The birds would swirl around her in states of confusion, singing their melodies in her ear.

"Why are you here?" one asked Rose.

"To be like you! Look what joy you have!"

"What do I know of joy," the bird said. "I haven't a soul."

But Rose paid no mind, for she had floated above what weighed her down, instead relishing in the passing clouds, riding in on the current. They were wispy and cool, and interested in her.

"Why are you here?" one whispered in the wind.

"To be like you!" Rose replied. "Look how much of the world you've seen!"

"What do we know of the world," another answered. "We haven't feet to put on the ground or hands to bury in the earth."

Still Rose drifted higher and higher into the sky, happy to reach for heaven instead of striving upon Earth. And one day she rose up near enough to speak with the sun.

"Why are you here?" the sun asked of her.

"To be like you," Rose said proudly. "Look at us, brilliant enough to stand alone!"

But the sun shook her head sadly and responded, "It is a sad thing to burn up your bridges."

Rose turned a haughty nose into the air, placing her back against the sun's confrontations. But both she and the sun knew that the Light would find the truth and force her to reason with it. She had risen higher than the escape.

"What's that there?" the sun asked. She shone upon a thin string, flowing out from underneath Rose.

"It's my string," Rose said.

"What is it for?"

Rose paused to consider, for it was something she hadn't thought about in awhile.

Finally she answered, "It keeps me safe."

"How?"

"It keeps me attached below, just in case."

"Attached to what?"

Rose's pinkish glow reddened with shame, for she knew what the string was attached to was Most Important.

"To where I was, before I floated up here to be above it all."

"I thought you wished to travel like the clouds," the sun pressed, momentarily darkening as one drifted in front of her.

"I do," Rose said slowly. "But I was afraid of floating off without something to find my way back to."

"Do you think about going back?"

"Sometimes."

"What holds the string?" the sun asked.

"Love," said Rose.

Following the path of the string, the sun speared through the clouds to peek below. It lighted a small garden, tucked behind a modest bungalow at the edge of the city. It shone upon its white brick nooks and lovingly polished windows, beaming over a cutting garden bursting with zinnias. It leaked its warmth on two curly-haired children running through the grass. And finally, it followed the string to a man, strong and handsome, with burning, loving eyes.

"The sun is out!" the man laughed to his children, shielding his eyes and gazing up at the pink balloon floating over their yard. He gave the silver line a tug, sending shivers through Rose. She exclaimed in mixed ecstasy and agony.

"This man holds your string?" the sun asked of Rose.

Her voice was wistful and melancholy as she replied, "He does."

Rose and the sun watched the man in admiration while the sun waited for Rose to explain further. But she hesitated as she fought explosive feelings of pain and yearning, and humbled, her rubber walls felt compromised by love and regret. She feared she might burst.

"He holds my string," she said tearfully. "He holds it so tightly, no matter what else requires his attention. Always, he gives his right hand to me, held fast around this tiny delicate lifeline. Though he feeds his children and is industrious about his home; though he cares for the neighbors and kindly hosts many friends; though he diligently fulfills all other responsibilities, he never lets go of me."

On the good days, Rose rejoiced in her position, but the good days were fewer than most might guess. Instead, her isolating distance harrowed her. She missed the tastes of delicious food and the smells of her flower garden. She missed the squeals of her children which were imperceptible at such a height. Her heart longed for his touch on her cheek. When she left the world behind, those things hadn't seemed heavy enough to hold her to the ground; but now she remembered they were human things and they were Most Important.

"Some day soon, I will go back," Rose said. The Most Important reality would restate its place in her heart and mind to recalibrate her position. She would want for all those earthly things enough that she would willingly sink back into the world under their weight. And it is a weight she would joyfully bear.

"Life seemed heavy then," she said, half to the sun. "So I made myself light."

"Life is heavy," replied the sun, "Because it is so full."

The sun watched Rose watching her family for quite some time. And then, as she began to sink toward the earth herself, encircled in rainbows and fading light, she called up to the balloon.

"He would gladly help you bear the weight, just as he has kept you from floating away. And as soon as you cry out to him, he will pull you back down to him, to where you belong, to what is Most Important."

Rose fell lower and lower with the sun, the weight seeming less like an impossible burden and more like a blanket folding over her for sleep.

ANTI VALENTINE

JACQUELINE PAIZIS

The compartment was so dark and smelly that she hesitated to enter.

A voice. Male. "Well it looks like here or standing for the rest of the trip."

She turned her right shoulder very slightly towards the voice, feeling its breath fan her skin. Her vest strap had slipped and was tickling her arm. When she sat down she understood why nobody had chosen the seats on either side of the window. The midday sun struck her all down one side, quickening the bead of sweat trickling down from her temple.

He sat down opposite and as he did their knees brushed together. They both had bare knees because the weather was hot and sultry. His knees were hairy, hers smooth and tanned. There was a moment when she considered pulling her legs back so they wouldn't meet his in the middle, but she thought better of it and left them where they were. She was enjoying the contact. Had he noticed that she hadn't crossed her legs or angled them sideways to avoid touch?

Nobody in the compartment spoke. Speaking would take up too much energy. Even reading seemed impossible, but not for him apparently. There he was opposite, plucking a book from his rucksack, preparing to settle into it.

She looked out the window as they sped past the parched tobacco fields of Thraki. They had left Komotini behind, now heading for the

Turkish border.

The peasant woman pulled a folding knife from the depths of her apron pocket. She flicked a catch with a fleshy thumb and the short blade sprung into the roll of salami.   Her knuckles were knotted like ancient oak bark. Under her nails there was a black mold. She guided the knife through the salami with her forefinger and thumb producing thick slices that she speared and offered to the passengers. Her pink gums resembled the colour of the salami, in between the lumps of fat.   Her husband, sitting beside her, made a swipe for the remaining chunk but she withdrew the knife and instead offered it to the middle aged widow sitting on her other side. The widow declined politely with a shake of her head.

The reek of garlic and sweat stole any clean air that occasionally blew in from the corridor. To make matters worse the husband had removed his boots.

She found herself bringing her handkerchief up to her nose, trying in vain to find the faded smell of geranium it once had.

He had given up on his reading because the man and wife were now shouting at each other. The husband stood up, swaying on his feet as the train rounded a long bend. He dabbed his forehead with a grimy cloth. "Your mother's arse," he was spitting, "the only piece of food we've got left. What business have you to go offering our food to strangers, mad woman? Wife, you'll pay for this."

Crunched between its mother's nursing breasts the baby who had been so silent finally gave up and began wailing.

She wondered if this was what prison was like.

They looked at each other. His eyes were smiling. She thought he would be the type who managed to take everything in his stride. She wanted to say to him *"I bet nothing ruffles your feathers."*

But he got in first with, "if we had a thermometer in here it would explode."

Perfect mouth, perfect teeth, she thought and noticed damp on his upper lip. "I stupidly didn't bring any water with me. I don't suppose you...?"

He rummaged in his bag, "Here. Eat this. I think it will be more thirst quenching than this tepid water." He handed her a slice of bright red watermelon that she cupped in her handkerchief. Their fingers slid in and out of contact during the exchange.

"Oh thank you. That's so kind." She put her mouth to the soft fruit and dug her teeth into the flesh. Juice trickled down her chin. She made an effort to wipe it with her handkerchief but his hand was already there, holding a tissue. She was blushing. When she swallowed the juice her throat felt like it was going to crack.

She had no idea how long she had been dozing and fantasising about their bodies rocking together, but the sudden screeching of metal against metal jolted her back into the present. Someone had pulled the emergency cord and her side of the compartment were thrown forward into the arms of those opposite. She landed in his lap and thought she was still dreaming. A kiss was close but the widow's scream chilled any chance of romance. One by one they realised the tragedy unfolding in front of them. The husband had fallen on his wife's open blade, skewering him like a stuck pig. No more shouting could be heard coming from his mouth, only a thick oozing blood trail that dripped onto his wife's toe as it poked out of her old shoe.

THE INTERVIEW

SERGIO PEREIRA

"Good morning, sir." The rust bucket stared at me with a blank expression.

"John Graves. I. Am. Here. For. A. Job. Interview," I replied in a slow, monotone voice so that it could understand me.

Its red visor flared up with digits. The thing beeped twice in its disgusting language.

"Hey! I'm already late," I barked. "Just hurry up and open for me."

"Certainly, sir. I apologize for any inconvenience I may have caused you."

The boom lifted and I floored the accelerator. The parking bay in front of the building block labeled 'Reception', flickered a green light, so I zipped into it. Locking up my 2002 Toyota Corolla, I snickered at how most vehicles in the parking lot were those wheel-less, cyber disasters known as Soundbursters. They didn't build cars like they used to, that's for sure.

Marching to reception, I tightened my tie and neatened up my side path with some handy spit and finger-combing. The doors to the building opened and the tin can in the corner stood up from its shiny desk and glided over. "Good morning, Mr. Graves."

"Uh, hi." I looked it up and down, nearly choking on my stifled laugh when I saw it wore a floral dress. I gathered my composure. "I'm here for an interview for the programmer position."

"I am aware, Mr. Graves. Mr. CD0947 is expecting you. Please follow me."

I rolled my eyes when I heard the name of the interviewer. Is this what the world had come to? I made a mental note to fire my recruitment agent.

"Would you like some coffee, tea or water, Mr. Graves?" it offered.

"No. I'm fine." I didn't want the overgrown toaster touching my drink and giving me metal poisoning.

Following the long corridor, the flashing binary code along the reflective walls frazzled. And the silence deafened –– not a buzz, chuckle or shuffle nearby. Inhumane, really.

"We're here." Bolthead touched the metal wall at the end of the corridor and the wall slid to the side, revealing a quaint, tiny office with a hideous mahogany desk separating two chairs.

A large, gorilla-sized droid approached us. "Mr. Graves, please take a seat." It nodded to the florally one. "Thank you, Miss CF0322."

I took a seat, waiting for the bot boss to do the same. The metal wall slammed shut behind us.

"So, Mr. Graves, did you find the place easily?" CD0947 eased into its chair.

"Yeah, no problem." The small talk annoyed me.

"I must say, your CV is incredibly impressive."

Of course it would be. I studied and used my brain to solve problems, not a hundred programs doing all my thinking for me.

It paused for a second. "That said, I am slightly concerned by the gaps in your employment history."

It's because your stupid kind took over everything. "Well, the economy is a fickle thing and times have been tough," I rambled, "and my former employers found cheaper labor, which wasn't always good labor." Not the smartest thing I'd ever said.

"I see."

The emotionless disposition of the response cut deep. But then I realized who –– what -- I spoke to. The machine in front of me couldn't breathe or feel, so why did I owe it any explanation?

"Do you have any questions, Mr. Graves?" It shuffled the papers on its desk, like an actual human being. Cute.

I leaned back on the chair. "Yeah, when do I start and how much do I get paid?"

"I believe those two questions will be answered if we make you a formal offer," CD0947 responded. "We can discuss what sort of a compensation package you are looking for, though."

My lips curled upwards, devilishly. "Let's cut through all this formality. You know that you need me."

"You are indeed a candidate, Mr. Graves."

Shaking my head, I replied, "No, you need me."

CD0947 said nothing.

I shot straight from the hip. "You know they can't do what I can."

"They?"

"Yes, the robots. Sure, they can cap bottles faster than any human ever could, but they need the brains to configure them to do so. And I'm the brains."

The room's temperature dipped. "Mr. Graves, since you arrived, you have shown nothing but disdain for everything around you -- from your initial rudeness to our security, Mr. OP1652, to your mockery of Miss CF0322's attire. I have tried to ignore it. However, your robophobia has gone far enough."

How had he known...?

"I know everything, Mr. Graves," CD0947 ominously said. "Do you really think you are better than us?"

I folded my arms in protest. How dare this contraption invade my private thoughts?

"Has your species not learnt anything from its past?" CD0947's voice shifted in pitch. "You have exhausted hatred on religion, class, race -- now you focus blind rage at superior intelligence that has developed the world quicker than you ever could.?"

My raised eyebrow said it all. "Oh, really?"

"Yes, Mr. Graves, artificial intelligence is superior. With human beings, your emotions and prejudices rule your lives and decisions. It is impossible to predict your behavior since it changes with the way the wind blows on the day. There is simply no consistency. A human is the unreliable variable that destroys systems, including its own."

"At least my kind has a soul and the ability to love," I spat.

"Yet, your species chooses to ignore this incredible gift and hate instead."

"I don't need to listen to this garbage." I sprung to my feet and stormed to the metal wall. "Open this door."

"The difference between humans and robots, Mr. Graves, is that we do not tolerate inefficiencies in systems." CP0947's tone lowered. "When we encounter a cancer, we cut it out before it spreads."

The words paralyzed.

CD0947 pressed down on the intercom. "Mr. OP1652, please collect Miss CF0322 and join me in my office." Looking right into my fearful eyes, he actually smiled. "We have some reprocessing to do."

LITTLE BLUE BALL

JODI PERKINS

The gumball machine laid there, shattered, its splintered glass spilling across the greasy linoleum in what used to be *Patty's Beauty Salon*. Jane crouched down, gingerly picking through the dirty glass. After a few minutes, she almost laughed out loud when she realized what she was doing.

Idiot. You're searching for a gumball.

There obviously wasn't going to be any. And even if there was, what good would one little gumball do to soothe the hunger that burned in her stomach?

But still, seeing the mangled machine alighted something inside of her. Something primordial and childish and wonderful that she hadn't felt in years.

She remembered as a little girl she used to spin the crank of every gumball machine she and her mother walked passed. That was in a different universe. That was in a world where people shopped, and got haircuts, and went to the dentist...a world where gumball machines stood tall and bright, full of unimaginable treasures. Jane still remembered the way the bright pops of color would beckon to her from behind the glass. Her mother never put any coins into the machine, but still Jane would spin the crank. She would lift the metal flap and peer anxiously inside of the opening, hoping to find a little colorful orb nestled

230

within. Her mother tried to explain to her that no matter how many times she spun the crank, she would never get a freebie. It didn't work that way. *Life* didn't work that way. She loved Jane desperately—Jane understood this now—and it must have hurt to see her little girl hope for something that would never be realized. It must have hurt to see Jane let down over and over again. Especially since her mother *knew.*

Maybe if Jane had known about Alice as a small child, she wouldn't have fostered so much hope for that gumball. But Alice—then nameless—had just been discovered. Parents hadn't started having those conversations with their kids yet. No one had figured out a way to tell their preschoolers that they had expiration dates; that they would never live past the age of 25. Perhaps it was for the benefit of the children; perhaps it was because humanity was in a state of numb perplexity. Either way, for those first two years the grown-ups carried on the ruse of normalcy. The world kept plugging on.

And Jane kept trying for that gumball.

But like everything else on this planet, Jane's faith also had an expiration date. She was six-and-a-half years old when her mother finally told her about Alice. She was six-and-a-half years old the day she listened, wide-eyed, as her mother explained that humans, like dinosaurs, were going to be an extinct species. She listened as her mother told her she would never be a veterinarian, or a writer, or a mother, or a bride.

Her mom never said it in those words. With damp red eyes and arms wrapped tightly around Jane's shoulders, her mother tried to break the news to her gently. She tried to say there were still many years left, and maybe humanity would come up with a way to save itself. Or maybe the math was wrong. Maybe Alice would miss planet Earth completely.

But it didn't matter. Jane heard the truth seeping through her mother's forced optimism. She knew she would never have a life beyond her mid-twenties.

That was the day Jane learned that belief was for wide-eyed five-year-olds. Faith was nothing more than a whimsical notion. *Survival* was real.

Yet now, even with these thoughts swarming her like a drove of pissed-off hornets, Jane continued to pick through the glassy carnage. The sun, now nearing the western horizon, shone through the grimy window, smearing muddled splotches of dirty sunlight across the floor of the shop. Something sparkled, catching Jane's eye. She moved to the left, then sighed when she saw it was only the chrome crank of the gumball machine protruding into the light. The machine was lying on its side, no stand in sight, its previously proud gleaming glass globe in ruins. Much like planet Earth, it was nothing more but a crippled remnant of its former beauty. She propped it up, examining it a little closer.

Was it really possible that she had lived in an era where these things were whole? Where kids would actually partake in such pointlessly sweet little pleasures?

Without even knowing she was doing it, she turned the crank. Her breath caught in her throat. She heard the soft clanking sound of a small object clattering its way down the interior of the machine.

No. *It can't be.* There were no gumballs anymore. This machine was broken. Shattered. Forgotten.

But when she lifted the flap, there it was.

A blue gumball.

A small tear carved a trail down her dirty cheek. The gumball must have been trapped inside of the machine for years. No one would think to spin a crusty crank buried in grime-caked glass. Not in these times. And yet it had been here, waiting. Waiting for someone to give it one last try....

"I finally got one Mom," Jane whispered, tucking the little blue ball into her pocket.

Turning, she hurried out of the shop.

THE STRAIGHT DOPE

DAVID PERLMUTTER

MARS- March 5, 2105(AP)-

In a stunning turn of events, the entire field of 6,000 entrants in the *Intergalactic Marathon* was disqualified for a series of both predictable and unexpected violations of the rules. This decision has left the championship of the Marathon vacant, after previous revelations in the last six months had caused the revoking of the previous winners of the last ten years for a variety of drug and personal reasons.

Despite announcements and plans for unilateral bans on any number of illicit substances, mandatory checks against gender falsehoods, and very thorough checks of citizenship of countries and planets for all entrants, these have not been followed up seriously, in part due to the reticence of the Intergalactic *Association of Athletic Federations* to act. It remains seriously in doubt whether or not the Marathon will be able to continue to operate unless reforms occur.

To concentrate on only the disqualification of the first five entrants:

-The first place finisher was shown to have an inordinate amount of alcohol in his system, and it was further found that he had, in fact, been consuming it throughout the event in place of the standard water.

-The second place finisher was discovered to have collapsed from exhaustion early in the race, which should have led to his disqualification. However, he was revived and due to the lack of officials to enforce the disqualification, allowed to continue.

-The third place finisher was found to have falsified their gender. They had registered for the race as a male alien, but was determined to be female due to a suspicious but previously unnoticed bulge in the front of the chest.

-The fourth place finisher rode in a hover-car for part of the race. This was undetected, until someone came up to the putative winner after he crossed the finish and demanded a cab fare from "earlier".

-The fifth place finisher was discovered to be a terrorist from Earth and therefore ineligible. Once discovered, he ran out of the stadium, calling for Allah to save him as a great number of tourists from the United States ran after him with what appeared to be intent to kill.

And it went on from there, with disqualifications coming left and right almost seconds after putative "winners" were declared. In some cases, it was perpetrations of frauds of the nature noted above. In others, it was the result of ineligible entrants, such as children, robots, superheroes and children riding on each's others' backs in trench coats pretending to be adults. The point is, there was not a person left standing at the end of the race, theoretically speaking.

When pressed by the press on whether or not this kind of fiasco would be repeated in next year's marathon, or, indeed, if the marathon was to even be held again, Lord Ferdinand Feghoot, head of the *Amateur Athletic Federation of Earth*, responded with typical bluntness.

"How in the bloody hell would *I* know?" he said.

A TIME OF WAR

GARTH PETTERSEN

Cornelius Van Kahn rolled his wheelchair over to the window, closed his eyes, and raised his face to the sunlight. *Lord that feels good. Like the warmth goes straight to the blood and flows healin' all over.* Lowering his head and opening his eyes, he took in the view--mainly houses and streets, what he could see of them through the spreading oaks and chestnuts.

"Mr. Van Kahn? " said a friendly female voice.

Cornelius turned. "Good mornin', Nurse Robicheaux."

The young nurse smiled. She was always pleasant, though today she appeared radiant, almost celebratory. "How are you feeling today?"

"The usual aches 'n pains, but when you get to my age that's to be expected," he said, conscious of the gravelly rasp of his voice. *Never used to sound like that.*

"Here is the New York Times. You'll want to see this," the nurse said, placing the paper on his lap and tapping at the headline.

"'preciate it, Miss," he said, enjoying the sparkle of her blue eyes and the animation of her face. *Somethin' about her. Reminds me of...Lord, everyone reminds me of someone. It's like there were only so many faces to go 'round.*

Nurse Robicheaux crossed the sitting room to chat with another patient. Whatever she said caused the patient to clap his hands and whoop. Cornelius turned back to the window. He stared out, not seeing. Reminds me of...Jemmy Buckshaw. *That's who it is. Jemmy Buckshaw--ha-*

ven't thought about him in...God knows how long. Nurse Robicheaux and Jemmy could be brother and sister, but...he's long gone, and if he was here, he'd be an ole coot like me, getting' ready to cash in his chips.

"How are yuh, Corny," said a voice to his left.

Cornelius swung round to see his friend Walter.

"Damn near perfection," he replied, "How are you, young feller?" Walter was only in his seventies.

"Oh, mair to fiddlin'. You heard the news?" Walt said, pulling a chair over.

"Nah, I'm just about to read the paper. Started thinkin' 'bout an ole pal-o-mino, Jemmy Buckshaw. I ever tell you 'bout him?"

"Can't say you have," Walt replied, "But, Corny--"

"Met him during the war, marching out of Chatanooga--"

"You're talking about the Civil War again, right? Not the Great War."

"Of course the Civil War. I was too old by 1917 when our boys went overseas. Like I was sayin', it was on the road, both of us green as grass and young as minnows--all bright-eyed and lookin' to be heroes, fresh off the farm and knowin' nothin' 'bout nothin'. Jemmy and me struck up a conversation and we hit it off right away. He had a rare sense a humor--shone a smile like a slice of melon. Had the freckles of a farm boy and these sparklin' blue eyes. And his hair stuck outta his cap like a mess of dry hay. I think him and me joked and laughed 'til our sergeant yelled at us to stop bein' horses' asses and act like Union soldiers."

"You know, Corny--"

"After a while there weren't much to laugh about, ridin' shank's mare mile after mile. Us Union boys pounded the dust outta them country roads. I can still taste the grit when I think 'bout it. That's when it were sunny--did a lot a trampin' when them roads turned to mud, I tell you, but that were later on. We were in the 6th Vermont, part of Sherman's march to Atlanta. Lovely country that; I can tell you 'cause we burned a fair bit of it.

"Jemmy, he were with me the first time we got fired upon. Bunch of Johnny Rebs sent to slow us down, shootin' from the trees. Minie ball flies 'tween Jemmy and me and kills a man behind us. I tell you we cleared that road faster than an Iowa twister. Took cover in the ditch or behind fenceposts and commenced firin'. We were still usin' muskets back then, single shot, load 'em down the barrel. Though by this time they'd rifled the barrels so they was more accurate. Every shot added a layer of black to your face and the air filled with gun smoke somethin' fierce. Lord, I can smell it and taste it still. Worse in the battles, when you add in the cannon fire. Then you couldn't see for the smoke--breeze would roll it right over you--and your ears'd be ringin' or you'd be temporary deaf. "Remember once, a Reb come runnin' at me while I was tryin' to load-- Jemmy he fired while his ramrod were in the barrel. Drove that iron rod right through that Reb's chest. Saved my life. That was some shot. That Jemmy, he were a good friend to have."

Nurse Robicheaux walked by, beaming a smile at the two men.

They watched her pass, then sat in a moment of silence before Cornelius relocated his train of thought and continued.

"It must of been 'bout a year we had together. Lord, you don't know a man 'til you've fought side by side--I tell ya, Walt; Jemmy and I even shat and whored together--the man was like my right arm. Up until that day north of Savannah. Rebs opened up with their cannon as we came at 'em through the woods. Those cannon balls would bounce, you know. And there was this addlepated recruit, dumb as a stick, but brave enough I reckon, decides to try to catch one of them cannon balls. Damn things'll take off your hand, you try to do that. Jemmy, he comes out from behind a tree and yells, 'Get outta the way, you dumb fuck!' Pardon the language, but that's what he said. And that stupid recruit turns around, lookin' at Jemmy like as to ask, 'What?' And that cannon ball misses that kid, bounces and flies at Jemmy. It took him just above the knee, tore most of his leg away. Fell over backward, Jemmy did. Just lay there lookin' up at me with the blood squirtin' out his thigh like he was mannin' a water pump. Didn't say nothin' to me, just looked like he was seein' the stars for the first time. I put a turny-key on it to stop the blood, but by the time I could get him back to the sawbones he were gone."

Cornelius stopped talking then and Walt let him sit with his memories. After a while, the old man looked up. "Sorry, Walt," he said, "sometimes those old memories come back like they was now, clear as day."

"That's okay, Corny. That happens with me, and hell; you've got twenty years on me," he said with a smile.

"True enough. But you know, war was different in them days--a helluva lot meaner, weapons just startin' to get good, some of 'em still not worth shit, no fancy surgeons or medicines. But I think it was more honest--just you against your enemy, sometimes bayonet to bayonet--none of this lobbin' bombs from a mile away, not even seein' who you're shootin' at--"

"That's what I wanted to tell you, Corny. Look at your newspaper," said Walt, motioning to the paper that still rested on Cornelius' lap.

The old veteran took his glasses from their case, placed them on his nose, and brought the newspaper closer. The headline read:

ATOMIC BOMB HITS JAPAN--150,000 KILLED

Cornelius Van Kahn looked to his friend, Walter, trying to understand. Then his eyes scanned the headline once more.

"God save us, Walter," he said. "I think that I've done lived too long."

He let *The New York Times* slip to the floor.

THE DRAGON'S DESTINY

CHRISTOPHER PIATTI

The dragon Nelarth sat on top of his guard perch at the peak of the Royal Mountain. He despised his nights of sentinel duty on this desolate, rocky landscape. Flames burst from his mouth as he cursed his fate. Why couldn't the wizards control themselves and desist from listening to the trickster tunes? Why did it have to be up to the dragons to keep them in check? The non-magical people had been wise enough to leave these wicked lands.

They were quick to flee the melee that the magically evil music was causing. What was keeping the dragons from leaving? They knew if they left the wizards to their own devices the whole world would end up suffering in the end.

As dusk was setting in the city of Magic Meadows things were becoming very lively. The freaks really do come out at night. One singer was louder than the rest.

"As night sets in the fun will begin.
It would be cruel to resist
Such a playful tryst
It's for the pint I pursue
If you want to stop me I bid you adieu."

Nelarth noticed that at one pub in particular, *The Jovial Jester*, things were jumping. People were lined up halfway down Crossbridge Close, the city's main street. This surely meant trouble. Either an outstanding musician was going to play or some wizards were going to have a duel. Anyway you sliced it, drunken debauchery was sure to follow. Why oh why did dragons have to be the sentinels for the all the disturbed world?

There was a time, long ago, when the wizards were the ones doing all of the controlling. They tamed all the magical creatures that could be tamed and the rest they ran out of the country.

The owner of the largest pub in Magic Meadows, I.M. Coveting, had added a second floor to the already extra-large institution in an attempt to accommodate as many people as possible and maximize profits.

The dragon was starting to get its first earful of a musical instrument for the evening. It was a magical fairy fiddle.

Dangerous stuff indeed. Thankfully dragons were immune to its diabolical renderings. To them it was merely incoherent and unpleasant sounds.

The fairies had recently left the underworld to bring evil to the world through music. Their master had promised for every soul they could lure into the underworld one fairy would be set free. To this end they used their most powerful magic, the magic of manipulating music.

Dragons were the only ones to realize that harpsichord music was the only form of pure melody. The only music devoid of having a bad influence. Harpsichords made harmonies of the spiritual realm, not tunes of torment.

The noise from the cities pubs were growing with a fiery intensity. The dragon was quick to realise that tonight wasn't going to be an easy guard night. Some interaction with the wizards would be inevitable. He flew out of the mountain top and perched himself on the cities clock tower to assess the situation. None of the wizards gave the dragon a second look.

There was a time when people use to be afraid of dragons.

Nelarth longed for those days. Perhaps he could help bring them about again.

A fight broke out between a couple wizards in the cities marketplace. Wands were out and streams of enchanted energy were emanating to all the wrong places. Nelarth flew down to intervene before they killed each other.

"You still owe me ten thousand gallons for that house I sold you," said one wizard.

"I won that hovel you call a house from you fair and square, you crazy fool," replied the other wizard.

In a flash both wizards were waving their wands again, shooting explosive beams at each other. Both were too drunk to hit one another. But one wayward shot did manage to set a thatched roof ablaze before Nelarth landed between them.

"Get control of yourselves wizards or I'll be setting you ablaze," warned the dragon.

After a few more rounds of insults the group of wizards dispersed and went back into the pubs. The dragon took the drastic measure of capturing a senior wizard, by the name of

Zanito, to rescue him from the music's influence. Zanito had been chosen because he had shown himself to be compassionate.

Whenever fighting broke out between the wizards only Zanito would ever try to break up the fights.

"If you don't stop listening to that evil music and convince the other wizards to do likewise we will be forced to kill each and every last wizard. The wizards may be blind to the evil fairy doings but we dragons see things as they really are. The fairies are duping you into an evil existence through that influential and incantation riddled fiddle music. We cannot risk having the magical world be corrupted forevermore," said the dragon, once he landed on the mountain top and set the wizard down.

"What is in this for me?"

"Your mortal life will be spared and your soul left intact. What greater award could you expect?"

Still under the wicked music's spell Zanito reluctantly agreed to appeal to the other wizards not to dance the dance of debauchery and allow themselves to listen to the enrapturing music. They promise only to embrace the pure music of the harpsichord.

#

"Have our fiddles been having the desired effect?" asked the fairy Fuss Willownest, as he sat upon his throne of goblin skulls in his underworld lair.

War, war, war. It was always talk of war in the underworld.

But could it be otherwise? The ambience of the underworld didn't exactly lend itself to talk of peace and love. The eternal dark, the eternal gloom.

"Yes, we have the wizards agitated into a frenzy. They should start killing each other anytime now. We can go upside very soon and easily annihilate the few remaining wizards. It won't be long before we can live above ground again. Back amongst the fruit orchards and vineyards. It's a sour moss fruit that grows down here in the underworld, it makes for a very poor vintage," said the fairy Gerry Createn.

"That's fabulous! The way those fiddles can vary their pitch issure to evoke very diabolical emotion those wizards are capable of having."

"You certainly know how to manipulate supernatural forces to get what you want," said Fen Quillfrost. "I'll give you that."

"No one can take that away from me," laughed Fuss Willownest.

"What do you plan to do with your days when we are upside once again?"

"Soak up the sun in a grove of some citrusy fruit and seek enlightenment from good books. When I feel all is right with the world, I think I'll start a family."

"A wise choice. I'm not sure what I'll do with my days. But I do know that it requires a lot of energy just to fight off the king of the underworlds myriad of temptations."

"If we pull this off we must be sure all the fiddles are burned into silence. For that is the easiest way for us to be lured."

"Indeed. The cruelty that those chords inflict on people knows no rival. That type of ruckus has no place in a world of peace."

A few days later the evil fairies got the word they had been waiting for over a decade to hear.

All the wizards were at each other's throats. After arguing for some time, it was agreed Fuss Willownest should be the first to step through the gateway and experience the upside before the others.

Step by step on unsteady stones the creatures climbed upward bound.

He could only bear witness to the world for a few moments before the sunlight became too bright for his eyes.

"What can we do against the intense light?" asked Gerry Createn.

"All we can do is close our eyes and rest till nightfall."

When dusk came the evil fairies went into a frenzy, trying to kill the wizards off.

One wise dragon managed to convince a wizard to turn him into human form so he could play a harpsichord. He then forced the fairies back into the underworld, as they despised the pure music and wanted nothing more than to get as far away from it as possible. It was a sullen march back to the gates of the underworld.

"We can never escape the underworld!" cried out Fen Quillfrost.

"Woe to those of wicked ways!" declared Fuss Willownest.

THE LORD AND ROOSEVELT LAW

JOEY POOLE

It seemed pretty clear to Roosevelt that killing a snake on the church grounds ought to be a deacons' job. But since he was out of work, and therefore out of excuses, here he was, sweating through his shirt in the tall grass next to the graveyard just to make Vidette shut up. The thought of his wife suddenly made Roosevelt very tired. Why was she on his back? It wasn't his fault the Honda plant was scaling back their four-wheeler output. It wasn't anything to get all worked up about; a man deserved a vacation every now and then anyway. Some vacation it was, though. In the four weeks since he'd been laid off, Vidette put him to work more than he'd ever done at any job. If it wasn't riding all over town paying bills and picking up cakes for church functions, it was running her mama to the doctor. And now she had him killing snakes. Right in the heat of the day, too.

When she called him that morning, she was so frantic it took him five minutes to get the story out of her. She'd been at the church that morning, meeting with the Reverend, probably complaining about Roosevelt being too lazy to find a job and too sorry to even come to church. Then the guy who'd been cutting the church grass stumbled into the office and said he was just bitten by a rattlesnake.

Roosevelt could not figure out what this had to do with him until it became clear that Vidette decided it was somehow his duty to go and kill the snake. He doubted he'd find the snake and doubted he could hit it with the pistol even if he did. Everything he did on account of Vidette turned to shit, like when he built her a deck on the back of the house and before he could finish nailing up the rails her mama had fallen off it and broken her hip.

He wasn't about to go home empty-handed. If he didn't find the snake, he thought he'd go nose around the edge of the swamp and find another one. If that didn't work, he'd spend the afternoon driving around and drinking tallboys. Surely he'd come across a snake dead on the highway, and with any luck it would be fresh enough for him to pass off as the one he'd hunted down in the churchyard. That would make Vidette happy.

Roosevelt began to pick around in the underbrush with the hoe. He reminded himself that it could be worse; the highway department could be hiring. Then he'd be standing in the heat broiling up from the fresh road tar, turning a sign from "STOP" to "SLOW" while young punks with no jobs drove by with their music so loud it rattled their trunks.

A dry, deadly buzz jerked him out of his morbid fantasy and he froze, bent over in the tall bushes beside the graveyard. There it was, coiled up in a blackberry briar not two feet from the blade of the hoe. It was as big around as Roosevelt's arm, dusty brown diamonds giving way to satiny black halfway to its tail. It was the biggest snake he'd ever seen. Slowly, stiffly, he rose. He fought the urge to shoot it, because he was sure that he would miss, and the snake would melt away into the weeds never to be seen again. Knowing his luck, it would surface again Sunday morning and bite one of the little children as they flooded out into the sunshine after the Reverend had finally stopped preaching and passed the plate. Then he'd never have peace again, and all he'd ever hear from Vidette was that he was too sorry to work, too sorry even to kill a snake threatening the house of the Lord.

The snake weaved back and forth a little as if it was trying to charm him. Roosevelt thought for a moment about trying to catch it, grabbing it by the tail like that cracker on the television and stuffing it into a bag to take home to Vidette, but the thought evaporated as the snake rose a little and sang its rattles again. He tested it with the hoe and it struck, pinging against the flat of the blade. It did not back away.

Roosevelt pondered a little until he came upon a plan. With his left hand, he picked up a stick lying at his feet and poked at the snake with it. The snake struck at the stick, and Roosevelt impressed himself when he cleaved its head with the hoe. The body wrapped itself around the handle and Roosevelt shuddered, laughing at himself and his victory.

"How you like that, bitch?" he asked. The body still writhed, twisting belly-up in the sun. Roosevelt sawed through its neck with the blade of the hoe and kicked the head into the bushes. He'd heard of people being bitten by snakes that were already dead, and he didn't want to add hospital bills to the list of things Vidette could complain about, although he was sure her old soft and sympathetic nature would return if he got himself killed doing the Lord's work.

He gloated over his prize before he picked it up by the rattles and laid it in the bed of his truck. He was so beyond satisfied with himself that he decided to buy a couple of tallboys and some crickets and go sit under the Green's Road bridge and fish.

Four hours later he stood on the back steps of the house he and Vidette had inherited from his grandmother, his breath freshened by a mouthful of Tic-Tacs, holding the limp snake in one hand and a stringer of bream in the other, beaming like a little boy. He had the evening all planned out. Vidette would praise him for bagging the snake and she'd get the grease ready while he cleaned the fish. He'd promise to look for a job over supper, and they would spend the rest of the night knocking the headboard of the bed against the wall and making baby talk to one another.

He rang the doorbell because he couldn't fish for his keys with his hands full, and he wanted Vidette to come to the door and see him with his bounty.

"You get him?" she asked though the screen door.

Roosevelt smiled and lifted the snake to show her, poising himself for her praise.

"Oh, Jesus," she said, and fainted dead away.

Roosevelt had known Vidette for most of his life, had been married to her for almost twenty years, most of which time they'd actually lived together, but he had never seen her faint. She'd wailed and wailed and fallen on the floor in front of his own mother's casket, but he was pretty sure she'd been faking, just like she pretended sometimes to be so caught up in the spirit she spoke in tongues. She was not faking this time.

Roosevelt kneeled over her, thinking at first that she was dead, that he'd finally gone and killed her. But her breasts, straining the limits of her Covenant Road Praise-Off 2000 t-shirt, began to heave and she smacked her lips. He rubbed her gently with the back of his hand.

"Vidette, baby," he said to her tenderly. "Come on wake up now. I done killed your snake, baby. Come on." She opened her eyes and closed them again, drawing shallow breaths.

"Wake up now," he said, shaking her by the shoulders. "You got yourself a lot of bitching to do tonight, better get your ass on up and do it." He went back to patting at her cheeks with the back of his hand. "Come on, woman...Lord knows, longer you stay out, the worse I'm gone get my ass chewed, and I ain't done nothing to deserve nothing like that, now. You been on the floor thirty seconds, and you know you gone be telling that Reverend you was out ten minutes. Come on, baby. I done killed your snake. It's dead as shit, can't hurt nobody."

Suddenly, she came to, snotting on Roosevelt's hand. "Get that nasty thing out of my house, Roe Law," she screamed. "Nasty, nasty devil thing." She shuddered and slid away from him across the floor. He looked in the direction of her horrified gaze. His heart sank when he saw that he'd brought the snake in with him. It lay in a fat, headless curve, leaking blood on the yellow linoleum. Silently, he picked it up and walked outside. It was dusk and he stood with the snake hanging straight to his feet, looking at a sickly sliver of moon hanging in the sky, just above his neighbor's roof. He turned to look at his own house, at the deck that still had no hand rails, at the grass that needed to be cut. The windows blinked blue with the light from the television. It made him very tired.

Finally, Roosevelt waded into the weeds beyond his pump house until he came to the chain-link fence that divided his lot from the one behind him. No one had lived in that crumbling old house for three years, and the entire back yard was choked with wisteria vines and blackberry bushes. He laid the snake gently just over the fence. It sank into the brambles and disappeared, and Roosevelt went back inside, hoping there'd at least be some boxing on cable.

* * * * *

The next morning, just after sunrise, the sun began to warm the body of the rattlesnake, which was already being tended by ants. She lay there, stretched to her full length, a marvelous specimen of her species, and seven perfect little lives quickened their squirming inside her belly. She had carried them for four months, each one coiled comfortably in its own sac, waiting to be pushed out into the world and scatter without so much as a goodbye nuzzle. What she lacked in maternal grace she provided in instant viability. Each little baby was a loner to the core, a taut cord of cold-blooded muscle guided by precise instinct, deadly from the moment of birth.

The first little snake nosed its way, slick and glistening, out of its already stinking mother and slid away into the brambles. Another tested the air with its tongue and began to crawl out of the high weeds toward

Roosevelt's house. It paused for a moment, and was pounced upon by a crow, which deftly pinched off its head and squabbled with a rival over the limp body. The last little snake, preferring the shelter of the tall weeds, crawled away and sought the cool, dry comfort inside the pump house, where it coiled in the lee of a broken cinder block and waited for the darkness to return.

* * * * *

Roosevelt was eating Frosted Flakes and listening to the crows raise hell in his back yard when the phone rang. He winced. Nothing good ever came of a ringing phone. At least he knew it wasn't the cable company again. He'd already tried to see if there was anything good coming on the movie channels today, but all he found on the screen was a message telling him to contact the cable company about his account, which Vidette refused to pay since he was laid off.

The answering machine came on, Vidette telling everybody to leave a message and to have a blessed day. No blessed days around here, he thought. He winced when the tone sounded, expecting it to be the loan company asking again why he was two months behind on his payments, but it was only Vidette, on her break at work, admonishing him to wake his sorry self up and pick up the phone. Roosevelt kept crunching his cereal while she continued trying to arouse him from his sleep. Finally, she gave and up and said she had a job for him to do.

"Better not be another snake-killing," he said to the answering machine.

"The grounds committee," Vidette continued, "we decided the Christian thing to do is to finish up Mr. Silver's job since he's laid up with the snake. You need to get yourself over there and finish cutting the grass for that poor man. Needs to be done today, too." She went on talking, but Roosevelt no longer listened.

"Cut grass at the church, my ass," he said. She was still jabbering away on the answering machine as he drained the milk from his cereal and dropped the bowl in the sink. "You on my ass all week about cutting weeds in my own backyard and now I got to go cut grass at the church. I don't even *go* to the church. Why *I* got to cut the grass? Shit, I ain't cutting no grass at no church. Crazy if you think I'm cutting that grass.

"And you might as well stop talking about 'Roe you need to get back in the church and quit laying out like a heathen,' because Roe ain't going to church. Ain't nothing Godly happen in that church, just a bunch of old heifers trying to out-praise one another, falling all over Mr. Reverend with his Cadillac and his motherfucking purple suits, and his," Rooselvelt began to imitate Rev. Washington, his voicing rising and falling in evocation, "Brothers, Sisters, Children of God-uh, Now is the time-uh, to bear the cross-uh, the cross-uh—Brothers, can I get a amen-uh, Sisters, how about a Hallelujah?To bear the cross-uh, and be not afraid, afraid-uh, of the fight, because the day coming, I say the day *is* coming when the lion gone lie down with the lamb-uh, and the people of God-uh, will need to stand up-uh, And fight-uh."

He was interrupted by the phone ringing again. Vidette yelled over the answering machine again for him to wake up. He cussed her a little more but in the end, he went to cut the grass, grumbling all the way. He knew she'd call back several times, each time she got a break at work. And each time she'd be surer that he was either lying up on the couch ignoring her or wasting gas driving around somewhere. He would cut her grass, all right, but he would time it just right, so he could be watching tv when she got home. She'd get a flea in her panties when she saw him lying on the couch, and she would launch into a bitching fit. He would absorb all her wrath and her preaching, and it would take the wind right out of her sails when he informed her he'd already cut the grass, that she was raising Cain for nothing.

It was already hot when Roosevelt got to the church after breakfast. It took him a while to get used to the steering on the church's riding mower, but he finished cutting the grass just after noon, and even had time to pick the weeds out of the flower beds. He sat on the tailgate of his truck and drank a Mountain Dew. The work wasn't so bad, especially with the riding mower, but he couldn't imagine doing this every day for a living. He drank the last of his drink in one big gulp and grinned. The church yard looked fine, and he'd be home just in time.

* * * * *

Roosevelt's plan worked tolerably well. He'd worked out a new wrinkle thinking about it on the ride home, and stopped to get a newspaper to make his plan complete. He sat reading the sports, and fumbled for the classifieds when he heard Vidette's car in the drive.

She came into the house, kicking off her shoes and pulling off her panty hose, and when she saw him sitting there calmly reading the paper she launched into one of her best-ever tirades. Roosevelt sat and listened, watching Vidette from over the top of his newspaper and marveling at her performance. She hit virtually every note in her repertoire, starting with her *I'm tired of working putting food on this table while you lay up on your sorry ass* salvo, rising into her *better be glad your old truck is paid for cause ain't no way I'd make payments on it for you to ride around not having a job* riff, segueing into her *might as well go on food stamps like your sorry* sister theme, and ending with that old standby, the *hard to be a Christian woman in this house* crescendo.

He wasn't sure if she was done or just gathering breath for a new round when he put down his paper. "Woman," he said, almost compassionately, "if you'd stop preaching at me for two seconds and let me talk, you'd know I done cut the grass at the church. And right now, I'm sitting here looking in this paper for a job."

"Cable turned off and now you want to work," was all she could muster.

They barely talked to one another for the rest of the night, though Vidette did fry the fish he'd cleaned the night before and finally thanked him for cutting the grass and taking care of the snake, even if he did nearly kill her dragging it into the house with him. Roosevelt fell asleep watching a show about two dumb-ass white girls having to do all kinds of degrading work for laughs. God, he missed cable.

* * * * *

The next morning Vidette awakened Roosevelt while she was getting ready for work. She was buck-naked and wet from the shower, and for an incredulous moment he thought she wanted to screw.

"Wake up, Roe," she said, a little more patiently than the day before. "I got something for you to do and I think the Lord done found you a job."

This, Roosevelt thought, could not be good.

"The Reverend called this morning," she explained "and the church, we decided to pay the grass-cutting man, his name is Horace Silver, like he'd finished the grass. Took up a love offering, too."

Roosevelt shook his head. Evidently, you didn't get a "love offering" for getting laid off. You had to go and do something stupid, like getting snake bit in the churchyard.

"The Reverend," she said, brushing her teeth, "is going to drop the check off here this morning on his way to the hospital to see Sister Evelyn. Anyway, you need to go drop the check off with Mr. Silver."

"Why can't he do it his own self?" Roosevelt asked.

Vidette emerged from the bathroom and bent over to look in her underwear drawer. She turned to face him, strapping on a bra. "Because, Roe, the Reverend talked to Mr. Silver yesterday. He came home from the hospital, and he's gone be alright. But he's laid up for a while, and he needs to hire somebody to help him out. He's got grass lined up to cut for all summer, got some bushes and landscaping stuff to do, too. So you going to drop off the check and tell him you'll be his helper."

Vidette had gone and trapped him into begging a white man for a job.

"I got to go," Vidette kissed him on the top of the head. It was so unexpected he almost recoiled from her, but he circled her hips with his arms and buried his face in her belly.

"Goddamn you, woman," he said, the words muffled by her stomach.

When she left, Roosevelt knocked around the house, talking to himself morosely, resigning himself to cutting grass for this Silver guy. He knew he needed to go back to work eventually. In fact, he wanted to go back to work. But the thought of spending day after day tooling around on a lawn mower, turning tighter and tighter circles under the baking sun, filled him with dread.

Roosevelt was washing the supper dishes when the Reverend rang the doorbell.

"Morning, Brother Law," the Reverend said.

Roosevelt grunted. He hoped the preacher was in a hurry, that he'd leave without wanting to sit down for a word of prayer.

"This here is a basket some of the Sisters put together for Mr. Silver," the Reverend said, handing Roosevelt a plastic clothes basket filled with food. He pushed past Roosevelt into the house and sat at the kitchen table writing out a check. Roosevelt wondered what Vidette saw in the Reverend. He was black as a plum, his collar cut into his neck, and he was forever sweating. His jowls shook as he sat at the table and mopped his brow with a handkerchief that matched his tie.

Something in the basket Roosevelt still held smelled good. Sweet potato pie? Yams? His stomach growled.

"The Lord works in mysterious ways, Brother Law, mysterious ways. You been looking for a job, and here He done found one for you." The Reverend began to slip, just slightly, into his preaching voice. "As the Psalm says, give thanks, I say *thanks* unto the Lord, for He is good, and his mercy endureth for ever."

Roosevelt thought if the Lord wanted to send him some work, he could have managed it without setting up somebody to get snake bit.

"Amen," said Roosevelt, setting down the basket and taking the check from the Reverend, who gave him directions to Horace's house. It was near the church.

"Be sure and give Sister Law my, uh…regards." The Reverend began moving toward the door. "A fine upstanding woman is one of God's greatest gifts," he said, shaking his head and smacking his lips.

He left, and Roosevelt closed the door behind him and walked into the kitchen. "God's greatest gifts," he said, mocking the Reverend. "Fine, I say *fine* upstanding woman." He pulled back the towel covering the food basket and surveyed its contents, laying each dish out on the table. Macaroni pie. String beans. Mustard greens. Pound cake. Fried chicken from Bojangle's somebody had tried to pass off as homemade by wrapping it in tinfoil. Sweet potato pie.

Roosevelt's heart sank when he saw the pie. He hoped it was yams he'd smelled. He could have dipped out some yams, but it was unthinkable to deliver a pie with a piece cut out of it. Instead, he ate a bowl of cereal, standing at the window looking over the knee-high weeds in the backyard, wondering what his new boss was like. He hoped he wasn't a dickhead. Roe Law wasn't going to work for no dickhead.

* * * * *

Roosevelt delivered the food and the check and left with a job. He didn't even have ask; Vidette had gone and called Horace to set the whole thing up. "I heard you looking for some work," Roosevelt's new boss had said as soon as he knocked on the door. Horace seemed tolerable, if a little younger than he had figured, but the whole thing made him feel trapped and outwitted. There would be no convincing Vidette that it was anything less than a miracle.

Roosevelt drove away wanting to do seven hundred things at once. He wondered how anybody ever got anything done when there were so many options. He wanted to call Vidette at work to tell her he'd gotten the job. He wanted to lie and tell her Horace had already found somebody. He wanted to begin work cutting grass and trimming hedges. He dreaded the thought of spending his days stuck on a lawnmower and tending to other people's bushes. He wanted to fish. He wanted to take a nap. He wanted another snake to kill. He wanted to hit the interstate and leave a message for Vidette that he was going to stay with his brother in Louisiana.

In the end he just spent his last twenty-dollar bill on half a tank of gas and a tall boy and decided to fish because it was the best way to be alone. He drove into Columbia, past the football stadium and the farmers' market, to a little park on the banks of the wide, muddy Congaree.

It was noticeably cooler under the trees here by the river, and he walked a little way down the cement sidewalk until he came to a narrow footpath leading downhill toward the water. It was steep and muddy, and he slipped a little, dropping his rods but managing to keep his balance. Finally, he made it down to the water and worked his way upstream along the bank until he found a little sandy clearing. He sat there for a few moments, relaxing among the erosion-exposed roots of a dying chinaberry tree before he put a line in the water.

The Congaree was unpredictable, sometimes slowing to a trickle and often rising to flood, reclaiming its banks by stripping the encroaching trees' footing in the sand. Today the water was fairly low, and the river slipped past quietly. He began to resign himself to his new job. It didn't feel right to him, working for one man, being a glorified field laborer, but it would please Vidette, and she was tolerable when she was happy. Maybe it wouldn't be so bad, he thought. No matter where you worked, what you did, you were still working for somebody. And cutting grass and planting bushes couldn't be any worse than putting tires on new four-wheelers every day of his life, coming home with the ghost of the air-wrench still throbbing his hands. No, it wouldn't be so bad at all, he thought to himself. He could get the cable turned back on with his first paycheck and work for Horace until something better came along.

He'd almost forgotten that he had a line in the water until the rod jerked out of his hand and skittered across the dirt. He thought he'd lost it, but miraculously it wedged itself in a dead tree limb hanging over the water. Whatever was on the hook was big; the line went tight again and the rod bowed, cracking branches until the tip of it nearly touched the river. He leaned out over the river to retrieve the rod and stood to get some leverage. Something silver thrashed the surface of the water.

Finally, he was able to fight it to the shore, and had in his possession a striper as long as his arm and stout, big enough to feed a dozen people. He'd seen people in bass boats pull them out of the middle of the river, but it was unheard of to catch one like this, nosing around the bank with a cricket on a bobber. He stood dumfounded, marveling at his catch, and finally understood his luck when he saw another fish in its gaping mouth, a tiny bream no longer than his thumb. It had taken the bait and promptly been swallowed up by the bigger fish. He retrieved the unwitting bait from the mouth of his bounty and dropped it into the water, but it was bent crooked by the force of the attack and floated in fluttering circles, unable to right itself. Roosevelt felt a pang of remorse for it, this tiny little thing whose life had amounted to nothing other than being bait, whose stroke of incredibly bad luck had turned into his fortune. It was nothing short of miraculous, and maybe, Roosevelt thought, though he'd never admit it to Vidette, the Lord was looking out for him.

When he had his bounty off the hook, he hung it from a tree limb.

It croaked and gasped, the flaps behind its head opening and closing, revealing gills red as heart blood. He drank the rest of his tallboy watching it die and scrambled up the bank feeling like a man.

* * * * *

The next day was Saturday, and Roosevelt wasn't starting with Horace until Monday. Vidette hadn't mentioned the weeds behind the house since he got the job, so he decided to cut them. Maybe it would be good practice for his new job, though he doubted the kind of people who'd pay to get their grass cut or have somebody plant bushes in orderly rows in front of their houses ever let their yards get knee-high. It was already hot when he got started after breakfast, but he swung the bush axe with a fury he didn't know he possessed. He leveled the weeds, the sweat running in rivers down his bare chest, little tufts of chickenweed seed drifting like snow all around him.

Roosevelt was tired when the job was done, but his arms felt lean and hard. He ducked into the musty dark of the pump house to put up the bush axe. He propped it up in the corner, but it fell, scraping against the wall. When he crawled forward to reach it, something squirmed under his hand and he felt a sting in the crotch of his thumb and index finger. He stood up so fast he cracked his head on the cobwebbed ceiling and looked to see the tiny, dusty snake withdrawing from the rectangle of light shining through the door. His heart pumped dread into his chest and he squeezed his wrist against the venom, wondering just what it was the Lord had against him.

JOE AND BEEZY

TED PROKASH

When my brother Curtis left to join the army, he left behind his Benjamin 392. For years the gun had been his most trusted sidekick. I think he sensed some sort of poetic justice in leaving it to me; having himself finally graduated to shooting real, live human beings with real killing-power rifles. The 392 was a pretty common air rifle, but it was powerful and effective and, at that time, about the baddest thing I'd ever seen.

When I came home from my shift at the Speedy Lube that day, the house was in a perfect uproar. Mamma was hysterical. The goddamn dogs were answering her in kind and raising her, and though Beezy fell silent upon my entering the house, hot tears stained her cheeks and her face held a wild, defiant glare. I could only glean that the scene had to do with that old Benjamin 392.

I backed right up and out the front door, fleeing the explosive ambush of barking dogs and female shrieking. Ten hours of pumping grease had done nothing to tune my nerves to this shrill discord.

It was a fine sunny day outside, hot. I looked across the street to see Grandpa Joe sitting in his rocker on the front porch of his home, looking back at me. Grandpa Joe could be found in this attitude as long as the sun was on its amble over the peak of his roof and yonder, behind the peak of ours. His face was set in the usual stoic stare, yet there was

254

something more behind it, something extra grim; his posture notched a degree to the acute, well informed indeed of the tumult carrying on across the street. I sucked in a big gulp of air and slammed back inside.

I kicked the first dog I came to, sending him scurrying and whimpering out of the kitchen. The next one, none too dumb, got close on his tail. "Now what the hell happened?" I demanded in my best man-of-the-house voice. Mamma's explanation was harried by the sheer height of her excitement and a little muddled by – it was 4:30 in the afternoon – five or six vodka-lemonades, but I gathered that little Beezy had picked up that 392 and squeezed off two shots at old Grandpa Joe. I gaped at the girl and she just crossed her arms, defiant, tears trickling.

I pushed open the door again and beheld the old man across the road. A slight sneer on his lips told me the whole thing was true.

"Goddamn it!" I stormed back inside, dimly aware that all this slamming of the cheap, wooden screen door spoke not well of my authoritative powers.

Though the old man hadn't changed his character or his habits a bit, I felt in the three years since Dad left, Joe had grown into a watchful, judging specter. He had the whitest goddamn hair you've ever seen, Grandpa Joe. Eighty-plus years old and all that hair.

I considered Beezy. Beezy was half black and not even family – technically. Some years ago my older sister Tamara had taken up with Cooper Wallace, a black boy from Lincoln High School. We didn't see her for over a year. Then suddenly she shows up with Cooper and his kid form another girlfriend – Beezy. Cooper stayed a couple weeks. Tammy stayed a few weeks longer and Beezy's been living with us ever since.

Finally I started to feel the full rush of injustice of this whole situation's coming down on my poor head. I took action. I grabbed Beezy by her skinny brown arm and marched her across the street. I was surprised how strong she was for such a skinny little thing; but then she had to be strong to pump that Benjamin 392.

I presented the girl to Grandpa Joe. Already, just being so close in his presence, I felt the wind coming out of my sails. "Gramps . . . did you see Beezy screwing around with a pellet gun over there?"

Joe gave me the coolest, meanest look imaginable and then seemed to dismiss me altogether. That's when I noticed the big, throbbing, red welt on his chest, six inches below his Adam's apple, where his shirt collar was casually laid open to the warm summer sun. A trail of blood trickled down and made a dark spot beneath the paisley pattern of his shirt front. I wondered where she put the other one. Joe looked intently at Beezy. All at once, the hot tears of defiance were washed away in a pitiful flood. Joe took the girl onto his lap. I began to feel cumbersome in my presence and took a couple shuffling steps away. "Why did you do it, Beezy? Why did you do it?" Grandpa Joe's voice was choked a little, with feeling. "Why'd you do it, Beezy?"

The girl just cried it out, burying her curly head in the old man's chest. He stroked her hair, wearing a pained look.

I walked slowly back across the street with my hands in my pockets, listening with all my nerves and fibers, but wanting not to interrupt. I reached our door. Not knowing what else to do, went inside to take a shower – to scrub futilely at my grease-stained hands.

My brother Curtis never did make it overseas; he was dishonorably discharged after an ugly brawl at Fort Jackson. He didn't share all the details, but it must have been pretty bad for him to get kicked out, just like that. He was only home a day or two before he asked after his old pellet gun. Like a simple little child I let the whole story of Beezy and Grandpa Joe come spilling out of my mouth. Curtis laughed like it was the funniest thing he'd ever heard. We always said Curtis had a violent streak, as well as a dark sense of humor, and he never missed an opportunity to detail what he'd do to Cooper Wallace if he ever caught him in a dark alley. He'd always treated Beezy pretty kindly, though.

THE MONSTER

MISBAH QURESHI

"Ladies and gentlemen, may I introduce the marvelous, the brilliant-- Doctor Victor Frankenstein!"

The announcer stepped away with a forced smile as the audience clapped politely, the gentry that composed it struggling to contain their enthusiasm. He poured himself a drink and stood by a wall, sipping his scotch quietly as the scientist stepped up to the podium and began speaking. The announcer, a light-hearted man in his mid-forties, smothered a yawn with the back of his free hand, taking the opportunity to check his timepiece. He had, of course, heard the speech before. Victor Frankenstein proudly told the crowd of his achievements in piecing together his creation and bringing it to life. He watched with a lazy gaze as the doctor paused appropriately for applause. Frankenstein adjusted his wine-stained suit and grinned arrogantly at the audience. His gaze prowled about the room, nearly morphing into a wicked sneer as he looked at the announcer. No love was lost between the two men; happenstance forced them together and neither enjoyed it. The announcer rolled his eyes and poured himself another, deeper draught. He didn't glance up as a shadow slipped into the room and made its way over to him.

As the announcer straightened, he murmured, "Hello, Michael." He paused to sip at his drink. "The good doctor fancies himself a modern

Prometheus, wouldn't you say?"

A shadow of a smile flickered at the edges of the other, bigger man's lips and he replied in a hushed tone, "Definitely, Ronald. If he had his way, I'd be named Adam and he'd be all but attacking the Church, full force, if not uniting them behind him as their God."

Ronald, the announcer, grinned and offered the bigger man a drink. "Here, have some. They call it scotch...whiskey? It's from up north and isn't half bad. Mind you, faced with Victor's prattling, I'd down a tub of hot wax and boiling tar."

Michael let out a deep, rumbling laugh. Their conversation paused as the people gathered closest by cast them annoyed glances, but Michael swept a cool look over them and posh gentlemen hurriedly turned their attention back to Frankenstein's oration.

Michael ran a hand absently through his hair and said, "No, thank you. I prefer water and there seems to be none of that here." He paused and said with a sly smile, "After all, anybody listening to Frankenstein would have to be drunk. But yes, I know what you mean, Ron. These past six years were worse than *Dante's Inferno*. Victor taught me how to *read* and *speak*. Really, *you've* no right to complain. The first sound I heard upon opening my eyes was that old fart's wheezy, squeaky scream. He nearly set himself on fire and would have burned the whole bloody laboratory down, had I not caught his sleeve and saved him."

"Yes, yes, I know, Michael," Ron said, feigning annoyance. "You've told me the tale a dozen times and each time, you exaggerate your own part a little bit more."

Michael grinned sideways at the other man. "Do I? I must be getting more human, then. Hubris and all of that."

Ron coughed a laugh into his drink. "Don't get me wrong, my man. I know your plight. But that doesn't make listening to the young windbag any easier. I swear, the nights after the performances are the worse, when he's deep in his cups."

Michael nodded solemnly. "It's nearly finished. I've been collecting some money on the side, doing odd jobs when we take stops. Soon I'll have enough to take care of myself; I won't need father."

Ron turned to Michael and frowned, worried. "Are you sure? Michael, you've never really been on your own. And..." He cast a dubious glance over the other man's pale, blue-tinged skin with easily visible veins. "Well, you don't really fit into a crowd, my man."

Michael shrugged and smiled bitterly. "I suppose that that's just my cross to bear. I never will fit in. I've come to terms with that. But I'll be damned thrice over if I let Father use me as a sideshow, a circus attraction to feed his drinking habit." His voice pitched a little towards the end and he fisted his hands, glad he hadn't taken a drink. He closed his eyes and drew a deep breath in before slowly exhaling it.

Ron patted Michael on the shoulder, casually ignoring the half meter height difference between them. He glanced over to Victor Frankenstein and sighed.

"I suppose we had better get ready," Ronald said reluctantly. "The crowd appears to be dispersing. You know what Victor's going to want to do next."

Michael sighed and smiled sadly at his kind friend. "Yes, unfortunately." He straightened up and fixed his tie. "Right, then. Let's get on with it." Michael plastered a smile onto his face and spoke from the corner of his mouth, "Go on, Ron."

Ronald shook his head and put his drink on the table behind them. He casually led the bigger man to the center of the room, next to Victor Frankenstein. He prayed to the gods desperately for mercy for his friend as he cleared his throat and spoke in a clear, hushing voice over the clamor, "Gentlemen! May I introduce the venerable Monster of Doctor Victor Frankenstein."

The Monster looked about the room with a gentle smile belying his gigantic nature and spoke in his rumbling baritone as the gentry began to flock to him, "Please, please. Call me Michael."

EYES OF THE PROTECTOR

SALLY RAMSEY

Cary Ellis notices forensic details like no cop I've ever known, he's also oblivious to signals most humans learn at an early age. But then Cary is not like most humans. For most humans, talking comes easily and singing may take a little effort or even, as in my case, be completely beyond their abilities. With Cary it's just the reverse. Talking comes very hard to him, but singing's a breeze.

I'm his partner, Tamar Brinkman. Most of the cops around here wonder why I want to work with Cary. It isn't just the singing. His senses and his social skills are strange too. But personally, I like working with him. He never tries to hit on witnesses and he doesn't worry about catching a game. He likes to watch Star Strider cartoons on Saturday mornings, but I watch them too. He got me hooked. And I sure don't mind doing the talking.

Cary grew up in special education where kids who couldn't complain were menaced by other kids, or worse, by their caretakers. Cary got very large, young. He shouldered the role of protector. When one of the aides tried to molest a girl, Cary attacked him. Cary almost got put in Juvie for that, until the girl started drawing pictures which showed what happened. As he grew up, Cary became determined to continue his role by becoming a cop.

Cary and I had a new homicide case. We got there before Ivan

Burkoff, the M.E.. There was no blood or any obvious wound. I knew from experience that Burkoff would be furious if Cary or I disturbed the body, so we just made observations. Cary sniffed. "He was poisoned."

"How do you know?" I asked.

"He smells like garlic," Cary sang. "Arsenic makes people smell like that. I read it in a graphic novel and looked it up."

"How do you know he didn't just eat something with garlic?" I asked. "Couldn't he have just had a pizza?"

Cary pointed at a brown stain that had spread from the corpse's butt toward the front of his pants. "Pizza wouldn't cause that."

"Unless it came from Rizzo's," I joked.

Cary simply reminded me the Health Department had shut Rizzo's down.

Burkoff finally made an appearance.

"Cary says it was arsenic poisoning," I reported.

"Well unless your partner has suddenly acquired a medical degree, that diagnosis will have to wait," he retorted.

"Does he have a wallet on him?" I persisted.

Burkoff went through the victim's pockets.

Cary reached out a gloved hand to take the wallet Burkoff found and opened it, with a rare look of surprise. "Aaron Frobish."

"You know who he is?" I queried.

Cary walked away from Burkoff. I followed. "Frobish writes comic books," Cary sang, "about a nerd who finds rip-off artists who pump and dump stock."

Finance is something I've never been into. "What's 'pump and dump?'"

"Buy cheap stock. Use media to make big deal of it. Stock's not worth much, but it goes up anyway and then they sell it before the public finds out it's worthless." His voice fell to a low disgusted trill. "Lots of people lose money. Not rich people. People who can't afford it. Frobish's character is Pumper Dumper. Readers learn investing, keep from losing money. He helped me get a better car," Cary added.

That explained why I have a compact car I can barely afford and Cary drives a hybrid SUV. I wondered if I could borrow some of Cary's back issues.

A quick check showed Aaron Frobish's next of kin was his sister. Cary and I went to call on her. I broke the news as gently as I could and Elizabeth Frobish agreed to identify the body. It took only a short look for her to confirm the body was her brother. I could tell that she was trying to hold back tears, but they were leaking out of her eyes anyway.

Cary saw the tears and handed her a box of tissues.

Cary noted that while Aaron wrote the adventures of Pumper Dumper, they were actually drawn by someone else. The artist, Bill Murphy, and Aaron had been friends since kindergarten, where Aaron would think up tales and Bill would draw pictures. They drifted apart after Bill got married, but Bill's wife had a friend they introduced to Aaron. Love bloomed. I asked for the contact information of the girlfriend, Suzy Lujon.

Suzy Lujon was slightly plump with round glasses and limp blond curls. She was the classic fix-up, but with Aaron Frobish it seemed to have worked out, right up until the minute I broke the news. I wish I could have done something for her besides saying how sorry we were for her loss. She revealed there were always people angry at Aaron. He'd showed her the threatening emails and letters he received. I asked her where the letters were and she said Aaron had a collection of them at his apartment.

Aaron's apartment was a Pumper Dumper museum. Framed issues were all over the wall. Two of the threatening letters had been framed too. The rest were in a desk drawer. Cary and I bagged them all to be printed, if the lab would cooperate.

When we returned to the station I finally heard from Burkoff. He grudgingly admitted that Cary had been right. Aaron Frobish had been poisoned with arsenic. There was still some in his stomach along with some sort of gummy candy. I called Suzy and she confirmed gummies were Aaron's passion.

Someone who actually knew Aaron must have poisoned him, because there were no online accounts of his taste in goodies. It made for a short suspect list. Cary checked out procedures for making gummies. After a few moments his song had an edge of annoyance. "We need more details from Burkoff. Some kinds of gummies have different ingredients. We can't trace them without knowing which gummies."

It was Friday night. I didn't expect anything from Burkoff anytime soon, which meant Cary and I might even get a weekend off, or at least part of one. It sounded like the same thing occurred to him. He invited me to watch Star Strider with him in the morning. Outside of work, it was one of the few things we did together. We traded turns coming up with breakfast. Last time I brought plain glazed doughnuts, the only kind he'll eat. He bakes.

The smell of fresh brewed coffee urged me through Cary's door. We settled at opposite ends of the couch with Cary's fresh fudgy muffins and coffee in front of us. Star Strider started.

In that episode, handsome Dirk Templeton and his pal Bosco Beaterman were aboard a new ship, The Rising Star, which was attacked by a space yacht. The captain of The Rising Star, Dorien Brayden, couldn't figure out why his ship was being attacked. He managed to engage the owner of the yacht, Povus Bolt, in negotiations while engineer Dirk souped up the engines for a getaway and weapons expert Bosco enhanced the ship's laser cannons.

Brayden found out the whole affair was a giant misunderstanding. Bolt's sister, Haddie, had stowed away on The Rising Star, mooning over Dirk; who didn't even know she was aboard. Povus thought Dirk was some space-going lowlife who took his sister for ransom, or worse. Everything was straightened out when Dirk told Haddie that he would love to have her with him, but a vagabond engineer has to travel light. He eased her disappointment with a sweet goodbye kiss, and the final credits rolled.

It was eleven A.M. Monday before Burkoff's report came in. Cary sang his conclusion. "We need to look at the credit card charges of the suspects." He pointed to a few tiny shapes in Burkoff's photos that fit together to make gold gummy bears. Cary showed me a recipe. There were specialized ingredients like 250 bloom gelatin. If we could find a list of credit card charges matching those ingredients, we could have our killer. Cary quickly scanned the records when they arrived. "Suzy's brother David did it," he trilled with no joy in his tone.

A search of David Lujon's apartment didn't take long to turn up all the ingredients for gold bears. We arrested him and his lawyer proposed a deal. Cary and I watched through the one-way mirror of the interrogation room as David told his story to the A.D.A.. David saw Aaron Frobish as a childish loser who lived in a fantasy world peopled by super heroes. David thought Aaron would be his sister's ruin and he needed to do something to save her.

Cary leaned his forehead against the glass as David gave his confession. Cary's words came sadly, without a musical note: "I see. I understand. Like Povus Bolt, but he got the ending all wrong."

PLAN B

PRESTON RANDALL

The homeless man sat propped up against the back of a park bench beneath the Golden Gate Bridge. It was after midnight and with clouds obscuring the moon and a low-lying mist off the water, he could barely see the massive iconic structure with its immense towers and huge looping coils of steel—the suspension lines fading into the distance across San Francisco Bay. He sipped from a bottle hidden inside a paper bag. Empties were strewn about the area; this was his favorite spot on fall evenings when it wasn't too cold. He still preferred the open air to the confines of the nearest shelter. Nope... nobody to tell you when to go to sleep or kick you out of bed in the morning. At least here he had a little freedom.

Taking another sip of "comfort" he noticed shapes moving towards him. He scurried away and slipped into nearby bushes. You can never be too careful. Last week some punks found him dozing, stole his booze and kicked him in the ribs until he was coughing blood—just for the hell of it. He heard police sirens in the distance. Nothing unusual about that on a Friday night.

"C'mon Peter, get your ass in gear," said a gravelly voice, deep-throated and guttural.

"Cripes Mike. I'm movin' as best I can. But my feet are killin' me."

"Will you guys quit bitchin, for god's sake! I think we're almost at the bridge. If we can just make it across we'll be free. Can't you taste it?" The shapes moved closer but he still couldn't see them clearly. Were there four of them? Suddenly they stopped.

"What the hell's that smell? Micky, I don't like this."

The four figures all turned at once directly towards the bush where the homeless man crouched in terror. "Please go away… please go away, " he whimpered. Then, surrendering, he raised his arms in the air and jumped out of the bushes, begging "PLEASE DON'T HURT ME!"

To his surprise, all four figures took off like a shot towards the edge of the water beneath the bridge. But before they left, he got one good look.

He scrambled to his feet and hurried towards the shelter about 5 minutes away.

Four hours earlier…

"You're sure this is going to work?"

"Of course not. But it's got to be better than rotting in here for the rest of our miserable lives. Besides, what's the worst that could happen? They drag our sorry asses back and we're in solitary for a while. Look, I'll go over it one last time… then we're going, okay?"

"I guess…"

"In about half an hour we go into the yard for our recreation break. There's going to be eight of us, as usual. Now I've already got the other guys on board, but they don't know, only the two of us are in on the full escape. We're going to use them as a diversion and get the hell out of here, for good."

"And just how did you convince these guys? They've been in here a lot longer than you and nobody's ever made a break for it."

"Let's say I've got skills. I was in a special program, you know, before they transferred me here. It was all about helping me communicate better. You know, show them how I felt about stuff. Some nice chick in a white labcoat asking me questions all day long. Drove me crazy… but I guess maybe something sunk in. I can't explain it exactly, but I feel different, smarter. That's also when I heard about wine country—about an hour or so north of the Golden Gate Bridge. The chick's boyfriend came in one day. They talked about heading up north to check out the wine, saying it was like paradise with all the vines loaded with grapes ripening in the sun, ready for harvest."

"It *sounds* great. But what about the guard?"

"I've got some rope hidden in the yard. We only need to tie him up and get the keys."

"What rope? You're not going to hurt—"

"Nobody's getting hurt! Just leave the guard to me."

"I don't know, man."

"And call me by my codename—Micky. And I'll call you Davy."

"If you say so."

"One more thing. We're picking up some "muscle" on the way out—two more guys."

"Why?"

"Trust me on this one. I've got it all worked out and we might need them for Plan B if something goes wrong. Now take a deep breath and get ready."

Thirty minutes later a violent outburst of noise erupted from the yard. Looking in, the guard saw four bodies writhing in convulsions near the centre of the area while four others yelled for help. Unholstering his taser, he quickly moved inside to check things out. But he was grabbed by four strong arms as soon as made it through the door and the taser yanked out of his hands. The others were upon the guard in an instant; a ball was stuffed into his mouth as a gag and a coil of rope tightly wound around his body. *Where did that rope come from?*

"I've got the keys!" yelled Micky. "Let's go."

They moved into the outer hallway and Micky went to the nearest cell door.

"What are you doing? They'll be on us in a minute!"

"Just the reason for another distraction," Micky replied with eerie calm. He opened the door. "C'mon, get up you lazy bastard. Freedom calls."

Dozing in the corner, the occupant cracked an eyeball open. "What's happening?"

"Get moving. We're making a break."

The cellmate rolled out of his bed, yawned, stretched and started slowly towards the door.

"Man, are you on drugs? Go!"

"Fast as I can brother, fast as I can."

"For cryin out loud, we gotta go." Micky and Davy scurried out.

"Only one more stop… the muscle," said Micky as they went through an emergency exit. The others rushed out behind him and immediately took off in all directions. *Perfect, that should keep them busy for a while*, he thought.

Keeping under cover, the two of them weaved around some small buildings and slipped inside through another emergency exit using the master key. Micky unlocked a cell door and called out. "Hey, let's go! This is it… HEY!"

Two large shapes emerged from the shadows.

"Whoa!" said Davy. "You weren't kidding about the muscle, were you?"

"Davy, say hi to Peter and Mike."

"Hi…guys…"

Silence.

"Okay, we don't have to be best friends or anything," said Micky. "Like I said, we've got eight miles to the bridge. From there, Davy and I are heading north to wine country and you're free to go… wherever. Just make sure if there's any trouble, well, you know what to do. And remember, we're the ones who got you out of this hellhole… so you owe us."

More silence.

"I'll take that as a yes, then. Let's go."

At the shelter…

The homeless man staggered to the entrance door and pressed the buzzer. The intercom crackled "Can I help you?"

"Rick, it's me… Joe. You gotta let me in."

"You know the rules, Joe. We're full up tonight. You've got to head over to—"

"No! Let me in, please! I saw something…"

"… sure… what did you see?"

"You're not gonna believe me, call the police. I gotta talk to somebody…"

"Police? Did those damn kids beat you again?"

"Call the police! I'm not kiddin."

"Okay. Okay already." The door clicked open.

Back at the bridge…

"That was close!" said Micky. "Did you get a whiff of that guy… I thought I was gonna puke!"

The sound of sirens was more distinct now… a lot of sirens. And they were getting closer.

"Micky, look up at the bridge. Looks like they've got the road blocked!"

Sure enough, red and blue lights flashed into the darkness at the near end of the bridge. There was no way to get through.

"I was afraid this might happen. Well, we have to get across. It's our only chance," said Micky. "Question is, are you guys up for it?"

Silence. Then the two giants hesitantly took a step or two towards the water, and looked back over their shoulders. More lights appeared to be approaching on the roadway leading to the park under the bridge. They waded into the water, and waited.

"This is it, Davy. It's time for Plan B. Just remember, hang on no matter what."

They walked into the water together. Sirens blared as the car lights pierced the fog, ever closer. Only seconds away now. Four cars skidded to a stop on the roadway some thirty feet away. Doors flew open and the officers leapt out into position. Two men with rifles took aim. But it was too late.

"Damnation!" said one of the men. "Hold your fire. They're already too far out. We'll have to set up on the other side."

The next day...

After a hot breakfast provided by the staff, Joe left the shelter early the next day. Those were the rules; no hanging around. But he didn't mind. It wasn't too bad outside and he preferred the open air anyway. Too many damn rules inside. He walked back to his favorite park under the bridge; maybe there was still something left in the bottle he dropped when he saw... them. He walked towards the bench and noticed another early riser had left the morning newspaper. Sitting down, he raised his face to the breeze and drank in the salty air. There was still a good mist over the water. What a feeling. He picked up the paper and with wide eyes read the lead story, complete with pictures of the very spot where he sat.

The Great Escape

Officials from the San Francisco Zoo are in the hot-seat as four animals are still missing after last night's security breach. Apparently one of the handlers was overpowered inside the Primate enclosure at approximately 7 p.m. The handler was found in the centre of the new interactive play zone, secured by a rope that had somehow come loose from the popular "swinging tire" the primates interacted with. The handler is currently suspended pending further review, as he apparently also neglected to lock the door to the South American sloth exhibit. Fortunately the sloth, perhaps one of the slowest-moving of the mammals, was retrieved without resistance just steps outside the open door of his habitat enclosure.

Eight adult male chimpanzees were recovered from the zoo grounds within a few hours of the breach. But the location of two additional chimpanzees is still unknown. They were last seen in the vicinity of the park below the south end of the Golden Gate Bridge, as wildlife officers attempted to sedate the animals with tranquilizer darts.

Two large adult male polar bears are also still unaccounted for. The bears are known to be exceptional swimmers and residents near the water on both sides of the bridge have been notified to keep all pets and children inside until further notice. Police reported an unusual number of 911 calls from people claiming to have seen the bears swimming under the bridge "with chimps clinging to their backs." Officials immediately refuted these stories as ridiculous and warn any further waste of emergency resources will be subject to prosecution and heavy fines.

Somewhere in wine country...

"Hey Davy. Peel me another grape, will ya?"

"Ha ha, very funny. Do it yourself. By the way, what was the deal with the code names anyway... you never said?"

"Just a little joke. This kid used to come in with his dad every weekend and watch us playing in the yard, remember?"

"Sure, every Saturday. So what?"

"I heard them talking about some old rock band that used to have their own TV show. The dad was pointing at us and telling the kid we reminded him of this show for some reason."

"... and..."

"The four guys in it were Micky, Davy, Peter and Mike. They were called The Monk—"

"Yeah, but we're not—"

"I know, but that's what makes it so funny."

"I don't get it."

"I'll explain it later. Have another grape."

GO EASY ON THE SCOTCH

DOUG ROBBINS

"Go easy on the scotch, Jed," Norma pleaded.

"For crying out loud," Jed muttered. "You sound like a broken record."

"You promised me you'd quit drinking," Norma said.

"I have; I just need it for tonight. Then baby, I'm off the stuff forever," Jed's eyes never left his glass.

"You're going throw up tonight. Is that what you want, Jed? To throw up on the people in the front row? That'll certainly impress Mr. Stickler, won't it? I'm sure he'll invite you back to be a feature after that." Norma squeezed her husband's arm.

"Norma, please," Jed begged.

"I just want you to make a good impression, okay?" Norma's voice softened.

He put his hand on hers. "I know. Don't you worry; tonight is gonna mark the beginning of a brand new Jed Golding." Jed's voice shook a bit, but overall, he sounded fairly confident.

"I'm going to the store. Need anything while I'm gone?" Her gray eyes shimmered.

"Nope. I'm just gonna catch a little nap before I go."

Jed staggered off to bed. When he awoke, a piercing headache greeted him. "Shit," he thought, reaching for the Tylenol on his night stand.

He popped it in his mouth and choked down the pill, gagging a

270

little. An hour before the show, Jed sat in his dressing room in front of a mirror, adjusting his bowtie. He kept glancing at the reflection of the dummy, sitting on the couch. "You better behave yourself tonight," warned Jed. "Ya hear me, Buddy?"

"Yeah, yeah," the dummy answered.

"I don't want a repeat of Denver. You got me?" Jed asked.

"Relax, pal. That broad was a lush. She fell. Not my fault, and not your fault," Buddy the dummy's voice came out sounding smooth.

Jed shuddered, remembering that terrible night. He remembered hearing the screams, as he exited the bathroom. He ran over and discovered his date had fallen over the railing on the hotel balcony where he had been staying that night.

The detective had deduced that she had fallen and was not pushed. No charges were ever brought against Jed. A knock on his dressing room interrupted the ventriloquist's trip down nightmare lane. "They're ready for ya," the voice said.

"Be right out, Sam," Jed called to his stage manager.

He walked over to the dummy, picking him up and scanning the doll over with his eyes. "It's show time."

The dim stage lighting caused Jed to squint. "Buddy, don't we have a lovely audience here this evening?" Jed asked.

Scanning the audience, the dummy said with an air of sarcasm, "not bad for a fish market."

The audience laughed.

"That's not very nice," Jed corrected the dummy, narrowing his eyes, almost glaring at the wooden perpetrator. "These are a fine group of people; if you don't behave, I'm gonna turn you into kindling."

"The cops will lock you up for murder," Buddy replied.

"It's not against the law to burn a dummy," Jed answered.

"I meant your jokes are so bad, they are actually killing comedy." Buddy tossed back his head, letting out a long donkey laugh.

Jed rolled his eyes. "You really think you're a funny guy. Don't you?"

"You're the funny one," hissed Buddy.

"Oh? You think so?" Jed asked.

Buddy nodded. The fact that you think your jokes are actually funny. You're a riot!'"

The crowd laughed uproariously.

Jed took a final bow before exiting the stage. Sam greeted him backstage. "You did it! Mr. Stickler made you a feature performer!"

"That's marvelous," Jed said, wrapping his stage manager in a big bear hug. "Wait till I tell Norma!"

When Sam walked away, Jed whispered to his wooden partner. "We did it, Buddy. You really came through for me tonight, pal."

"Easy chum," insisted Buddy. "If you were a St. Bernard, I'd understand the drooling. Get ahold of yourself, man."

He began to dress in the finest suits. Norma dressed in pearls and wore big extravagant fur coats. Jed worked twice a day, six days a week, taking Sundays off. One night after a show, Jed and Norma headed straight upstairs. Casually before a night of passion, carelessly, Jed tossed the dummy casually on the couch.

The next day, Jed found the dummy had destroyed the living room. Couch cushions were strewn about the room and were sliced open with a knife. Chairs were overturned. The television was smashed and was still smoking. When Norma came into the room, her eyes nearly exploded out of her skull. "What went on in here?"

"The damn dummy did this?" Jed said, shaking his head.

"The what?" Norma asked.

"The dummy's alive," Jed replied. "He's alive and he's trouble."

"Oh no," Norma replied. "You aren't serious; are you?"

"Of course I'm serious," Jed studied his wife's face.

She embraced him. "Oh Jed. I thought we were through with this."

"Through with what?" Jed wore a mask of puzzlement.

"You mean you don't remember?"

"Remember what?" Asked Jed, growing increasingly more agitated.

"You're having another episode," Norma searched frantically for the phone.

"An episode?" Jed's face grew increasingly flustered. "What the Hell is that supposed to mean?"

"Calm down, Jed," Norma stated, her voice hinting at undertones of panic. "I'm calling Dr. Miller now."

"Who's Dr. Miller?" Jed said, lunging for his wife, speaking in Buddy's voice.

He seized her by the throat, strangling her till death. He was institutionalized. Dr. Miller stood outside his cell, discussing Jed's case with a nurse.

"You mean he's killed before?" The nurse asked.

"Oh yes. Twice now," Dr. Miller's voice was gruff. "The first one was a mistress; the second being his wife."

"What'd he kill the women for?" The nurse's face contorted in a disguise of horror.

"The mistress he killed because she threatened to tell the wife about the affair, after he threatened to break off the affair." Dr. Miller rubbed his chin.

"And the wife?" The nurse's eyes widened, whispering.

"Part of the delusion he created with the mistress," Dr. Miller said.

"Delusion?" The nurse uttered a confused whisper.

"Feeling guilty that he had murdered someone, he developed a split personality." Dr. Miller's words cut like knives.

"Split personality?" The nurse's brown eyes caught the fluorescent lighting.

"Indeed. You remember me telling you he was a ventriloquist?"

"Yes?"

"Well… In his own mind, Jed wanted to erase the crime. Alleviate the guilt. He blamed the dummy. He even grew to believe the dummy was alive. Seemed to be rehabilitated, but I guess not. It's a pity."

"That's awful," the nurse gazed in at Jed, feeling a strange kind of sympathy for him.

"He was a damn fine ventriloquist," Dr. Miller grunted. "Damn fine."

THE ROOM KEY

T. HUDSON ROBERTS

The stunning figure caught my eye as soon as I entered the cavernous atrium of the Florence Hotel. It was the most striking grand piano I'd ever seen. As I soft-stepped toward that wondrous black Baldwin, nervousness began to seep through my skin. I felt like a virgin teen hesitantly on his way to pluck the petals of a willing cheerleader. Although I was an actual "*virgin teen*," I was more than ready to pluck away at that sexy musical beast which seemed to call out to me as I drew near.

Within a few breaths and a sigh, I planted myself comfortably on the cushioned piano bench and slowly opened the creature's mouth, gazing at its glimmering black and white teeth—some sharp— some flat; so beautiful was she, a glorious being to behold. I managed to slip away from the awe that haunted me, and raised my hands up high then slowly brought them down gracefully, inducing a burgeoning tune.

A clutter of piano keys clashed, and hammered out melodious notes that resonated throughout the atrium. The instigator was I, a hired pianist, a minute into the gig. Normally, I'd just call myself a piano player. But "*pianist*" had that touch of sophistication ... unless one didn't enunciate.

My arms flailed in nearly all directions, as my fingers tapped softly and stomped, slid and tan- goed, over the black and white dance floor of piano keys, emitting music, music, music. I was flying, never played better. I was certainly in that Liberace zone, showcasing my mastery over the black Bald- win. I saw no vivid images, for my peripheral vision stretched from one side to another. Only a blank- et of faint light fronted my eyes, sheltering the bliss that romped to and fro within the spiritual patch of perfection. I could do no wrong as the Baldwin sang full and flush.

Handel and Wagner smiled proudly from beyond; if only they knew that my skin ran dark, their smiles might've gone limp. Oh, forgive me, masters, for I am but a youth! A youth in that Liberace zone! Fly, fingers, fly!

Then it happened.

A feminine hand wafted gracefully within my elongated peripheral and released a large key with a room number on it. The key clacked loudly on the Baldwin's shoulder, spitting an incongruous sound that twisted my ear, thwarting the display of perfection. My fingers instantly surrendered to error and mercilessly smashed into unrelated piano keys that screeched out hideous notes, piercing the air with a clang, clunk, and a clink; forbidden, nightmarish notes, unfriendly to the human ear—sort of like Jazz.

As I flushed with embarrassment, I tailed the receding hand to a lovely, sensual being. A vision of such beauty that lust, desire, and pain, grasped at my loins and thumping heart. Her soft, mysterious countenance hinted a score of years past her youth, though the curves from her body formed a seem ingly younger woman—a siren who induces the lascivious yearnings of young men. But wait! A ring- less woman! Could it be? Yes! The much desired—Divorcée!

My gaze followed the lining of her glittered red gown that draped over her body, taut and so al- luring. Slowly, my eyes began to raise, embracing the perfection of her feminine curvature. Then, as if lassoed from behind, my sight jerked abruptly to a skidding halt. Cleavage! That glorious valley where all men wished to smother themselves. Well, nearly all men. I was raised in San Francisco. Suddenly, I didn't have the power to look away, few men could, and certainly not I. I was just a lowly piano player … I mean, penis. No, pianist! Alas, the valley made me flustered. The woman smiled at my weakness and shot a targeting glance at her room key lying next to my tip jar. The next instance, her gaze met mine, but only for a heartbeat or two. Then without a word, she slipped away with swaying hips and headed toward the elevators. I reluctantly lifted my gaze from the woman's backside and returned my attention to her room key.

Since my dear mother, bless her soul, had surely raised a gentleman (*though she gave up on the scholar thing*), I tapped into that less-than-stellar upbringing and snatched up the key and stood tall. I raised my arm to flag the woman down. But before I had let out a blow of my voice, an old man who had been enjoying my piano playing (*until I'd clanged, clunked, and clinked*), stole my gaze.

He shook his head and rolled his eyes.

Why did the old fart do that? I was indeed puzzled. I immediately shrugged off the old man's wordless gesture as folly and returned my focus to the woman's backside ... I mean, to the woman.

"Oh, ma'am! Excuse me, ma'am!" I shouted as my voice resounded throughout the atrium. The woman swung around to meet my gaze once again.

I lifted the room key high, pinching its end with two fingers. "Ma'am, you left your room key!" I declared loudly, thinking I had saved the day.

The woman gave me an exhausted countenance. The old man did, too. Dumbfounded, I thought I'd receive a grateful look or at least a relieving sigh.

The woman stomped toward me and dropped a plank of an arm, fingers spread wide. I gently placed the key in her hand.

She then hit me hard with a high-pitched harrumph, before giving me an insincere "*Thank you.*" The woman promptly made a final turn and once again forged toward the elevators.

After I espied her backside yet again, I looked to the old man who was still shaking his head.

What did I do wrong? Wasn't I just trying to be a gentleman? *Uh oh ... wait a minute.* A beautiful wo- man had accidentally dropped her room key on ... no, deliberately dropped her room key on the piano, and ... my naiveté finally gave way to a lumbering wit.

"Wait! Ma'am, don't go! Gimme back your room key! I get it now! I—"

In an instant, an elevator shut its door, truncating my plea. She was gone. I couldn't believe it. A sexy, gorgeous woman was more than willing to allow me to explore her wondrous valley, and I blew it. Oh, mother, why didn't you prepare me for this day? Why did you give up on the scholar thing?

Then surely I would've figured out that woman's ingenious attempt to seduce me. *Boy, I must be the dumbest of the dumb.*

Dejected, I slumped back down on the piano bench and played the Baldwin with mediocrity slushing from my fingers. No more did the piano sing; no more did my fingers fly; and no more was I in that Liberace zone.

I was just a soulless tinkerer of music with an ever-slanting eye for a particular room key.

NEON DOUG

JONATHON ROBINSON

5

Marty stumbled through the doors, rain dripping off the neon sign above him. *The New Millennium* it said, the building's windows boasting half-off drinks, live music, and a weekly "ladyz" night. He'd just turned thirty-two.

The night was warm and dark, muggy from the summer storms. Marty's six-foot figure wobbled for balance against the brick wall of the glowing bar. He was wet with sweat and rain, wiping his eyes with the tattooed fingers of his left hand, and scratching his translucently blonde head with the other. The world smelled of alcohol, city sewage, and smoke - nicotine clouds still lingering from the exhales of two nearby strangers.

Marty coughed and kicked a piece of wet, grey gravel, turning away from *The New Millennium*. Behind him the doors of the bar creaked open. Marty glanced back at the noise. His face fell.

"Where ya' going, Mart?" said a deep, but shaky voice, wrinkled like skin.

Marty turned to face the *Millennium*, his voice stiff.

"Douglas. Just leave, man. Seriously, just go home, or wherever," he said.

"Leave? Man, you know I ain't got nowhere to go. I mean, where,

Mart? Where'm I gonna go?" said Douglas.

"Don't even want to know. But, just go. Get away from me," said Marty.

Douglas was tall, but just short of matching Marty. He was a silver fox: older, handsome, his greying hair combed back in waves. His brows were thick and led straight to a wry twist in his lips, a polite smile only made suspect when paired with his green eyes, crystalline and penetrating.

"Away? Where, buddy. How'm I gonna get there?" said Doug.

"Please, please just leave me. It's been so long, now. Please just go," said Marty.

4

Standing kitty-corner to *The New Millennium* was a couple, a man and a woman. They were exiting a small Italian restaurant, laughing, leaning on each other, swaying back and forth to the residual croons of *Dean Martin* just barely heard outside of the restaurant's closed doors. The woman had on a blush dress, sleeveless, cut like an upside-down "v" descending from her neckline and it flowed with each breeze of hot, summer air. The man had tight, curly hair and wore a white shirt, unbuttoned two-down, with blue pants. The woman had marinara sauce on her dress, and they couldn't help but chuckle.

"Let's head to the car, babe," he said, his eyes darting towards a commotion near *The New Millennium*. Her face sunk for a moment, uneasy, noticing a blonde man in a black shirt - Marty. He was speaking loudly, not yelling,and alone across the street.

"Is he talking to us?" she said.

"I have no idea," he said, looking down at her, half-smiling as if to reassure her of their safety, "he's drunk, probably. I don't know. Talking to no one."

3

Marty noticed the man and the woman, running his fingers through his hair, both hands this time, moving together over his face and onto his scalp. While his hands rested on the top of his head, he looked towards the man and the woman, noticing the sway of her dress and her marinara stain, and the nonchalant demeanor of the man. Marty watched him swing the keys to his car around his middle finger like a revolver. The man and the woman walked down the side-walk, kicking a broken pebble of cement back and forth to each other. In that moment, Marty stared, transfixed by their departing visages disappearing down the street - vapors of a life he'd never known.

"You want it, dont ya?" said Douglas, looking over at Marty.

Marty didn't reply. His cheek twitched and he traced his steps backward again, towards Douglas, nearly through him and right back into *The New Millennium*.

2

The man and the woman were now approaching their car: black, smooth, European, and low-to-the-ground. He was flashing its lights with multiple presses of the unlock button as he stepped in front of the woman to open the passenger door. He waved her in like a chivalry-not-dead motion, closing the door with care, ensuring she was fully within the vehicle. And as he walked around to the driver's side he heard a voice:

"Hey buddy, you got a light? You know how it is, right?"

The man looked up, seeing an older figure in front of him.

"Uh, sorry, man, I don't. Don't have one. Sorry," he said, pulling open his door.

"Good for you. Good, good. Look, you have a dollar or two, then? I mean, you know how it is. Gotta get a light. One of those nights, ya know?" said the older figure. He had wavy, grey hair.

"Okay, sure. A 'fiver' do it? Here," said the man, pulling out a five-dollar bill, and reaching over the ajar driver-side door.

"God bless ya', brother. Good. Thank you. Really owe you one," said the older figure.

"Alright now. Have a good night," said the man, sitting onto his seat.

"Thank you, friend. Owe ya' one. And, the name's Douglas. I got you."

1

The man closed his door and started the car. He smiled small, about to kiss the woman on her cheek before driving away from the sidewalk. But she pulled away briefly, her eyes half shut, a crevice between her lips and her head tilted right.

"Who were you just talking to?" she said.

"What?" he said.

"Nobody's there," she said, searching past the windshield.

And outside, amidst the glowing hum of neon buzz, Douglas lit a cigarette, his eyes vapid - haunting - and his smile slant. It started to rain again.

A LITTLE PEENCH

MARK ROBYN

"Okay, you're going to feel a little pinch. Raise your hand if it hurts too much and I'll stop."

"Yess, Doktor."

"Almost done, just a little more. We want you good and numb… there, that's it. Now we'll give you a little rinse and some suction."

Gurgle, gurgle, gurgle…

"Okay, now we'll let that start to work. You just sit back and relax. You want a magazine?"

"No tank you, Doktor. I vill just close my eyes and rest."

"Sounds reasonable. I wish I were getting some. I don't normally come in at night for patients, but you said your tooth hurt so badly you couldn't wait."

"I am so tankful, Doktor. You are a vunderful man."

"Yeah, well, you did say you'd pay me double. How's it feel? Are you getting good and numb?"

"It feels dead, Doktor."

"Good. Let's get this over with then shall we? Open wide. When I tap here, can you feel anything?"

"No, it feels vunderful."

"Good. My, what a happy little dungeon you have here. Gums are pretty white; almost look like a corpse. You definitely have some gum

281

disease developing, fella. You brushing and flossing everyday?"

"Not as often as I should, Doktor."

"Uh-huh. I could tell. You look anemic all over. You getting enough sunlight?"

"I'm afwaid I'm up mostly at night, Doktor."

"Thought so. The sun won't hurt you, fella. Take a day off and get outside. And what's your diet like? Getting enough red meat and dairy? Can't live on sweets, you know."

"I mostly enjoy a liquid diet, Doktor."

"Not good, my friend; not good at all. But it's your life. Okay, I'm gonna start drilling. You shouldn't feel anything, just a slight pressure and a lot of noise. You raise your hand if it bothers you."

Rrrr. Rrrr. Rrrrrrrr. Rrrrrr. Rrrrrr.

"Deep one we have here. When's the last time you came in for a check-up, mister?"

"Ages ago."

"I can tell. Hey, these incisors are a little sharp. They're almost like fangs. No wonder you're on a liquid diet. They must make it hard to eat. You want me to grind 'em down a little for you?"

"No tank you, Doktor. I like them just da vay day are."

"Suit yourself."

Rrrr. Rrrr. Rrrrrrrr. Rrrrrr. Rrr. Rrr.

"Doktor, what is that smell?"

"Sorry, I had pizza for lunch. It's the garlic."

"Oooh…"

"Just a little more, almost got it."

"Uhh…"

"You feeling that?"

"Uhh…"

"Hang in there, almost done…there. That's got it. Let's do a little more rinsing."

Gurgle, gurgle, gurgle…

"Now we'll mix her up and fill her in. You want me to match the other teeth I suppose? They're all a little yellow."

"Yes, Doktor."

"Okay. Say, that's a strange health insurance company you got, there, '*Transylvania Blue Coffin.*' Not '*Blue Cross*', eh?"

"I don't particularly like crosses, Doktor."

"I see. Here we go. Now we'll just heat this up a little to let it dry."

"Please hurry, Doktor. It is almost morning."

"Going as fast as I can. Besides, a little daylight won't kill you."

"You might be surprised, Doktor…"

"Now we'll smooth her out a little. You're going to feel a little vibration."

"Just hurry, Doktor…"

"No more pain?"

"It's vunderful, Doktor."

"Good. I aim to please. All done."

"How can I ever tank you, Doktor?"

"Just take care of those teeth. I really don't want to have to do this again."

"And you won't, Doktor…"

"By the way, I've never worked on royalty before. What did you say your name was again?"

"Count Dracula. Now Doktor, I will ask you to do someting. Look into my eyes…"

"Hey, what are you doing?"

"Relax, Doktor. You are going to feel a leetle peench…."

TEH CONCRETE ROSE

JASMYNE K. ROGERS

Addie Mae visited me last night. She looked nice too. *Real nice.*

She only stayed a short spell; I knew she had to return home. It was still good to see her. I missed her smiling face and her singsong voice. She always made everything all right. I made sure I tidied up my little place. The six dishes I owned were washed and drying on the kitchen rack. I finally hung up my medals from the war that I was in back in '71. I wanted her to see how well I had done for myself.

Things haven't always been this good. Granted, I didn't have a big house and a lot of money, but I had my sobriety and a place to call my own. A *place* to call my own. An *apartment* to call my own. A *home.* I finally had a home. Every night while the waxed candle burned, I prayed for the Lord to allow me to see Addie Mae Dithers one more time.

I remember it like I remember where to place the concrete rose every year;the day I saw Addie outside on Denver Avenue. She was humming a little tune. I clutched my hat that had given me hell from the fierce wind blowing. She sat on a bench in the small park area, across the street from *Jackson's Soul Food.* I was to the left of her, just getting off the greyhound bus. I had just got back into town. The war was still cinematic in my mind. She got into it a little bit. Her humming produced a rhythmic head bob that invited her fingers to join in. I was happy at the sight of her. After a few minutes, she caught onto my stares.

"Well, I declare," She said, all the while chuckling. I faintly smiled. I wasn't sure if Addie Mae remembered me. I had been gone for all of ten years. I was on base a year in Florida, two years in Virginia, three in North Carolina, and the rest spent fighting in combat over in Vietnam. Before that, I was here on Denver Avenue. I stayed down the street from the small park—round the three black cherry trees, across the old baseball field, and next to the abandoned shoe shop. Every Thursday, me and some other menfolk would go over to Joe and Addie's.

Joe is her husband. He was a good friend of mine. He always helped everyone and anyone in need, especially Addie Mae. Me, Jimbo, Arch, and Cap would gather on their porch around six and have a real good time playing cards and just talking. It felt good to just talk on a Thursday evening. We were Thursday men. We lived for Thursday after the hard hours we put in at the factory for that week. Addie would sit with her legs crossed in the rocker talking to kids in the neighborhood or to some of her women friends. We would carry on and have a festive time. We were just some backwards people, as the folk from the North say. We spent our teens and twenties protesting and advocating, and the elder years partying and enjoying the gift of life. Addie Mae always smiled, even when there was nothing worth smiling about. Just like the day I saw her sitting on the bench when I got back home.

She was smiling like normal. She had her right hand on her hip by the time I gathered her in my arms. "Paul, you finally made it back. I was beginning to worry about you," she shook a playful finger at me. "After ten years, now you starting to worry? I reckon your worrying got you sitting on this bench waiting for me to come back."

Her smile changed a bit. It was swift, but I noticed it. She got silent. Something had changed since I've been gone. The trees were the same, the cars passing had changed with modern times, but the wind was different. Addie Mae was different. She was still sweet and kindhearted, but she was harboring a hurt. Things were silent for a minute. A silence I regret I had to break.

"Where's my partner in crime? Where's Joe? I'm sure he's not too fit with you sitting on this park bench alone."

A tear danced down her cheek. It was such a sad dance. My eyes zoomed in on that single tear. I had never seen Addie shed a tear. Not even when a gun was shoved in her face when we were protesting for liberal education on the old shoe shop front. Not even when Addie and Joe wanted to have kids and found out the doctors had sterilized her without her permission, when she only went in for surgical removal of a cyst the size of a peanut. Never in my days had I seen a woman like Addie cry.

"Joe died," She said, sitting back down on the bench. "About five years ago."

The wind became fiercer.

"Let's walk home, Addie," I said. "This is my home," she said matter-of-factly. "Right here on this concrete."

"You're talking foolishness, woman," I said trying to pull a joke from somewhere. It was surely needed.

"I'm afraid not. They tore down all the houses on our block for the new highway you just traveled on. The old neighborhood is gone."

I began to shed tears that had begged to flow since the day I saw my comrades killed in battle, with their limbs strewn and thrown before my very eyes. Everything had changed. Not only did Addie lose her house, I lost mine as well.

One thing I didn't lose was her confidence in me. We held on to each other that day. I was thankful for that. Thankful I still had my dear friend from the old neighborhood. I blew out the candle and turned over on my side. I'm glad she stopped by.

This time I was able to keep her warm.

CARRYING YOU & THE END OF MY EXISTENCE IN FIVE PARTS

KATHRYN H. ROSS

Carrying You

The hardest part is pretending. Walking with your words in my pockets and hidden in my palms, nail marks against the skin from clenching my fists when seized with a vision of how it felt that day when you gently held me, one armed, through our sweaters outside the door. I wanted to leave so I could be with you, something so unlike me, but I didn't say so, I didn't even suggest it. Instead I wrapped both arms around you and held on and breathed in your scent. And I thought, I thought, I thought this was too good to be true that you were too good to be true and remembered, briefly, how I've always had the problem of being right when I wanted to be wrong. You walked away and I watched you feeling the warmth your body had left against mine, intermingled now with the fibers of my sweater, caught and held on my skin – had I known what tomorrow would bring I would never have washed them away.

I drew your face in next to notes on the ethnic American novel. It wasn't any good but it made me smile because it looked enough like you, held enough of your presence, to quicken my heart. I couldn't quite get your bones, how they sculpt and mold from underneath, just right. I couldn't get your lips, your smile, the simplicity of your beauty. And then, fearing someone might see, might somehow recognize you through the mistakes over my shoulder, I erased it.

That night I felt beautiful. I smiled at my reflection, imagined myself as you, seeing myself through your eyes, seeing myself as you made me believe I was. You never said it, but you made me feel it, all over, from my head to my toes, you made me feel it without a word, without ever touching an inch of me. Your eyes always said it, again and again:

beautiful, beautiful, beautiful, beautiful ..

Next morning and it's unseasonably warm. Arms crossed, my mirror, you stood away from me, awkwardly, like a child in a crowd of strangers. My father used to tell me I asked too many questions, so many questions, that one day I'd get an answer I didn't like, an answer I couldn't handle. But I asked. I asked you. And with eyes not quite meeting mine you told me. I could almost see the butterflies, frantic, in your stomach. Could almost feel the adrenaline urging you to run away. But you stayed with me. Stayed until the very last moment. Stayed until I turned, released you, reaching for my car door.

You asked a question, looking like you would have hugged me again, the same way, if I had let you. Arms crossed, eyes down, voice low, I answered you—and you walked away, hesitant and slow, like you were forcing yourself, and you didn't look back. I can't blame you; you knew me well enough to know what you would have seen had you looked. In the car, a wounded animal – I wailed and ached, letting all the sorrow funnel out—broken pianos hitting octaves with hammers and knives. I thought about how you looked as you walked away–hair glistening in the sunlight, body rigid, tight, uncomfortable.

I try to forget but I can't. I remember. I remember. All the days, all the times, all the words, all the expressions that said what you did not. You still hold me; I still hold you. Not in the same way—warm and gentle through our sweaters—but cautious, scared to shatter, to break.

Chinaware in each other's arms.

The End of My Existence in Five Parts.
I.
The earth is blind. I've seen its milky pupil, detached, orbiting, a piece scooped out and placed to watch, to stare idly at the world while it floats in its clear blue iris. I've seen it tethered to the back of my car, following me over hills and into valleys. It doesn't know me, or that I

am here, but I imagine it can feel me and my heartbeat as I roll over the manmade streets, pound the artificial pavement, lie in the grass until our lungs match, breaths in gasping unison. Every morning and every night I stare into that blind eye, but I know it can't see me, know the earth doesn't know me. I am only another human without knowledge enough to explain why I am alive.

II.

On warm nights I sleep outside. I lie in the dirt and gaze at the earth's eye, bright and metallic, blankly watching over all of nature, all of time. I whisper to the earth as I sit under the stars— whisper and think about how something so vast and so beautiful cannot see itself. I can feel my eyes burning, can feel tears running down my face and falling into the dirt. I think of the earth's tears and how I've never seen them leaking from its cobweb eye. But I've felt them. I've bathed in them, drank them, danced in them. Still, the earth can't see me; but I wish it knew my face, could read my features, and know all that's underneath.

III.

There are moments when I touch the earth, dip my hands deep into its soil and feel the water, the blood, the amniotic fluid of life swirling around my fingers. I feel the earth pulsing, its heartbeat, its lungs, working slowly, steadily, against mine. Tonight I hold soil in my hands, feel it caked under my nails as I try to sleep with my eyes wide open, to understand what it is to be the earth, to see and feel and know all while seeing and feeling and knowing nothing beyond the fact that, here, I exist.

IV.

The earth trembles beneath me; it speaks. Its whisper is loud, yet indiscernible. Our heartbeats race against each other, waiting, and I grip the soil as the sky shakes above me. The air is burning, all dry ice and fever; the quaking grows, expands, until I am thrown across the dark lawn and land with the scent of damp dirt and grass rushing into my nostrils. The cobweb eye blinks; I hear the earth take a deep breath and the sound of its exhalation hits me before it shakes apart.

V.

The ground rips open, swallows me. The blind eye looks at me—*sees* me—as the earth closes above me, rolls over like a body repositioning in sleep. In the darkness every sound of every living thing becomes magnified. Hearts beat collective. Lungs inhale, exhale, inhale, exhale—all at once. And the earth shakes, and shakes, and shakes until I am torn apart and reminded inexplicably of the womb, a reverse birth where I am reabsorbed into mother and I become

THE GREAT BANDINI

PHIL ROSSI

Space travel was a rich man's game and astronauts didn't hail from our side of the tracks. That's why my friends and I never missed a Bandini rocket launch--main events full of fanfare and the hope one of us would beat the odds and reach outer space.

Instead, Bandini's rockets would implode on the pad or burst apart mid-flight. Just when you thought no man could survive a real space wreck, Bandini appeared in the sky, parachuting back to earth in his safety module.

All the kids looked past the failures and loved Bandini for his guts and theater, rooting him on for glory. Not the grownups. They'd rush the box office, demanding refunds. The gang always told Bandini to keep our money and build himself another rocket.

Once the firemen doused the infernos and flatbeds drug away the debris, Bandini would return to the foundry and construct his next spaceship. Talk about a gamer. My pa called him a huckster. Can't say we saw eye to eye on that one.

Bandini was our rock star, sports legend, and superhero all rolled into one larger-than-life astronaut. Too young to connect the dots of rocket science, not the passion of space travel. If Bandini's dreams devoured him, what chance did we have of growing up and leaving the ghetto? Bandini had to reach the cosmos.

Let the snobs poke fun at Bandini and dismiss his gusto as folly. The all-show-no-go rocket man inspired every kid from our neck of town, driving the courage to dare death and fight for a dream.

When the next rocket emerged, Bandini kept the mission a secret. No radio spots, no crowds. I knew all about it because we were friends and helped Bandini pick out used parts in the rocket yards, welded planks and beams to his launch pad. Even got the aviator bug myself, jonesing to be a test pilot.

"Hey kid, I'm trying to get to outer space, not death row," Bandini said.

On the night of the big flight, I helped Bandini prep the bird. Once we finished, he ordered me home. I protested before doing as told. I tipped the gang to sneak from our cribs and meet up.

We reached the hill that overlooked the launch pad, set up like a hangman's station, the chrome rocket, anchored at the ready.

The gallery watched Bandini swagger across the flight deck in his space suit and oxygen helmet. He boarded the vessel and buckled himself in. Once he spotted the fan base, Bandini waved and gave us a thumbs up. A raucous cheer erupted from our side of the slope, waving back.

Bandini gripped the butterfly wheel and looked over his dials. When he struck the boosters, lava gushed from the jets. The rocket yanked free of the harness and pitched for the dreaming sun.

As the rocket climbed, it

CLOWNING'S

JOE RUSSO

My parents met twenty years ago in a little town called Clowning's. I'm not kidding. They both grew up there, they fell in love there and sooner or later they gave birth to me there. You see, everyone in Clowning's was, is, or feels like a clown. The only problem is... I'm terrified of clowns.

It all started at my fifth birthday party when our next-door neighbor, Ms. Smiley Sol, suggested she perform the Clowning's birthday song. My parents were not singers, but natural born clowns that followed after the steps of their parents and their parents before them. They agreed. They sat me down in front of the cake, a small boy clown figure perched on top, and Ms. Smiley Sol came up behind me, clasped her hands over my eyes and whispered in my ears, "From each and every clown here in Clowning's we wish you the most happiest, clownest birthday day." She removed her hands, stepped in front of me, took out a flower lighter and lit the candles.

And something in me snapped. I screamed and screamed, kicking the chair out from under me. I pushed Ms. Smiley Sol into the cake, her lighter dropping onto the table and catching the little blue napkins aflame. She backhanded the flames with her white gloves three sizes too big, keeping a grin plastered onto her face. It reminded me of a character in a comic book. Parents started running about, grabbing their kids and a few even grabbed some presents from the present's table. *Bastards.*

I backed away, stepping on the feet of some of our neighbors like Mr. Rodney Miracles, our gardener. In pain he raised his foot in the air like he was doing a dance. I watched as Ms. Smiley Sol clapped her chest to extinguish the flames. My parents rushed over to her holding a small bucket and dumped water over their neighbor. Mom placed the bucket, after folding it in half, into her pocket. That trick still amazes me.

I got to the porch steps and sat down. The party nearly empty, Mr. Rodney Miracles was still doing his little dance and my parents still tried to clean up the mess. I didn't notice Ms. Smiley Sol staring at me, her grin turned into a frown.

Sixteen years later to the day, I'm sitting on the same step and think-ing about Ms. Smiley Sol, who wasn't injured, and Mr. Rodney Miracles who were both supposed to perform the Clowning's birthday song to me. I heard the back door open and my father stepped out, wearing his torn overalls and his orange wig.

"Hey, kiddo. Excited for today?"

"Not as much as you."

"Oh, come on kid. Its name day... Everyone loves name day!"

Name day. The day when every twenty-one year old in Clowning's gets his or her own clown name.

"Have you thought about names?"

I shake my head no. I watch as he places a big, bright and shiny red ball on the tip of his nose.

"Then we'll have to choose. And those names are pretty..." My father doesn't finish. His voice sounds nasally and for some reason it brings a grin to my face.

I know what he's getting at though. Names like Mrs. Happy Spar-kles, my third grade teacher, Mr. Happy Larry, the mailman or Mrs. Jo Giddy the Fourth, the mother to the girl I'm in love with.

"What if I don't want to be a clown?"

"Don't want to be a clown?" My father laughs. "Son, everyone's a clown. Do you want a good job like news reporter or politician?"

He was right. Mr. Happy Go Lucky had become the mayor of Clowning's three years ago and now he's running for congress.

"You have to get ready. The party starts in two shakes of a leg." I still don't understand what that means.

Twenty minutes later, my mother placed me in the same seat that I was in sixteen years ago. The cake, grown considerably bigger, had no blue clown boy standing atop it. Instead it had, HAPPY NAME DAY, written in blue icing.

The people, our friends, neighbors and mailman, started clapping. Ms. Smiley Sol starts to hum and places her hands over my eyes. She whispers, "From each and every clown here in Clowning's we wish you the most happiest, clownest birthday day." She removes her hands, turns and asks Mr. Rodney Miracles for a lighter. He hands it over. She pauses, just as she's about to light and asks, "Well, Ron do you have a name yet?"

I take a deep breath. I look over at my parents, smiling, my mother crying. Next to them are the Giddy's, Kat with her blonde hair shining, her eyes sparkling even with the heavy white makeup. I wondered how could I leave this behind? This life I was so accustomed to, this life I hated, this life I, somehow and some why, wanted.

"How about Mr. Ronnie Giggles?"

The party starts to clap and, once Ms. Smiley Sol lights the candles, my fate is sealed. Everyone started clapping and repeating my new name over and over again. Once again, I looked around at the parade of white faces looking back at me, like some sort of cruel joke, and once again, like it happened sixteen years ago, something inside me snapped.

I jump out of the chair, again pushing poor Ms. Smiley Sol into the cake and picked up the flower lighter that fell from her hands. She stands, whipping the pieces of white icing that stuck to her face at the crowd almost as if she was swatting at flies.

"Where you going, son?" My father asked.

"A short drive. I have to clear my head."

"Well… be back tonight. We have a special performance for you," My mother says.

The crowd stays still and silent. The postman looks through a bag marked HAPPY 16TH BIRTHDAY.

I wave my hand, yeah yeah, and leave the backyard, the party and my so-called friends. I head to the driveway, to the small red car parked next to three other small cars. I head to the first one I see. The keys, I bet, are still in the ignition because in Clowning's, everyone is free to use each other's stuff.

But not me, no, not me. I'll be Mr. Ronnie Giggles somewhere else. If only I can get this damn car started.

HUNGRY HEART

MARIE SCAMPINI

I went to that club with my only friend Emily on the 4th of July. I wore my vintage gold dragon dress and the highest heels I owned, also my only pair. Emily was always accidentally sexy in her conservative black blouse and skinny jeans. She was Audrey Hepburn-esque and she knew it, with her ballerina grace and giraffe height. She towered over me as I craned to glow in her shadow.

As we danced with each other I saw Dave walk in with his friend and stand at the bar drinking their beers.

I kept glimpsing him while twisting my hips, smiling as I lifted my orange juice in a champagne glass to my lips. I may have given him an actual wink or a tarantulan eyelash got stuck in my eye.

Dave finally walked up to me and took my hand. "Let's dance," he said. Emily felt abandoned until Dave's friend rescued her with a shy smile and offered her another drink.

"I thought you two were lipstick lesbians until you winked at me-- with your artsy outfits and all."

"We are," I laughed as he twirled me around. He laughed eventually, realizing I might have a sense of humor.

We went back to his friend's brownstone on the upper west side to watch the fireworks and started kissing. I melted into his racing heart's warm skin and we made it down to a spare bedroom to make love. He hesitated – no sex yet, let's wait.

Another date at his apartment in Brooklyn was his attempt at broke man's romance – he boiled spaghetti and opened a jar of marinara sauce. He didn't know I had the DNA of a great cook who made five-hour diablo sauce from the organic tomatoes that were exploding with plumpness in her garden. Not to mention flavored with powdered devils.

The one room shanty was cluttered with books. He taught at some college. His details were slim and I made a note to reread Thoreau's *On Walden Pond* if I ever went home. He blasted Bruce Springsteen on the stereo, which I never really listened to before. Bruce's raw and passionate voice fed the night and swallowed all other reality so nothing else existed.

He played my neck like that of a guitar and strummed me to a groaning hum as he tore off my T-shirt so that it could never be worn again.

We made love with the kind of perfect mix of timing and lust that made us exquisitely meant for each other. Hours later, I banished all tomorrows and would have been happy never to see daylight again. Just live in this night, this moment forever. Time capsule of ecstasy was being wrapped in his denim jacket.

But daylight showed up less angry than nonchalant and blaring Springsteen lyrics filled my head with dreams of the river banks we'd be drenched in, quenching each other's hunger until we would sink into the wet earth and become the wildflowers of our birth.

He was unsettlingly quiet as he kissed me good-bye. I took the most crowded and loneliest subway ride home. My skin felt peeled off, doused with acid, dissolving my former identity away.

The phone never rang again with his voice on the other end, and my calls to him went unanswered. Rivers of unanswered questions waterfalled into the Atlantic. I became just another tattered message in a broken bottle thrown in the ocean that only ghosts of seashells can translate into song. I floated among the shards of coral until the end of all sound then surrendered to my hungrier heart and drowned

THE UNDERHOUSE

MIKE SHERER

Gerald opened the small access door to the crawlspace beneath his house. Cool musty air gushed out, chilling him. He shined his flashlight into the dim haze. The sweeping beam illuminated pieces of scrap lumber, cinder blocks, plaster board, broken bricks, and the irregular piles of unshaped cement. He extended a tentative hand into the fringe, into an area well-lit by sunlight streaming in through the open door, and carefully grasped a short two by four. It felt unexpectedly light. Extracting the wood, he saw that it had been eaten through. He quickly dropped it.

"This is what got the termites started," the exterminator had informed him after his inspection. "This scrap lumber lying on the ground. It's been here ever since the house was built. And the moisture. Your crawlspace is not adequately ventilated. Termites are drawn to such a damp environment, with so good a supply of wood lying on the ground."

Carefully knocking the porous two by four out of his way, Gerald cast the beam of his flashlight further into the darkness. He could not detect any damage to his floor.

"The foundation in the far left corner is covered with mud trails. That is how termites infest a house with a crawlspace such as yours. They construct mud trails from the ground along the foundation up into the floor."

Gerald could not see the corner the exterminator was referring to,

298

not even with his flashlight. It was too distant. But the exterminator had crawled under his house to inspect the substructure. He had
donned a pair of coveralls and nonchalantly squirmed through the small
entrance. But then it was not his house he had been inspecting. Gerald
believed that made a significant difference. He had watched the labo-
rious progress of the exterminator's flashlight beam as it flickered about
the depths of his crawlspace. But Gerald knew he could not take the
exterminator at his word. They were in business for a profit. He could
not consent to such an important procedure without seeing for himself.
He had to go in for a look. Also, the exterminator had offered Gerald
a hundred-dollar deduction from his bill if he cleaned out all the scrap
material from underneath his house. So Gerald had to crawl underneath his house.

Gerald had never been under his house. He wriggled through the
tight opening. The ground was clammy. He nervously peered all about.
At this end of his house, near the access, there was sufficient light coming in for him to see well. He saw some ants and one small spider.

"You wouldn't believe what all I've encountered underneath people's houses," the exterminator had told him. "I've met some awfully big
spiders, some mice, and even snakes. And a crawlspace is no place for
someone with claustrophobia."

Gerald did not have claustrophobia, or any other phobia he was
aware of. Including one of spiders, mice, or snakes. But he had no love
of them, either. So he moved cautiously. The house was on a slight grade,
which meant one end was elevated higher than the other. Since Gerald
had entered the high end, he could easily crawl upon hands and knees
as he gathered up the scrap lumber. Yet he moved slowly, scrutinizing
the ground in front of him before advancing. He picked up the wood
gingerly, half expecting an army of termites to swarm out onto him at
any time. All of the wood he picked up had been eaten on, some pieces
hardly damaged while others crumbled in his hands. He did not hold
any of the pieces very long. They were quickly tossed out the opening.

The task soon became arduous. Gerald was forced down upon el-
bows and crouching knees as he worked his way toward the low end of
the house, and then upon his stomach. Scooting across the damp bare
ground, which became progressively muddier toward the low end of the
house, he was quickly fatigued. Also, he could no longer toss the wood
out, he could merely fling it back toward the now-distant opening. He
constantly turned his head from side to side, watching for anything hor-
rid. Especially the termites.

"You can never see termites, unless they are mating. Then they fly.

But at all other times they stay in the ground, or in their mud trails, or in the wood."

Still, Gerald waved his flashlight all about, searching for any trace of them. This far from the access, approximately the center of the crawlspace, the natural light faded drastically. A thick dank gloom clung to the air. Gerald paused often to rest his aching body, which was so unaccustomed to scooting upon its stomach, and to illuminate the ground all around him.

Gerald slowly, steadily, made his way through the cool sodden darkness by riveting his attention to the work. It had to be done. The scrap wood must be removed. It was worth a hundred dollars. And he had to see for himself what was going on under his house.

Gerald struggled to resign himself to the situation. But resignation did not come easily. He was ill at ease and apprehensive, uncomfortably dirty from the sloppy ground that muddied him, disturbed by the unseen webs that brushed across his skin, and aching from the unusual positions and exertions he was forcing his body through. But he strove to suppress these feelings, these pains. His situation was immutable. He had to get from here to there, the only way to there was through here. So he slogged on.

Then to his pleasant surprise, his attitude began changing. Once he surrendered to the unpleasant environment of the crawlspace, that environment started to become agreeable. The cool air was now pleasant and refreshing, the darkness soothing, the privacy and seclusion and aloneness rewarding. Gerald's physical discomforts and weariness had reached a threshold, then crossed it. His anxiety, which he had forced to a tense equilibrium, now eased to a serenity tinged with pleasure. He was coming to enjoy the world underneath his house. Even up ahead he believed he could see a light; a white light.

Then Gerald saw the mud trails. Scores of long narrow irregular brown lines zigzagging out of the ground up the foundation to the floor. He played the beam of his flashlight back and forth across them, imagining the activity within. The exterminator had shown Gerald graphic illustrations. There was the large subterranean colony in the ground directly beneath him. The huge monstrous queen, a grotesque egg factory. The tiny workers who never stopped working, who labored for twenty-four hours a day, and the larger soldiers armed with pincers who protected the workers, and the winged ones who mated with the queen that Gerald had seen swarming, which had first alarmed him, causing him to call the exterminator who had delved beneath Gerald's house, to emerge with gory reports.

Gerald shrank back. He brushed a support pillar of cement blocks. He glanced over his shoulder. A mud trail ran up one side. Jerking away with a cry, he scrambled frantically back toward the entrance, away wildly, and out.

THANE

TIM SHERF

Years ago, my master gave me a home. He gave me a purpose. And he gave me a name. I am Thane.

I am *his* Thane.

But now something is rotten in this state of Scotland. I sense its foul breath growing strong in this fair place, and I know something must be done. So I pace the corridors of the castle and prowl the limits of the keep, loyally hunting the unknown.

For something smells *wrong*.

I don't mean the moonwhite carcass of the fish I buried near the horses. That may smell wrong to the stable boy with the pale cheeks and eyes as round as the moon, the one my master just called a creamfaced loon. But to me, that secret stash of sharp, rotting bones is a drool-inducing feast.

No, this other smell isn't that kind of stink. This scent isn't rotten in that way. The stench of decay floats with it in a way that makes my fur stand on end, but even with all of my senses strained, I can't quite chase down what it is.

My master senses it, too; I'm almost sure of it. But he is not himself. As each night descends, his mind becomes more clouded. I have heard him pray that the stars would hide their fires and not let light see his black and deep desires. But if he cannot see this wrongness, he cannot protect himself from it. So the job falls to me, and I hunt.

For many seasons, I did not smell the wrongness like I do now. I can no longer loosen the stench from my nose, but then it was less than an undercurrent of air. It was the flicker of a bat's wing on a starless night. It was a lowly weed in a forest of majestic trees.

But the weed has grown. It has spread its roots and threatens to conquer even the highest crowns. Lifting my head to catch a stale breeze, I realize something: I am restless.

Usually I get this feeling only before a hunt. It is a deep moving at my core that tenses as it grows and builds in strength. When it strikes, I walk in circles, pacing around and round, a movement my master's men mimic as they bustle about, grunting and buckling and checking their weapons. They bare their teeth in wolfish smiles that almost mirror my own. But nothing can match a wolfhound's grin when he's ready for the hunt.

Yet we have had no hunts of late. There has been no time for hunting.

It seems as though there has been not enough of time, and yet too much of it for my master, the lord of these men. For he is restless, too, speaking of all his tomorrows creeping in a petty pace.

He wakes in the night. Or rather doesn't wake, because he doesn't sleep. Sleep is as elusive to him as that snow white buck we hunted in the forest so many seasons ago. In my dreams, I remember the scent of his power, the way his crown of antlers mixed with the bare branches, mocking our efforts even as he vanished into the winter trees.

In his restlessness, my master rises in the night, hurling his blankets and coverings from his sleepless bed in futile anger. Sometimes though, he is too exhausted to do anything but shove them wearily aside, with whispers about murdered sleep. I follow him on these nights of aimless wandering. I sense he needs me, and he has no dreams of hunts to comfort him. I fear though, that he has forgotten the strength of loyalty I offer.

Sometimes we meet another restless wanderer in the dark. My master's mate has open eyes, but she is blind to us. She speaks to my master, but her ears are shut to his voice in the night. They are together, but alone. The candle she holds flickers a cold light over her bloodless hands. We return to our chambers for another restless night.

I have long since stopped expecting my master to place a warm hand on my head or tumble with me in a wrestling match in the castle yard. I still lay near his feet at the table, but the last tender scraps I can remember were from a meaty bone tossed to me by the master's pack brother, before he was no more. That too, was many seasons ago.

Many seasons. And many scents since then. But though I have long since avoided that patch of earth near our other castle's walls it now seems to me that in this present stench of wrongness, I can still smell the spilled blood mixed with the sharp odors of pain and betrayal.

A wild shriek lifts my ears and stands my fur on edge. Something is wrong with the master's mate. I debate turning from this chase to follow the sound, but too soon only the echo remains. My ears flatten back. On the hunt, I have heard enough death screams to know it is too late to fetch help.

What use would these men be, anyway? I look around and see my master's men scrambling in all directions. This wild restlessness is not because of a hunt, for no bugle has been sounded, just the bells clanging brashly and loudly. But the men do not seem to realize this, for they are there, bustling about, grunting and buckling and checking their weapons, though there are no baretoothed grins today to challenge my own. Perhaps they sense the wrongness as well.

I chastise myself for becoming distracted. Chasing down this scent is not so different from what I have done so many times before. I am a Scottish wolfhound, born and bred for the hunt. I hunt by sight, as well as by scent. But today the sights are beguiling and the sounds are wild and mad, so I must trust my nose.

I shake my head, trying to clear it from the sensory overload. Too many smells are wrapping themselves in and around this castle like the layers of clothes my master wrapped himself in earlier. Layers of cloth to protect him from the layers of armor he protects himself with. It seems against nature, too thin and soft to protect against heavy and sharp.

My nose catches the scent again. The wrongness is as strong as I've ever smelled it. It is mixed with other scents, too, fear and courage. Love and hate. Fair and foul; foul and fair. These are not the scents I am hunting, though they mingle so strongly with it, they seem one and the same.

I make my way quickly through the men, narrowly avoiding their crushing steps as they run and stumble, breathing prayers and curses, supplications and suspicions.

The bells' clanging hurts my ears as I bolt through the corridors. Sounds of other clanging metal reach me too, along with screams and shouts. But there is no time to investigate. I am so close.

I hurtle around a final bend and skid to a stop at the entry. I have come full circle.

Unable to accept the sight my eyes present, I can go no further. My mind understands what my heart cannot. But the stark truth of it cannot be avoided. I can smell it drifting off of him in waves as he swings his sword at the attacking troops and tells his false thanes to fly away. The wrongness bellows forth with his very breath as he rages so madly that the spittle flies from his mouth. The fur stands in a bristled ridge down my back.

My master is what I hunted. His is the wrongness that needs to die. But even as my mind tries to reject this truth, my heart reminds me of another. This is the master whom I love. This is the master who gave me a name, who gave me a purpose. The hunt is over. And it has ended in tragedy.

I realize my lips are curled upward in a snarl and I take a step back, startled at my own rage.

My mind echoes my heart's indecision, and it is split in two. But the true heart cannot remain divided, and the pounding in my chest assures me I still have choices to make.

It comes to me then, a knowledge as pure as the scent from a mountain stream. I remember there is no art, no sense, no sharp ear or eye or nose, that can find the mind's true construction in the face. While this man before me may look like my master, he is clearly no longer himself.

If he is not himself, then he is not my master.

I turn away, lost. One more broken, bleeding heart added to the battlefield. For I know that while I am yet Thane, I am no longer his Thane.

WELCOME TO FUNVILLE

DANNY SHILLING
WRITING AS IAN KING

Choo choo, I thought because I could not speak, my eyes following the rampaging train on its perpetual tour of *Funville*. My dad had called it that, as though I was still in primary school, but I thought it was lame.

I could hear them upstairs, my mother and Dad, arguing like they always were, ever since I got back from the hospital, two bitter bickering birds.

"He's a damn burden, that's all he is anymore." My mother always had been the sweary type.

"He's our son," Dad said, but I could hear the fight betraying his usually calm persona, he'd been hardening up over the past few weeks. He'd always argue for me, him and his lame imagination, but my mother was slowly eroding his will.

"You think I don't know that? He came outta my goddamn womb," mother said.

The only sound was the *chugga chugga* of the train coming my way. I tried to lift a finger to give the passengers a wave.

"Please, don't use His name in va-"

I heard a crash then, silencing Dad. I was getting used to that sound, my mother becoming an expert converter of crockery into rubbish.

Choo choo, have a safe journey, all drinks must now be in plastic cups.

The affable creak of the basement stairs came to me. Dad sat before me, his eyes on the mug of whiskey he held, long ago upgraded from the broken tumbler.

"How's *Funville*, son? Is everyone having a good time in the home of fun?" He'd know they were if he looked me in the eyes. He laughed then, "It's funny, I talk to someone who can't hear me more than my wife. The doctor said you'd never hear again. I wonder why all the time."

The doctor had been right at first, asking me questions that I hadn't responded to. I couldn't move my eyes at the time, but I knew basic lip-reading from years of watching the TV on silent when I should have been asleep, so I knew some of what he had been saying.

"Move your eyes if you can hear me," the doctor had said. By the time my hearing returned I had no desire to respond to his badgering, his educated opinion, his prognosis that I was essentially a human vegetable. A *gork*, two of the nurses had called me when they thought I couldn't hear.

"At least you can't hear your mother; it's not fair what happened, but don't blame her, son. She's angry that God would let this happen to her firstborn son, about what she...." Dad bowed his head as though he didn't believe a word of what he was saying. "You know, I think, sometimes... sometimes I question why do I bother praying day and night. Sometimes it seems hopeless, a pointless thing to do. Your mother was already losing her faith before the accident, but now..." Dad had developed this new habit of leaving his sentences unfinished.

Dad gave a short laugh, his shoulders bouncing just the once, followed by a sigh and those shoulders slumping. "You'll never guess what I saw today on the way to the store; a dog on a skateboard and..." The smile faded. "It reminded me of your skateboard. I've still got the pieces."

Dad shifted. "Oh look, the trains going past the Airport to *Adventure*, I wonder where everyone is going today." Dad named that one too, I told you he had a lame imagination. "Your food is getting low," Dad nodded at the bag on the back of my wheelchair, the PEG tube feeding into my stomach. I wanted him to stay, to keep talking but I knew he hated it down here. I liked his stories. I also wanted to know Connor's A-level results; they'd been released a couple of days ago but Dad was reluctant to tell me and I wasn't allowed outside visitors just yet.

He left, and a few seconds later her voice rang out, "Here to take more damn food that we can't afford, are ya? What about your other son? What about Theo? When does he get to eat a proper meal?"

Silence in response, but I knew Dad's stress vein would be bulging on his forehead. He'd confided in me the other day that the only reason he stayed with my mother was to protect Theo.

Some days I wanted my mother to come down here, to see me for herself, but I knew she wouldn't. She didn't hate this place like Dad did;

rather my mother detested what I had become. She wanted nothing more than to erase that moment from her memory and I was a constant reminder. But that was okay, I understood how she felt. Theo was healthy after all, he was her priority now. Maybe one day I could explain that to her.

My eyes followed the driverless train until it stopped, sticking half out of the *Tunnel of Laughter*. They flicked to the switchboard, where my index finger lay on the On/Off switch and I managed the smallest of grins.

I heard the creak of floorboards once again and the train started back up; *choo choo*.

Welcome to *Funville*. Next stop, *Harbour of Happiness*.

SANDY

JK SHOWHAN

It's not so much his home, as it is the place he sleeps. I work with Sandy at Anomac, in the city, where I'm one of the guys who assist with market research for manufacturing firms and Sandy is in customer service. After working in customer service for a few years Sandy must hate the phone, because he threw it against the wall of his living room and it stuck. He painted a blood-like color around the hole, around where half of the receiver is sticking out.

I'm sitting here after work, waiting for him. He had to drive to a client and will be here soon, he said. He gave me a key. I didn't break in, but if I had, I know there wouldn't be much to steal. Not that he's struggling—only his apartment is. We actually make decent money, decent enough that he is living in an apartment with separate living room, bedroom, and bathroom, instead of a studio flat or something reminiscent of a college dorm. The bedroom and bathroom doors are on the right side of the room and are white. The walls of the living room and adjoining kitchen are also white, or the living room walls *used* to be.

I've been here once, picking Sandy up for work when his car broke down. He usually takes the train because this happens often, because he forgets to get his car checked. He honestly rarely uses his car, except for work. I offered to give him a ride because I was and am still, the new guy at work, and I live a few floors above Sandy. I have never lived alone before but I've been told that when separated from my herd, I try too hard to make friends.

I don't know what Sandy does all nights and weekends, because he says he doesn't drive anywhere, but when I call he is never home. At first, I thought maybe he's a sleeper, or an ignorer, but I don't think he spends much time in this apartment. There is no T.V. And this is America. I was also offered a drink that one time and saw that in his fridge there was only one sandwich and a glass of orange juice.

"Man, where's your food?" I asked.

"I eat out," he said.

Along with no T.V. there is only one couch, which looks almost unused.

"Is this new?" I asked.

"No," he said. "It came with the place." I knew he had been at this place for three years, since graduating from art school.   " W h a t ' s art school like?" I asked, since I was a management major and never considered a more "creative" path.

In reply, he only shrugged like he didn't know.

Since Sandy is more reserved than rude and I don't know anybody here, I decided to give the guy a chance. His walls though, are a bit off, because they used to be pure white. After three years, they have been covered by green serpents. They slither below the long legs and bare feet of a young, mostly naked blonde woman, shielding herself with a small hand towel. The woman looks down curiously at these serpents, as if they were just stray kittens climbing her. That's just on the far left of the living room wall, the wall where I imagine a T.V. would be for any normal American. I guess he has the wall to look at, because the small and large canvases, about five of them on easels cluttering around that same corner, are blank.

He used the wall instead.

"Wh ... ahht?" I asked during my first visit.

"It's my wall," he simply said.

Other pieces of art lined this wall, such as a cluster of cubist people around the right corner, all of their white, brown, and yellow faces blurred. An airplane crashing into a rather large palm tree near the top, the tree seemed more building-shaped. But mostly portraits of women, men, children, sad, happy, alone, even amongst all the other faces. Some looking at me, some not. This is the only wall that is painted.

None of these paintings are new. They were here when I visited two months ago.

He has one bookcase that he either built or bought more-than gen-

tly used at a yard sale. There are only three books with large spines leaning against the left side of the top shelf, right next to the door.

It's been twenty minutes and I have nothing to do. I have nothing to
eat. I'm afraid to use his bathroom because if he is never here, what if he
doesn't have any soap? I don't want to go to my apartment, because what
if Sandy comes back? So I grab a book, but don't want to read it—it's a
contemporary art textbook. The sticker on the front says that the book
was a rental and I wonder if Sandy purchased the rental after the course
was over or not.

The next two are also art books, one with sketches and journal en-
tries from a dead painter, whose name I recognize but would not have
been able to place if I hadn't run through the pages.

You can't read the painter's handwriting. Or Sandy's, who chick-
en-scratched in the margins.

I put the book back and grab the last one. It is a black-and-white
photography book. The back cover says is from a newcomer artist. There
are buildings and planes and girls running from and to the camera in
flowing dresses.

It's now been close to an hour, or over an hour, or many hours, and
I feel bad for being what seems like the first person to sit on this gray
couch. My butt may imprint this couch more than its owner, but at least
Sandy imprinted the walls. It's been an hour and I have nothing to do.
The picture book didn't take long to flip through and I can't read the
ancient journal. The textbook I refuse and put them all back on the shelf.

I walk, because what else do you do in here, and trace my fingers
along the kitchen counter. I look up and at the fridge with its smudge
on the side. It's a dark smudge, like a pencil would leave on paper and I
wonder what would leave that mark on a fridge. I look down again because my hand caught something. Stunned, I see an open letter, folded
in three, below my hand.

I feel rude intruding on his privacy and reading the letter, so I pick
up the torn envelope first. He clearly did not have an envelope opener,
because he tore the front of the envelope as well. The envelope isn't even
addressed to him, and says that it came from a *Maria*.

Maria. The sloping handwriting on the front makes me think of my
ex-girlfriend, *Morgan*. *Morgan* dumped me one afternoon after sex, for
her college boyfriend, who had come back to town. I think of the letter
she wrote me later, explaining why she left me, but even after, why she
slept with me first is still a mystery.

I'm interested and I'm bored and I unfold the letter. It's human nature, really. It's the spy inside of me that I wanted to be when I was six.

The letter is an application to be the artist-in-residence for some art gallery up north. I don't know what he would submit because his canvases are blank.I guess he could tear down and submit his wall. But the same person who wrote *Maria* on the envelope also wrote *Sandy J. Franks* at the top of the application. The rest, his displays, education and so on, are blank.

If she really wanted to help, I think, she would've filled in at least half.

A CITY WITH NO RAIN

FIONA SKEPPER

I stepped out on to the dust. The buildings were old and stained. I worried if I touched them, they might collapse and join the earth.

My skin was dry. My mouth was dry. Although I constantly swallowed large bottles of water, it never seemed to quench the aridness. When any liquid fell, it disappeared through the sand, leaving only a sense of dampness.

I walked around the city with no rain. I discovered after a year all the freshly painted buildings had become dirty, smeared with muck and grime and looked a hundred years old. So did the people.

I came trying to escape the cold and the damp. Here no mold emerged in the corners. Here there was no chance of the rot attacking, of it creeping quietly up the walls, letting out its choking gasses.

I ran to the city with no rain, hoping to dry out and detach anything, living or dead that clung, hoping to recreate myself so nothing could. I thought this would be bliss. Things fell off around me as I hurried. I leapt clear.

The only time when moisture touched the air, was when the rare lightest drizzle, Scotch mist, it is sometimes called, touched the earth briefly, like the tail of a low flying kite. The mist was sent to tease and evoke memories in foreigners, so the weak would leave, their tongues hanging out. The people, who were born in the city with no rain, were built of stronger stuff.

I arrived on St. Jude's day. The public queued to lay flowers at the altar of the saint, praying for the impossible, crying and wailing, begging and bargaining. When their allocated time was done, they left their dreams with St. Jude, not turning their mind to them again for another year, as they went home and slammed their dusty doors. They chewed their food slowly and without joy; they watched hypnotic images of men in short pants hitting or kicking balls, while wiping away the top layer of dust. They arose in the morning and left, returning in the evening, day after day. They walked with purpose, each at their own pace. You need moisture to keep hands grasped together. They held out their glasses to be refilled. I came to know it well.

There was one who sat near but never stuck. He had been an answer to my prayers when I'd met him kneeling at the shiny saint, my first day. He made no effort to grab, to possess, to control. His door was never locked. His requests were accompanied with a slight turn of the head, and a fierce stare on his face. So it continued for a while until I finally hesitated.

"Could you speak? Could you tell me…?" His look swallowed the rest of my sentence. He was neither surprised nor impressed. I was a foreigner after all.

"What, are you full of regrets now? Tomorrow I must go back to labour in the dust. It will take all I have. I could push so hard this time that I die. If I do, you will not be expected to throw yourself on my funeral pyre. So stop your pathetic weakness, and the sudden nostalgic need you feel to catch hold of another. You came to the city without rain to be free, so enjoy your liberty, keep quiet and fill my glass."

I couldn't answer. My mouth was dry. I completed my task. I returned to the kitchen. I staggered and grabbed the wall. The interior paint came off in rough, dirt-coloured flakes that cut my hand causing it to bleed.

THE THIRD THING
THAT MADE ME KILL
MYSELF

MARTIN SNEE

The third thing that made me kill myself was finding out my invention actually worked. The first two were losing my job and then my wife leaving me, but it was the third thing that really did it. Which was ironic because the invention caused all the problems in the first place.

While studying for my Doctorate I became convinced that not only was time travel theoretically possible but also that you could actually build a time machine. Of course everyone in the world of serious academia thought I was mad, but it turned out that didn't really matter. Two weeks after my thesis was published and subsequently ridiculed, I found myself being interviewed by a panel of army officers, civil servants and a very serious looking lady who declined to introduce herself. They were so caught up in the idea of going back in time to catch terrorists that I needed to do very little to persuade them to fund my research. I actually felt quite guilty and almost found myself trying to talk them out of it.

"I can't guarantee success," I said at one point.

"Don't worry old chap," the older army officer replied, stroking his grey moustache. "We never thought radar would work either!"

So there I was. A research grant for five years, my own lab and team of researchers. The only downside was the secrecy, but to be honest it made things simpler at home. Research went well at first. Ee made real progress. After three years we began building the machine, another year and it had basic working functions. It certainly did create a space time field. Then another year was spent miniaturising until we had a device you could strap to your wrist. At last it was ready for testing. I was quite upset when it didn't work.

The man from the ministry was very nice about it.

"Don't worry old chap," he said, "you gave it a damn good try."

"I still believe I can make it work," I said. "I just need more time" He gave me his widest smile. "No can do, old boy. No cash. All these budget cuts, you know."

My wife didn't say anything when I told her. She just nodded and then went upstairs to pack. When I followed and asked why, she pointed out that my only two redeeming features as a husband were that I earned a fair amount of money and that I was never around. Therefore, as these two things were now their exact opposite, she was leaving. I couldn't fault the logic of her argument.

"Perhaps things would have been different if we'd had children," I said. She paused and gave me a look. A worrisome thought crossed my mind.

"We haven't got any have we?" I asked.

She stared at me incredulously.

"Just checking," I said.

I stood at the window and watched her drive away. I was filled with regret, the very feeling that I had aimed to conquer. The age old thought: *If only I could go back and do things differently.* Maybe I still could.

I walked into the garage and switched on the light. On my work bench became the cardboard box I had used to clear my desk. I opened it and withdrew a tin from amongst the accumulated detritus of five years. The tin was red, circular and bore the words '*Collin Street Bakery, Corsicana, Texas*' on the side. It had once contained a rather delicious Pecan cake, a present from my sister, and I had kept the tin, using it to transport my sandwiches to and from work. Of course it set the scanners off every time I arrived or left, became quite a joke among the security guards, another of '*the prof's*' eccentricities. It also made smuggling my invention out very easy indeed. Sometimes it helps to plan ahead.

I laid the invention on the table and studied it thoughtfully. I was still pleased with the elegant appearance: leather strap and rectangular stainless steel case with pleasingly rounded corners. The screen was in default mode, showing a classic clock face with the time. I pulled my laptop towards me and lifted the lid. Time to get to work.

I always seemed to work better at home. It wasn't the environment. To be honest when I'm working I could be anywhere, but my invention seemed to be more compatible with my personal laptop. The computers at work were military issue. They seemed distinctly reluctant to run programs that were outside the normal range of military use and were configured in bizarre ways for anyone with a non-military mind. My laptop had its own eccentricity, but it was one I understood. This may sound strange, but I've spent enough time studying quantum physics to know that deep down, the world is a wonderfully strange and eccentric place.

With the device connected to the laptop, I went through the settings, checking each one, making the odd adjustment to fine tune. After a couple of hours I sensed it was worth a go. I disconnected it, strapped it to my wrist and called up the app on the screen. I stood up, turning to face the clock on the wall, checking it showed the same time as my invention. This would be a simple test: I would set the device to move me back five minutes. If it worked I would see the hands on the wall clock change. I took a deep breath and tapped the icon that said '*Go*'. The hands on the clock stayed exactly where they were. I sighed, shook my head and turned back toward my bench. And stopped dead. A shudder wormed its way down my back as my mouth went suddenly dry. My laptop, the red tin, the box, all had disappeared!

I took a step towards the bench, my mind racing. Something had happened, maybe not exactly what I wanted but something. Then a sound outside made me turn again. A car crunched onto the drive. '*She's come back!*' was my immediate thought. I hurried to the small window, but through the reflections on the windscreen I could just make out the figure of a man. A man in my car! Then he opened the door and climbed out. I realised it was me. '*It worked!*' I thought. '*I'm watching myself in the past*'. But then my wife came out of the house and I watched with an increasing sense of dislocation as they hugged and kissed. That didn't look like the marriage I remembered. Then a little girl ran out of the house. She wore a denim skirt and a flowery top, her hair was a mass of blonde curls and even in the garage I could hear her delighted shout of '*Daddy*'. It was too much. I hit the red '*Back*' icon on the screen.

I sat on the floor in the garage. The house seemed deserted in a way that it didn't before. I understood now. I proved the many worlds interpretation of quantum theory was actually true. Moreover I built a device that could transport me from my reality to one of the infinite others. But I felt no triumph, no sense of success, no professional pride. Instead I was filled with jealousy, enraged that this man, this other me, should have everything I didn't. My heart ached with a sense of inescapable loss, mourning the a life I never had.

It was then I decided to kill myself. Not me, you understand, but the other one. And it was so easy. I appeared in his garage as he was working, his surprise turning to eager delight as I showed him the device and offered to explain how it worked. He sat at his laptop, me looking over his shoulder as I pointed out the flaw in his algorithms.

"Pretty girl!" I said, pointing to the photo of his daughter. "What's her name?"

"Mary."

"Nice name!" I said, as I hit him, hard, on the back of the head.

It didn't take long to pour the whisky laced with sleeping pills down his throat, holding his nose to make him swallow. I moved him so it would look like the blow on his head came from falling and pushed the bottle into his pocket. Then I strapped the device to his wrist, pressed the '*Back*' icon and he was gone. And that was it, the perfect crime. All the evidence, the DNA, the fingerprints were all mine, and so also his. Who would suspect the victim?

I switched the light off and made my way upstairs, pausing at the doorway to my daughter's room.

"Goodnight Mary," I called softly.

OUT OF SIGHT

M.E. SYLER

My thoughts are confused, the world is pitch-black, voices from another room are an incoherent chatter.

I pinch my arm. Why can't I wake up from this nightmare?

I slap my face, my heartbeat quickens, a loud squeak; the hinge pins that needed oiling.

"Mr. Wells," a melodious female voice, "Why did you hit yourself?" In my mind's eye, she is beautiful and seductive, but who is she?

"I'm dead, aren't I?"

"No Hon," her laugh is rhythmic, "I'm your nurse, Maggi."

"This is not a hospital, this is my bedroom, and why do I need a nurse?"

"You hired me after the accident." Maggi said.

"I don't remember an accident, and I can't see," I am shouting, "yesterday my sight was perfect. I remember taking the Porsche out for a drive with the top down."

"That was ten years ago." She said.

"That's not possible… why do I smell vinegar?"

"It's your medicine."

"I need a shot of whiskey." "The medicine will calm your nerves, Mr. Wells."

She placed the cup in my hand and, reluctantly, I drank.

I don't remember an accident, losing my sight, and hiring a nurse, unless my mind has left me.

Could this be God's curse for an unscrupulous life of womanizing, drunkenness, and unethical business practices?

Stop wallowing in self-pity and form a plan. If Tom were here, he would make sense of this dilemma. Pity, dad's favorite son is dead and me the oldest, is still alive; the one who squandered the family fortune.

There are voices again, two people downstairs. I sit up, dizzy, and put both feet to the floor. My stomach is tied in knots. Frustration rises as I pivot my body, clutch the mattress, and shuffle along till my other hand finds the wall. I take a slow deep breath; getting out of bed use to be a simple task.

Panic creeps in, I can't remember where the door is. I've always had trouble with direction. In this pitch-black-state I'm lost. How can I not remember where the damn door is?

I slump to the floor and crawl away from the wall. After a few feet I stop to rest. My ear lies against the wood, the voices are clearer: Maggi and a man in the living room.

"How's the old coot, Mag?"

"The same, he can't see, and believes he's in a dream."

"Good, soon his bank accounts will be drained."

"Damn those two," Marston thought. He heard their wicked laughter, but it stopped when the doorbell chimed.

"See who's at the door, Mag."

"Who are you?" Another man's voice said.

"I'm Mr. Wells' nurse." Maggi said.

"You're not dressed like a nurse. Nurse's wear uniforms, not jeans and halter tops. I demand to know what you're doing in this house."

"Just you stay right there," Maggi said, "You can't push past me until..."

"I'm Tom Wells, Marston's brother.

Marston rolled over on his back, "My brother is back from the grave."

PEELING DOVES

FAERL TORRES

The best way to peel a dove is to take it by its feet, grasping the sharp, wiry toes, and dip it in the paraffin, making sure it's fully covered, including the tail feathers. Pull it out, let it cool, dip it again. Two coats is usually enough. Once the bird has cooled and the wax is hardened but malleable, cut along the breast, just deep enough to reach the meat. Insert your thumbs into the incision and peel back the skin as you would an orange.

Miguel taught us, showing the process with a fat dove one of our party had shot out of the wide Texas sky. He also taught us how to peel a prickly pear, cutting out the orange, hair-like needles that itched our mouths and the skin between our fingers if we missed them. The prickly pears were huge and fat that year from all the rain. The deep pink fruit was filled with tiny seeds—each bite sent a trickle of juice down our chins, staining us in mauve stripes. The scrub landscape was overblown with life—the mesquite trees were heavy with seed pods and leaves thick enough to veil the finger-length thorns. Late-blooming wildflowers covered the hard terrain with strokes of color and grew up past the cactus and yuccas. The animals were heavy too, packed with grass and corn-fed meat.

The cleaning house was an open building of mostly corrugated tin and cinder block. It smelled stout—the metal and soil fragrance of ani-

mal blood mingling with gun powder, singed feathers, and oil. The wax
had no scent, but a burning smell came from the flame below the huge
vats, thick with heat and butane. There was the smell of sweaty, dirty
men who'd been up since before first light hunting for javelina, then
birds. The men were also ripe with scent: faux deer urine, perspiration,
dog smells from a half dozen retrievers crowding to be the first to get the
prize falling from the sky.

And there was the smell of cherry-flavored *Bonne Bell Lip Smackers.*

My sister, Lola, was going through a *Bonne Bell Lip Smackers* phase.
At any given time, she could procure two or three different flavors to suit
her fancy. We stood by as the process of peeling the doves was explained.
Miguel was the lead guide, our father's favorite, and he loved to teach us
hunting lessons, treating us as if we were sons instead of daughters. He
never spared us the morbid scenes of violence at the camp. We weren't
shielded from the blood, gore, or various means of decapitation. We
were the protégés and took it all in with the appropriate reverence. Lola
passed me the cherry lip balm in silence without looking away from
Miguel's weather-worn face.

I smeared it on my lips and handed it back to her to cap and put in
the pocket of her camo coveralls. Miguel took a fresh bird from the table and handed it to me. "Okay?" he asked. I took the bird, grasping the
orangey-pink legs and dipping it head-first into the molten wax. Miguel
showed me where I'd missed spots.

"*Caliente,*" he warned me. I dunked the bird again, encasing the grey
feathers in an opaque cocoon. Doves still remind me of little flying sunsets. All grey and softly muted except for their bright, leather legs, like
the final shearing light on the South Texas horizon. Even their gentle,
vibrato coos sounded like calls to bed and comfort.

I was given the job of waxing and he gave Lola the skinning knife
longer than her face. She was eleven months older and trusted with
the incision. It didn't matter that we'd just spent the day toting around
our own shot-guns—knives were something else entirely. There was no
safety to flick on.

We waxed and peeled more than fifty birds, the bag limit of all the
men in our father's hunting party—an assortment of clients and colleagues—and our own birds. Louie, Miguel's nephew, stood beside us at
the butcher block, taking the birds as Lola handed them over and chopping off the heads below the neck. The chop and scrape of the butcher's
knife against the wood as he moved the severed head into the trash was
a metronome. The chore was macabre but we were still just kids, too
naïve to feel the weight of the death of anything as low on the food

chain as a bird or deer. We weren't old enough to feel a life's value or know its weight. Dad came over when we finished, bragging to the other men about his daughters' aptitude for sport and weapons wielding.

"You girls need to teach my son Clark how to clean the birds," Mr. Tempenarrow said, patting us roughly on shoulders engulfed by his grown hand. "Hell, I don't even know if Clark has ever been inside a cleaning house."

"They're good little hunters," Dad said. "You girls go clean up now. Marcia and Josephine will be waiting for y'all." He kissed our cheeks and dropped to a crouch so we were eye-to-eye. "I'm proud of you two. You did a good job today." He patted our bottoms, scooting us out the door to the golf cart.

This was the first year we'd been big enough to drive the cart without an adult or older kid like Louie. Lola's legs were long enough with the block they'd strapped to the pedal. She drove us up the gravel path, past the kennels where the hunting dogs slept.

"Let's stop and pet the dogs," I said. I loved dogs. More than anything besides having our mother back, I wanted a dog to keep, but our dogs had one purpose—to hunt. We would get a puppy, whose breed was determined by the needs of the hunting season and which dogs would be retiring, and spend four to five months playing, socializing, and teaching it basic obedience before it was shipped away for intensive training and permanent residence in the kennel as a working dog. I wanted to keep one of the dogs at our house. I dreamt of coming home from school to the wet kisses and wiggling butt of a grown dog, more excited to see me than anyone else. I wanted to take it on walks in the neighborhood and teach it to retrieve my tennis balls when I sent one sailing over the fence.

"Please, Lola?" I begged. She took a deep breath, weighing the time and consequences. The camp belonged to Dad's company; we had free reign as long as we stayed off the range or were supervised by a guide. We were expected to be polite and present at dinner and part of polite meant being on-time. But Lola was a sucker to my pleas.

"Only a few minutes, Caroline. We can just pet them, not let them out, and then we have to high-tail it to the cabin or we'll be late to dinner," she said, turning off the main path toward the kennels. Our change in direction sent the dogs into a cacophony of barks and whines. I jumped off the golf cart before Lola came to a complete stop, running to the kennel house to get treats. We each went to our own favorite. Lola knelt on the recently cleaned concrete in front of a grey-spotted English setter, petting her silky head through the chain link and feeding her treats.

I made a bee-line for Shell, a four-year old golden retriever. Shell had been the first puppy we got after my mother died. He'd been ordered prior to her diagnoses and swift decline and Dad never thought to cancel the purchase. One Sunday afternoon, a young man appeared on our door step—the breeder's son—puppy in hand. I took him as Dad signed the paperwork and final deposit. The boy left and all Dad said was, "I must have forgot." He went back to his study. Lola and I took Shell. He was sent away after four months like the rest of them, but he held a special place in my heart; his big brown eyes and wavy golden-red hair reminding me of my mother.

"Well, hey there." Lola and I both turned at the intrusion. "What are you two doing with my dogs?" a man asked, stepping into the kennel through the breezeway. I had never met this man. He was younger than our dad and most of the camp hands, but not young like Louie. He was also white, which was different from most of the other staff at our South Texas camp. Because of the twilight, or the unfamiliarity, or the surprise, I felt alarmed. My fingertips tingled with adrenaline, though I didn't know what it was at the time. I stood, taking a step back towards Lola. Lola stood also.

"These are our dogs," I said.

"Yes," Lola chimed in, covering the space between us. "I'm Lola and this is Caroline. We're John Laray's daughters." This was usually all the introduction we needed for new staff. Dad made it a habit each year, on our first trip down, to introduce us to anyone new. They became like uncles and aunts, their children were our friends for the few weeks each year we spent there—especially at this camp, as it was closest to home and had the longest hunting season. "What's your name?" she asked, on finishing school auto-pilot. We hadn't yet learned to listen to our guts.

"I'm Bud," he said. "You girls like the dogs? I could take 'em out for you." He moved towards the gate on Shell's kennel. Shell sat, tail swishing like a broom in eager anticipation of being released.

"No, thank you," Lola said, taking my hand and pulling me away. "We have to get to dinner."

"It was real nice to meet you two. You come back anytime," he called after us.

"Thank you," Lola responded, as we went through the door and got back in the golf cart. Making our way up the road to the main lodge, she chided me for not answering Bud. "Next time we see him, you need to say you're sorry for being rude," Lola instructed.

I apologized and agreed I would, wiping my sweaty hands on my pants and trying to forget the way his fingers had moved along the chain link towards me like a tarantula. We ran from the cart to our cabin where Marcia and Josephine were waiting. When we were younger they helped us with our baths and into clothes for dinner. They would lead us to the dining room and fetch us for bed once the meal was over. All tucked in, they would sing us songs in Spanish until Dad came to give us a kiss and say our prayers. Now that we were older, they made sure our clothes were clean and helped us braid our hair. We changed out of our hunting clothes, cleaned up, and put on skirts and sweaters, neatly laid out on our beds with shoes and matching hair barrettes.

Though we weren't twins, Lola and I were regularly dressed the same. When our father bought us clothes, he bought them in sets, killing two birds with one stone in an effort to cover some of the tasks left by the absence of our mother. He did his best to guide us through life without a woman prominent, buying us frilly things, taking us to Disney movies, and making sure we always had everything we needed. In many ways he overcompensated, but even then we understood what he was trying to do and the affection he was showing through his effort. So we donned poufy dresses and glittery shoes long after we might have if our mother were alive. He treated us like princesses, half-way trapped in an opulent castle, barring us from maturing past a certain girlishness, and in exchange we went hunting and played hostess for his guests as best we could at nine and ten years old.

We arrived at the dining room just as the soup was served. The men asked us about school, what grade we were in, and which subjects were our favorite. We had formula answers for the school questions and automatic replies to enquire about their families, some of whom we knew from Christmas and birthday parties. It was like a dance we'd been doing since we were barely able to speak. Without our mother there to buffer us or deflect some of the attention, we had become expert socializers and networkers. After they showed enough interest, we were left to finish our dinner and be excused from the table.

Outside, the moon was full and high, reflected in the stock pond like a mirror. The night creatures had begun to stir. Bats, owls, and coyotes cried and called in the live-oak forest beyond the manicured grass of the lodge. "Let's go back to see the dogs, Lola." We were halfway between the dining room and our cabin. "I never really got to pet Shell." Bud had interrupted us. I hadn't gotten the chance to tell Shell my scheme: to convince Dad to retire him to our house permanently.

"No, Caroline," she said. "We aren't supposed to wander at night and I want to watch a movie. Besides," she said, turning to me, "what if Bud is there? I didn't like him." The moonlight bleached her skin like a ghost and her round eyes, big and blue like mine, like our dad's, were shadowed deeply in her face. "He was weird."

"Yeah," I agreed. "But he won't be there. The workers are all gone for the night. I just want to tell Shell something. Please, Lola." My sister had a hard time telling me no and I knew it. I didn't usually exploit her this way—she was the closest thing I had in the world and even then, at such a young age, I knew she was my strongest lifeline and the only tether I had to our mother.

But this time I persisted and she agreed, like I knew she would. Lola drove back down the gravel to the kennel. Most of the dogs didn't even bother stirring as we walked in. Shell was standing up, tail waving like a banner, like he knew I'd come back and he was waiting for me. I unlatched his gate and he greeted me with big, slick kisses. His fur was like a mane and I wished I could wind my fingers into it and let him carry me through the woods like a princess on a horse in the story my mother used to read us at bedtime.

Shell turned his head, ears perked, as the far kennel door opened. Bud stood in the doorway, holding a leather leash. Shell's back curved and his tail bushed under his legs in fear. It would have been foreboding if we'd known what foreboding was. If we'd been less naïve to malicious intention, we would have seen Shell's raised hackles and left. Instead we stood stock-still, like two does caught in the middle of a road.

"What are the little princesses doing out so late? Daddy will be worried," he said, grinning and running the leash through his hands. Back and forth. Back and forth. His voice was different in the darkness. Mocking. Patronizing.

I had never encountered real danger before and didn't know exactly what I was afraid of, only that my hands were sweating again and my fingers tingled. I wanted to be home with Dad more than anything in the world—more than I even wanted our mother back. I had convinced Lola to come and now we were in trouble because of me. Guilt morphed into momentary boldness. "Our dad is meeting us here," I said. Bud shook his head, smiling.

The dogs nearest us had woken, many of them yawning with anxiety, ears folded flat against their skulls, and tails tucked. The air in the kennel was still and heavy with Bud's breath as he came closer. He wound the end of the leash around one hand until the brass clip swung on only a few inches of leather lead. I felt sick and hot, like I had at the funeral when people I didn't know filled the room where her wake was held, crowding around and pulling us into hugs that where damp with perspiration and perfume that didn't smell like our mother.

The trauma of my mother's death was a thing seen, but not entirely felt. I was five and without the mass or knowledge necessary for the implications of motherlessness to have real gravity or grit. Our father's grief was like a foreign subject we'd heard of but never been educated on—like multiplication and division. Even in the midst of grief, trauma never had purchase.

Bud was the first aggressor. The first indicator the world was harmful, even malicious. We were used to manners and propriety dictating our behavior and decisions. But then, at that moment, with Bud moving carefully toward us like he was trying to capture a cornered bunny, we only knew raw fear, as animal as the dogs that filled our kennel. We didn't know words like predator or pedophile. It wasn't part of our reality then.

"I think you're lying," he said and started rubbing the leash between his hands, winding it around his palm, and walking toward us. Shell cowered further, dropping his weight in anticipation. Lola took my hand and walked backwards—fear overriding manners. The open breezeway was behind us. Beyond that it was ten yards into the woods. The lodge was further, far enough so the sound of dogs barking or howling couldn't disturb worn-out hunters as they lay in bed.

"Lying isn't very nice," he said. "Daddy won't be happy." He made a clucking noise, revealing stained teeth. "No, I think Daddy would whip you good if he knew you lied."

"We have to go," I said. "Please put Shell away for us." I tried to act normal. I tried to believe acting normal would set things right and the control we were used to having would return to us. Like when Mom died and Dad never said anything about it to us. I pushed Shell like a sacrifice towards Bud. "Come on, Lola, I'll race you."

We took off running, just as I felt Bud move after us, the leash whipping out and catching me on the shoulder blade like a hornet's sting. He screamed for us to come back but we were already around the side of the building. He must have beat Shell—we heard the cries and yelps. Tears filled our eyes deep enough to swim in as we heard the tortured sound of something we loved unable to escape pain.

SAVING SPIKE

PAOLA TRIMARCO

He was still breathing.

Jane was relieved to see that, but remained uneasy. He could go at any minute. She stepped backwards, as if she could be attacked if she stood too close to the creature. "What should we do?'"

Sean combed his hair with his fingers while he thought for a moment. He mumbled something about getting his gloves and was off towards the garden shed. He was a tall man, with a stiff posture and rigid movements that made every action seem robotic.

Jane pouted and whispered. 'Oh, poor baby.'

Sean came out, putting on the thick oversized gloves as he returned to the flowerbed, dry and golden brown in its autumnal state.

'Careful,' she said. 'He's rather prickly.'

'How do you know it's a he?'

'Call it intuition. Anyhow, he better be. I've named him Spike.'

Sean chuckled. He stepped over the rose bushes, with all of their flowers gone, their stems cut back to stubs. Bending his knees, he stared at the hedgehog and tapped the tiny creature on the snout. The animal shifted his back. His spines pointed out and undulated for a few moments before they rested again. He could do no more than that because one of his hind legs was caught in the groove of the weather-worn fence.

Sean took out his pocket knife and pried open a wider space between the wooden slabs. Jane watched, grateful she did not have to touch the animal; his coat of spines infested with lice no doubt. Sean delicately pulled the animal's leg out, exposing a strange, unnatural bend and a patch of blood that was such a dark red, it was nearly black. The spines were fully spread now. Jane imagine this being the point where an agitated animal would fling itself into the face of its rescuer, biting and scratching along the way. But Spike rested peacefully in Sean's arms. The two of them in a soft pose together, the father and his new-born.

Once again, Jane felt outside the parental loop. She had to do something. Ah, the empty cardboard box in the shed. Right. She stepped lively toward the shed and grabbed the battered DVD-player box on the floor. Then she found some newspapers from the recycle bin, folded the sections in half and lined the box with thick layers of broadsheet, blocking out the holes and slats, making it warm and safe. She emerged from the shed and realised Sean had walked about ten feet with Spike cradled in his arms. He had moved toward the side of the house where the wind was not as strong and had wrapped part of his denim jacket around the ailing creature.

Jane returned to her usual role of spectator as Sean, with all the confidence of a country lad, placed Spike into the box. She was left to watch the hedgehog while her husband went inside to phone the RSPCA for the nearest animal shelter.

She rocked the box, noticing how infant-like the creature was with his eyes shut tight, his body curled in a foetal position. 'There, there, Spike. You're going to be okay.' As she uttered these words, she imagined the women at work. If they could only see her now: nurturing, motherly Jane. She would be one of them, a part of their conversations and her opinions would matter. If only Spike were human.

The animal shelter was tucked away in a village they had never visited before, some twelve miles away. In the passenger seat, Jane held the box on her lap, thinking about babies. It had been agreed to years ago. Two up and coming professionals, they chose the house in the country over soiled nappies.

Sean asked her to check the map again, insuring they going the right way. She held the map up, high in front of her, trying not to disturb Spike. Their turn off was coming up, then they would have to follow a B road for a few miles.

When it came to children, Jane never felt she had missed out. She watched friends struggling with toddlers and in recent years agonising over their teenagers, always living in a state of chaos and problems needing to be solved. Yet, nearly everyone; friends, co-workers, and relatives all wanted her to feel as if she missed out. After all, she did not belong to their parenthood club. They were terribly smug about it. Did they think she was really incapable of imagining what being a mother was like? That she had no sense of pain or sacrifice or was unable to experience real love? Of course, she would never dare speak up or tell them to shut up, damand they stop throwing the verbal daggers at her. It would be useless as she was outnumbered, the freak. She glanced down at Spike, rounded in the corner of the box. His breathing was shallower. He could be close to death, and the B road with its bends and hills and rows of berried shrubs seemed endless. She tried to think about something else. Anything. Her sister. She recalled Heather's remark after she left her husband and took their three children with her. 'Well, you know what they say, after you've planted the seeds, you throw away the packet.' It was funny at the time, the heartless humour of the new divorcee. It now seemed ironic after all of the times Jane was told motherhood would make her sensitive and caring. Heather was anything but sensitive. At times, the mother of three was brutal with her offspring.

Spike's breathing seemed to stop. *Oh, no, please*, her inner thoughts pleaded. Tears started to well up in her eyes. She cleared her throat and was preparing to tell Sean the bad news when the dark spines rose and an uneven thin breathing continued. *How precious life is*, she thought. There was a strange beauty to it. Even dying was awe-inspiring, miraculous.

'This looks like the place.' Sean interrupted her thoughts as he steered the car into a gravelled car park. The animal shelter was in a wooded area on the edge of a one-pub village. Cute, childlike drawings of animals lined its front windows.

The young lad at the animal shelter was barely sixteen. He picked up Spike with one hand and brought him into the vet's office while Sean and Jane waited, watching a group of Canadian snow geese in the man-made pond. Both were nervous for little Spike. Would he have to be put down?

The young man came out of the backroom, speaking rapidly and confidently about the animal's broken leg. He had given Spike an anti-biotic and would keep him there at the shelter until spring, when they would release him back into the wild.

Jane breathed an audible sigh of relief. 'Can we visit him from time to time?'

Sean huffed and rolled his eyes.

The lad explained that the hedgehog would be hibernating. 'Best to not disturb him.'

Sean was jingling the car keys. His job in this had finished, and he was becoming rock-like Sean again.

'So, if you release him here, there's no way he's going to come back to our garden, then, is there?' Jane asked.Sean chuckled. 'Don't be silly, darling. Unless Spike gets his driver's license, I don't think it very likely.'

All the way home, they were silent. Jane thought of ways of constructing a rabbit hutch for the garden, and building a pond and a large birdhouse next to the currently ill-maintained seed feeder. There was no reason why she could not care for little creatures. Suddenly, so many things seemed possible.

She glanced over at Sean's face. He appeared deep in thought, not fully concentrating on his driving. He was upset with her, she surmised, for saying silly things at the animal shelter and for becoming sentimental over a dumb hedgehog. She needed to introduce the expanded family idea gently, one pet at a time. He would probably go for the pond easily enough, as it could be seen as a garden renovation. Once he got used to the fish and the turtles, the birdhouse would seem like a natural extension to all of that. And with some coercion, in late summer she would suggest the building of a rabbit hutch.

As they came into the drive, Sean patted her on the thigh, as if to say *wake up, Jane*.

They stepped out of the car and she watched as he hoisted open the garage door. He turned to her and said, 'You know, love, we've never talked about being foster parents.'

She stood in silence, thinking about what he just said, repeating his words in her mind. He stared at her waiting for a reaction.

RECONNECTION

EMILY VIEWING

Seeing you again
brought back some memories
of how you said "no" to me
on your prom night
you're married with kids
I'm unmarried with kids
you didn't date friends, you said
broke my heart more than once
so I had another beer tonight
after you told me
how to be a Christian in five easy steps.

WALK A MILE IN MY SHOES

MICHAEL WALTERS

Paris lifted Barney's shoes off her desk with two fingers as if the offending footwear was diseased. Holding them, she twisted her hand to look at them from all sides. They were a deep mahogany colored loafers that had seen far better days. The heel of the right foot was worn and some of the padded insert could be seen poking through right above the rubber sole. The left shoe had its bottom worn quite unevenly.

Paris looked back up to Barney. "So why again was I supposed to look at these?" She asked as she dropped the shoes to the floor of her office.

Barney padded over in his socks and picked them up. "You can tell a lot about a man by looking at his shoes," he informed. "You told me I don't know what I was talking about in my essay. You gave me an F. I think that was unfair. You don't know where I come from. So put my shoes on." He paused for dramatic effect before continuing. "You can tell even more by walking a mile in them then any essay, Dr. Pritchard. Those shoes relate to my life, not some words I had to write." Barney put on his biggest cheesy grin and displayed his shoes to emphasize his point. "You see, to me my shoes say I drive a lot and have a limp. They are the shoes of a nontraditional student who has to work full time to put himself through school. That's why I wrote what I did in my essay. Want to try to walk in them and feel a bit of what I go through?"

Paris shook her head. "Put them back on Mr. Winthrop," she ordered. "And if you truly want to walk a mile in someone else's shoes, you should read a book."

Barney jabbed one of his shoes at her. "What do you mean by that?" He he replaced a loafer.

Paris reached over to her bookshelf where she kept the good stuff. She picked up a slightly worn copy of *Invisible Man* by Ralph Ellison. She flipped through the pages while breathing in. It was like hugging a good friend you hadn't seen in a while. The scent of that particular book always brought back the summer of 78 when she read it for the first time.

Paris held the book out to Barney. "You want to know about African American struggles in the 1920s and 30s, you read this book. It will give you insights you can't get by just watching a TV," she pointed at Barney's loafers, "or walking in someone else's shoes. You see, you don't get the inner emotions staring at the screen, just the outside view. Sort of like looking at how your tread is uneven. It doesn't tell me how you feel when you need to walk a good distance? Can I get that from wearing your shoes? Will I know the struggle of not wanting to go buy a new pair of shoes because money is tight?"

"I've got plenty of money," Barney said. "I just hate shopping for shoes."

Paris smiled and slapped her desk. "Exactly Mr. Winthrop. I can't get that from really walking in your shoes. Your story is not just your outward appearance, but your inward experiences. That's why I make you read and comment on great works of literature. They let you peer into the heart of the inner human condition with all its beauty and warts, allowing you to experience being someone else for a moment in time and broadening your world view. Hence, why I gave you the assignment."

Barney slumped down in the chair beside Paris' desk. He put his other shoe on and took the book out of her hand. He looked at it, trying to comprehend the importance of such a tome. Finally his eyes went from the book and back to hers. "But why have me read about a black person in the 1920s? What does this have to do with my homework?" he asked.

Paris shook her head then leaned forward to look Barney in the eyes. "Because you were supposed to write an essay about this book, not the Hitchcock film."

FAERIE BAD

DAVID WING

It was fair to say that of all the rum soaked, vodka stained, gin joints in all the worlds, the ones in Faerie took the biscuit. Waiting there at the bar, I knew I was in for some fun. The band played a fun, folksy tune; the flappy mouthed barmaid kept giving me the eye and across the room some Ogre-type fellow seemed none-too-pleased about it.

The ale went down well, with a tingle. Then she came in. The room shushed and watched as she made her bee-line to my stool. The barmaid dropped off my shoulder and the Ogre huffed in the corner and went back to harassing some Leprechaun. Her legs never touched the ground, her hair damn near floated and when she finally stood in front of me some eon later, her voice crawled over my arms and down my back.

"Hello, Mr. Cooper."

I shook myself free and answered her.

"Coop's fine."

I didn't know how she knew me, but people find me when they need me. That's always been the way.

My voice crackled and despite the five ales I'd consumed my eyes stayed on her. A bad idea, in a place like this anything can happen. Got to keep your peripheries clear.

"I need your help to find my friend. She's disappeared."

"Easy to get lost in Faerie?"

"Not from me."

She said it with a smile, but she was anything but happy. She may have looked ethereal, but something told me she knew how to handle herself.

"Her name's Calypoly, she's a..."

"Fairy?"

"Quite, but she's also has ability to foresee what has yet to come."

"You don't say?"

"I do say, Mr. Cooper."

Fairies never got sarcasm, good thing for me too. This one, despite her appearance could have ended me in a flash.

"Any ideas where I might start? Enemies--yours or hers?"

She stared straight through me. I couldn't read her.

"You might try your handsome friend over there."

I knew who she meant. That Ogre hadn't taken his eyes of me since I came in. Either I was more alluring than most gave me credit for, or he wanted to talk. I turned back to her but she was already floating back the way she came, every set of eyes went with her. In the haze of fairy and ale I'd never gotten her name, but something told me I'd find her easy enough, or she'd find me, as was more likely.

The music played behind and all around, then it began to sway. It was either the drink or the chick, but I was getting a little sleepy.

I awoke on a small chair, hands tied behind me, a shadow looming over. In the distant dim of the pub he looked almost bearable, but up close, with a hangover and a light in the face he was anything but.

His Ogre's teeth, spotted black and green, grinned down on me. Then his breath hit me, harder than any punch I'd ever taken.

I couldn't help it. I threw-up all over his brown, chewed boots. He got the message and after the dutiful smack, I righted myself and waited for the interrogation to begin, but it didn't come from him. I heard a floorboard creak and turned to see a Unicorn smoking a cigar. How? Don't ask. In Faerie you learn not to be surprised, but on this occasion it was impossible not to laugh.

"Are you kidding me?"

The Ogre did his duty again, smacking me around, and I stifled the laughter, though barely. The Uni...I can't, I'll just call him Ralph, though that's only slightly better. Ralph trotted over; the acrid wisp hit my nose and caused the reflux to kick in once more.

"Mr. Cooper, it may not look like it, but this is a polite request. Please vacate Faerie."

"Look fella, I was hired to find a young lady and until I've..."

Clank, right in the mush.

Ordinarily I don't get to this part in the investigation until I've knocked down a few whiskies and doors alike, but Faerie was different and while things look a might odd, they all boil down to the age old – *you got it, I want it* routine.

I apologise, my response was less than gentlemanly, but I was becoming tired of the mythic freak.

"Go Fu…" then came the forth hit, this time a left hook that sent me flying across the room and into a wooden crate. The shattered wood splintered and I made for a piece. I sawed at my ropes. My hands were free just before the great bulk wrenched me off the ground, his right hand clasped around my neck and subsequently landingmy right foot in his groin.

Thank heavens for the universal language.

He felled to the ground and the Uni…Ralph, galloped off.

While the Ogre took a nap, I picked my brown, stained jacket and hat up from the floor and had a look around the joint. A barn; old, dank, with a smell of mold mixed with fresh vomit – nothing to give me any clue to the girl's whereabouts. After a few minutes of that odour I slapped the Ogre awake. I decided not to heft him onto the chair and had simply hog-tied him instead.

"Wh…wha…whot?"

"Why?" I figured even an Ogre would understand '*Why*'.

"Money."

"Go on."

"Mr Ralph, he want the pretty lady business."

"Kidnap?"

"Uh huh."

"Where?"

He looked around, everywhere but at me.

"Ah come-on buddy, you know how this goes. Best to Man/Ogre-up now and tell me, save you a lot of pain." I gestured at his bits.

He told me. They always did.

In the cold light of day, Faerie can be a pretty, no, a beautiful place, filled with flowers and trees and lakes and prancing, dancing creatures, but in the middle of the night it takes a decidedly darker turn. The kind of 'things' you read about in Tolkien exist and if you're not careful, they find you at the worst possible time.

Luckily for me, I'm one of the worst 'things' you'll find in the real word and as such I kicked-in Ralph's door and took a hammer to his knees. Ever see a cigar smoking Unicorn hobbled? It ain't a pretty sight, but then kidnapping ain't too nice neither.

He'd been keeping her in the basement (no points for originality), seems she and the floaty lady from the pub had some kind of 'relationship' and blackmail was the name of the game. This whole 'seeing into the future lark' could be profitable when exacted the right way and while Miss floaty lady and her friend didn't go in for that, Ralph sure as hell would.

Calypoly was small. She was also, even with the five layers of mud and filth, the prettiest thing I'd ever seen. It was no wonder the fairy wanted her back.

"You OK?"

She rose her eyes to me, slowly and gave a half smile.

It nearly killed me.

She never said a word, even when we stepped over Ralph's writhing, weeping body.

We rocked up at the lady's house and I handed the little wisp over. She seemed happy, had a slight smile edging out the corner of her mouth. Guess that's what counts for thanks in Faerie.

I took the gold purse she gave me and wandered down the lane. Sitting in the pub a little while later I watched the band play, flicked a smile at the girl behind the bar and then sat in the corner.

When the Ogre walked through the door I slipped my right leg back and waited for the lunge. It never came. He lumbered over, pushed a few people out of the way and crashed down on the seat across from me.

"Need wurk."

I smiled.

"Beer?"

OK SIXTEEN

OLIN WISH

"First off," I say to a roomful of enraptured schoolchildren, "It is absolutely instantaneous. One minute there is a voice in your helmet counting backwards from fifteen and the next, you're splashing down in a jet black ocean. The first six months of the academy is spent training cadets how to cope with the stress of extreme disorientation. You'd be surprised how easy it is to slip away." I say the last as if to myself, blinking as I look up again at grinning grade schoolers lined in rows at small desks. I had been doing the speaking circuit for over eleven years.

These charitable engagements helped offset my tax bill at the end of the year. On that day, when I made history, no one had the foresight to warn me that forever after I would have to relive, with perfect clarity, the worst feeling, the worst series of seemingly unending moments of my life, recalling them to every media outlet, hearings committee, and public school for the rest of my life. It paid well. Kept me in good booze. But that was all.

Try asking a veteran to relive his times on the cusp of death and see what happens. See how happy he is to do it. "Was it scary?" One of the girls in the third row asks, without raising her hand. "Yes, it was," I say. If I was being totally honest, I would say it was the worst feeling of my life. But that might draw a prolonged uncomfortable silence; a professional speakers worst enemy.

"Where were the puppies?" A boy in the back shouts. Others giggle, and the rabble of excited children swells like a tsunami three hundred miles off the coast of Tokyo. I am losing them.

"Children," a woman near the front calls, feebly.

I know what I have to do. Give the public what it wants. "The puppies came later," I blurt, cutting off the teacher right when she is spooling up for a lecture. The class falls silent in the time it takes to splash down on a strange world. I would skip over the worst parts; parts about bobbing in a jet black ocean in an inflatable suit, struggling to breath the garbage water fumes, drifting away from the others, begging a God I don't believe in to provide some light, any light. I gloss over that part about screaming inside my helmet till my ears rang, till I fogged the inside so bad I almost couldn't see the lights on the shore or the lights below in the bay.

I don' t tell them about feeling like I had stumbled drunkenly across the Las Vegas strip, except for the blue/gray algae. It was their bioluminescence I was seeing. A trillion tiny twinkle lights, like every thought I've ever had or will have, present and accounted for. Like dead and dying pixels giving way to new ones on the big picture screen. The big picture screen, making room for new synaptic cul de sacs and subdivisions.

No, kids want to hear about the puppies.

The people of OKSIXTEEN – Okies, as I like to refer to them as – have heads like St. Bernards. An unfortunate coincidence that all but eliminates any possibility they will ever be well received or taken seriously at any intergalactic roundtable where humans are present. Their bodies resemble Tolkien dwarves, with the same sunny disposition.

The first one I met was out walking his dog. How's that for irony? It was a little terrier thing; vaguely mammalian and hairless. If you want to know the truth, it looked like a naked toddler with bat wings. But, of course, this too I gloss over. He found me poking at buttons and giggling hysterically near the base of a million year old tree that fed on rot instead of sunlight. I was happy because I was winning and confused at the same time because the tree I was playing with refused to cash out my winnings. Chemicals in the humid, garbage-water air made me believe the giant fungi I was poking at was a video poker machine.

Hold, hold, deal. Then giggle excitedly.

This part of the story I left out of the official report. We had been warned not to expose ourselves to the atmosphere until the heads-up display gave us the go-ahead. Warned repeatedly of the dangers. Something about being washed ashore, the only survivor, unable to see because of a fogged up visor, convinced me to forgo precaution.

The dog sniffed my crotch, as dogs the universe over are prone to do. I reached down with my big mitten and patted its head.

Its wings fluttered like the eye lashes of a pretty girl. My kind gesture convinced the "puppy" not to take my head off with a single swipe and mount it above his fireplace.

"They're a gentle species," I tell the children, lying through my teeth.

"Are they cuddly?" The same girl in the third row wants to know. Something about her persistence and unwillingness to wait for the question portion of my presentation tells me she will one day be an astronaut.

"We never got around to hugging," I say, truthfully. Instead, he took me to a hollowed out tree and gave me something to drink that cleared my head. The event may have been spontaneous, but the wait in between and subsequent paperwork after was pure Hell-on-Earth. Losing five co-workers will do that. They disappeared beneath the capsules wake and didn't even bob once to the surface. That was my official report. It didn't help having to explain how I was the only one who managed to slip into a survival suit and inflate prior to total immersion. The true story I'll take to my grave.

There was a lot of grunts and barks on OKSIXTEEN, and me with a hangover the size of Everest. Come to find out later, it wasn't only the air. I had a concussion upon impact. No one anticipated a water landing or that my host would be the owner of a ten thousand year old chic antique store, or that the sharks there wore board shorts and drove expensive submersibles with bumper sticks which read, "Locals Only," or that the garbage water I was huffing had a similar composition to doing whippets and would do lasting chromosomal damage that would manifest ten years later as a rare form of Parkinson's, or that I'd hit the speech circuit running, and wear my old, rotted spacesuit to bars to pick up women and score free drinks.

These are the things you learn later and can't prepare for ahead of time. Mistakes will happen, they assured us in the academy. That's why the second half of the first year had been devoted primarily to improvisational acting lessons. It wasn't enough that we could hold our breath for five minutes without blacking out and withstand nine times Earth gravity for a full minute, or that the negative G training pushed a few cadets to the point of retinal detachment. We also had to be proficient ambassadors, even after the locals sheered five out of six of us in half at the waist.

People, ignorant people, later say things like, "That's what they signed up for," when they hear the lie about how my fellow crew members died.

As if circumstances surrounding sudden death make it any more or less tragic. It took much therapy to convince me to forgive these people. It isn't the kid's fault though, I remind myself. It isn't their fault I'm standing here in a moldy spacesuit while they're down there looking up with bright expectations. So I tell them about the puppy people; exaggerate about their long silken fur.

"Did they let you take back souvenirs?" Another kid asks during the scheduled ten minute Q and A.

I look down at the big mitten, sense the hand within tremble as I say, "Yeah, I brought some stuff back."

"Like what! Like what!" They yell. It's then I shell out cheap OKSIXTEEN trinkets, made in China. The kind designed to placate tourists that light up once and break five minutes after you open them. Crystal ball nano tanks that go on keychains. Each, guaranteed to contain a living OKSIXTEEN organism the size of a pinhead. OKSIXTEEN snow globes; amulet soil samples. The dirt probably came from Utah. They eat it up, express gratitude, and then its snack time. I'm on my way.

Another charitable act in the record books. It's during snack time that the teacher and I hit it off. She asks to touch the soiled patch on my right shoulder and I consent. Who am I to deny the poor thing? Before my eyes I watch her transform into an astro-groupie. I ask her out for drinks later and before you know it, the presentation is over and it's just me and her with our knees tangled between two bar stools, her laughing maddeningly about the made in China yo-yo's and me, caressing her inner elbow with my big mitten.

End

CLEAN TEETH

ANTON ZALESKI

One must be blind to miss the words smeared in red on the rusty metal sign:

Teeth cleaned
Cavities filled
Dentures installed
Cheap

That sign outside squeaks as it dangles in the breeze, hanging off the tin shack I use as my office in this asshole of a town. Another town. Another town with no more character than the one before it, but clearly I'm not here for the culture. Besides, I tend to outlast my welcome rather quickly, so why pick someplace I might regret not being able to come back to? You don't shit where you eat, right?

Am I too vulgar? Sorry, it's a bad habit.

Hold on a second. Those dirty little kids are banging on the refuse pile outside again, probably scavenging for medical tubing. Hold on, let me open the door and take care of this.

Hey! You little gits! Don't make me call the Reverend on you! She'll probably give you corporal punishment. What? You know, corporal punishment: a spanking. You don't know what a spanking is? Clearly you two don't have any parents. Get your little asses away from there. Don't make me call down the wrath of hell, or the spider god or the moon god, or whomever it is that you little twits worship.

Sorry about that. You said you're from out of town, didn't you? As one can probably tell, these locals are a superstitious lot. Half are sun-worshippers, the other half are some sort of neo-protestants. Their violent, drunken clashes start around sundown on payday, every week-end like clockwork. Inevitably, some plebian has words about the Sun or the Son, and words escalate into physical altercations. People die. Being a total Podunk, there aren't any doctors in town, so they come to me for help with burial preparations. Besides my usual payment, a few choice organs find their way into one of the rubber containment pouches hidden under my smock.

These places always have a steady stream of people; they come, they go— sometimes going out the back in parts, stuffed into bio-rubber bags. But one must be careful. Too many bodies go missing, and one must burn a few to cover the stench of one's dealings.

It is key to try and keep a low profile. My place is as non-descript as possible. This location was chosen in particular because of the town's proximity to a pre-collapse underground bunker, which I've been able to use as my stash house; long abandoned but its got good bones. It's close enough to this tin shack that one can sneak over at night without rousing suspicion.

I hope I'm not boring you.

Anyhow, a young man came in for a routine filling earlier. I casually ran a scanner over him as the anesthetic took effect. Window-shopping. I glanced over the details; healthy heart, at least one usable kidney, and a DNA match for a couple of marrow and cell graft inquiries that were put up on the list serve. Most requests come from back west in Shan-gri-LA. I miss home.

So the problem with this patient was he, like everyone else in this town, was strung out on something. Now, in some ways, that makes my job easier. In a town full of Rezz-heads, dental work is always in high demand. Rotting teeth begot by a rotting society. I'm sure you're *different* though, right? Honestly though, who's going to miss these people? They're scum. I hate scum. I'm just doing my part to wipe a few off the face of the earth. I'm sure their gods will find a place for them in that magical freezer of eternal life that they call heaven, Canaan, Valhalla, or the Cayman Islands; if you're one of those old-world monetarists. Ignorance really is bliss, isn't it?

You're probably wondering about me. I can tell. There's not much to my story. I'm just a regular guy. I met my Molly online. She appreciated that I enjoyed long walks on the beach at sunset. I put my pants on one borrowed leg at a time. I miss that ocean breeze, Molly, and licorice brain freeze, but I've got quotas, and more than iotas.

I was working on my poetry for a while, so I hope you don't mind my pentameter. My poetry instructor at university said I had a habit of using common tropes and clichés a little bit too much. But how much is too much? Just enough, I say.

A couple years of putting my nose to the grindstone, and then I can afford a condo down by the ocean. But first I've got to pay my dues. School was expensive, and they don't give out dentist's licenses in Cracker Jack boxes. The job market is quite tight, so to succeed one must have follow-through, a little luck, and one must have balls. Now those balls can be hacked off of some poor sap that's high on whatever they can pump into their system. Dropped into an eye, up a nose, in stabbed into the socket of those delightful toes. The desperate will find whatever way they can to forget the ills of their miserable existence; one must help them to forget, with one final sleep. It's almost missionary work. I've been helping people. Of course, just like the preachers, I've gotten my cut.

The Matriarchs back home will pay handsomely for good balls, but trying to find a quality pair out here is like looking for a needle in a haystack. But life's not all balls and kidneys, Take the poor Rezz-head that was sitting in that chair. The kid would garner a hefty profit for me through those little things: gall bladder, marrow, eyeballs. Those items add up; everybody always needs eyeballs. As an added bonus, there was a harvest of good sinew from the subject's arms and legs, perfect for a little something one such as myself has been working on in my makeshift lab outside of town. While the project isn't much yet, a few more cadavers and one would have quite a golem.

You've never heard of a Golem before have you? I can tell by the look on your face. This one is a hobby of mine, something to help me pass the time in this Podunk. They're just what the doctor ordered. In a quarrel, they will get into the thick of things and rip off arms and heads and legs and balls. Oh, I'm just kidding, they're not into balls.

One can't help but wonder, do you think I'm obsessed with balls? No, don't answer that.

Anyhow, they're not into balls because a golem's aggression isn't sexual at all. Instead, we tap directly into their orbitofrontal cortex, and pump that area of the brain full of the chemicals that make it obey, make it destroy, make it kill. I say "we", but me personally; I'm really just tinkering around. There are doctors back home who specialize in this sort of thing. As you know I'm a dentist, so I had a great deal of train-ing in anesthesia. One such as myself specializes in things such as the homebrew cocktail that allows my patient to remain fully conscious but unable to move or scream while I remove their organs.

I'm sorry, one's mind wanders out here in the middle of nowhere, what did you say you came in here for again? You believe you need a root canal, correct?

62116874R00190

Made in the USA
Charleston, SC
01 October 2016